M000110678

"I Want

To Witness,

But What

Do I Say?"

"I Want To Witness, But What Do I Say?"

Easy Icebreakers to Get You
Started Witnessing to the Lost

By Rev. Susan Nazarewicz

Copyright ©2016 by Witness Publishing

Witness Publishing

PO Box 700382

Tulsa, OK 74170

Available from **Amazon.com** and **www.iwanttowitness.com** and other online stores and book stores and also available on Kindle.

Printed in the United States of America

Dedication

I dedicate this book to Christians of all denominations that believe we are all called to be salt and light to share the Gospel, but they need some courage and they need to know what to say.

I also dedicate this book to all the "on fire for Jesus" evangelists that are humble enough to admit that they do not know it all and these icebreakers and all the contents herein will help them witness to the lost.

Most importantly, I dedicate this book to all those who will become born again through the Christians that read this book and become doers of it. I wrote this book for you all of you. You are the reason for this book. God showed His love and proved His love for you by the fact that while you were all still sinners, Christ the Messiah, the Anointed One, died for you all (Romans 5:8).

Acknowledgements

"We don't accomplish anything in this world alone and whatever happens is the result of the whole tapestry of one's life and all the weavings of individual threads from one to another that creates something." — Sandra Day O'Connor

I give God all the glory for the publishing of this book. I thank the Holy Spirit for giving me the grace, the strength, the wisdom, the perseverance, and the anointing to write and publish this book to help bring in the end time harvest of souls. I wanted to thank the following people for the "weavings of your threads" into my life.

Thank you Pastors Kenneth and Lynette Hagin, Jr. and all the associate pastors at RHEMA Bible Church for all the anointed "faith–filled" messages that encouraged me, like Pastor Hagin often preaches: "I shall not be defeated and I will not quit." Thank you all for your encouragement and faith–filled messages that have encouraged me to not quit and publish this book for Christians to use in these last days. See: www.rhema.org

Thank you, Richard and Lindsay Roberts, for both being obedient to the Lord's vision to be a light in the darkness, "where His voice is heard small and His light is dim" and to bring the healing power of God to the nations. Thank you for your hearts for evangelism that really inspired me to write this book. I thank God for Oral Roberts. He touched so many lives through the healing power of Jesus. His message about "Jesus is coming soon" that he delivered before he moved to heaven in December 15, 2009 was instrumental in inspiring me to publish this book. It is an honor and a privilege working as a prayer partner and assistant supervisor at Oral Roberts Ministries at the Abundant Life Prayer Group since 2004. Thank you, Raymond and Sandra Forbes, for believing in me. You all are the best!

Thank you, Jayne Bowman, for being such a wonderful steadfast best friend. I pray that your practice, Real Solutions Christian Counseling will prosper and that many will be delivered set free, and emotionally healed and whole through your anointed counseling that is led by the spirit. See: www.real–soulutions.com

Thank you, Rev. Curry and Dawn Blake, overseers of John G. Lake Ministries, for ordaining me as a minister of the Gospel in 2001. Thank you both for believing in me and for being supportive of my prophetic gifting as well. www.jglm.org

I thank God for my friend/former roommate, Karen Fetty, who prays for me. I cannot thank you enough. I also thank Roberta Sweem for her prayers. Thank you Fran Steinke for your accurate prophetic words that came true and changed my last name!

I am always hungry for the Word of God largely because I pray on the phone 40 hours a week at the Abundant Life Prayer Group (for over 11 years). I wrote this book, which was a big deal, and arduously created my website, www.traintracts.com; and I have dealt with many disappointments and brokenness and obstacles in my life that have all made me very hungry for the Word of God. So I wanted to thank the following ministers that have encouraged, comforted, impacted and filled my hunger with their teaching and preaching of the word. I thank God for the following "threads" that have been woven into my life to make my life's tapestry beautiful:

Thank you, Joyce Meyer, for being a spiritual Mom to me. I discovered your ministry a year after my mother, Joyce Mulford, died of bone cancer in 1994 and you really helped me grow spiritually. Literally my real mom was named "Joyce" too, but she died of bone cancer January 5, 1994. But God has used you to spiritually "mother me" and grow me up in Christ. I have listened to over 25 tape series and have read over 30 of your books!

Thank you, Joel Osteen, for your hope–filled messages that uplifted me and for your opening jokes that made me smile.

Thank You Pastor Keith Moore. I had you for eight different classes when I graduated from RHEMA Bible Training College in 1995 from the Teacher's group. I loved Prayer and Healing School! I'll never forget your comforting messages that you preached after my mom passed away. Now I thank God for your church and your wonderful staff at Moore Life Ministries Thank you for sending me your music

CD – "Peace of God" and your CD teachings, "Have Faith in God. Thank for everything and for teaching me to trust in the Lord in the hard times of life.

Thank you Pastor Willie George for your anointed powerful messages at Church On The Move that have encouraged me many times to do what I am called to do. Thank you, Andy Chrisman, for your anointed praise and worship songs that lifted me many times. Thank you for your song: "We Will Not Be Silent."

Thank you, Pastor Craig Groeschel, for your uplifting, fun and encouraging messages at: www.life.church.

Thank you, Jim and Miriam Puleo from "Drink From the River", for opening up your house and making "an open heaven" for the Presence of God to soak us and bless us with His love and peace and joy, which gave me strength for the battle.

I give thanks to Betty Earls for help with editing my book.

To save the best for last, I especially wanted to thank my husband David Nazarewicz for his humor that keeps me laughing, his love and support, his wisdom and encouragement. I thank God for your spirit of excellence as well. You are my knight in shining armor. You are an Ephesians 3:20 husband

Table of Contents

Introduction

Statistics say that 95% of Christians do not share their faith in Jesus Christ. It is even hard for pastors. This is what a pastor admitted in his own words:

"Years ago I received a call from a church member explaining that her dad, Frank, was close to death. He occasionally attended our church with his daughter, but he did not believe in Christ and was skeptical of all pastors. His concerned daughter asked if I'd visit him in the hospital to explain the Gospel so her Dad would have a final chance to know Christ before he died. Not wanting to come across like a typical fire and brimstone preacher, I kept the conversation light. The whole time we talked, I looked for the opportune moment to shift the conversation toward spiritual issues. Frank loves the Redskins and hated the Cowboys ever since Tom Landry left. (No apparent opportunities for a spiritual segue.) He told me about his grandson, who is playing on the varsity baseball team as a sophomore. (No easy way to jump from baseball to Jesus.) We chatted about the unseasonably hot weather. (I considered mentioning the heat, but thought better of it.) The perfect moment to transition the conversation to a spiritual issue never came. I decided not to force it. I told myself that I had developed a better relationship with him and would return the next day to try and talk to him about Christ and eternity."

The following morning the pastor returned to the hospital. He couldn't see Frank because the room was packed with people. Instantly he realized what had just happened. Moments before he arrived, Frank had died.

"No one saw me, so I quickly turned around and walked back to my car, ashamed that I had missed a chance to impact Frank's eternity. I truly believe that Christ is the only door through which we enter heaven, but I failed to share Him with a man at death's door." (Excerpt from *The Christian Atheist*, by Craig Groeschel, Zondervan, p 196) Since then Pastor Craig has changed a lot and as of May 2015, there are twenty–four Life.Church (formerly called: www.lifechurch.tv) locations in seven states across the USA and many all over the world watch www.life.church online as well.

This is an honest story at how hard it is to just segue the conversation into the Gospel, even for a pastor. I have heard many Christians say, "I want to witness, but what do I say?" In fact, that was my question when the Lord prompted me to start an "undercover" evangelistic cell group at the mall. I say "undercover" because at the mall, you cannot solicit or pass out materials, but there is no law against talking with people in a friendly conversational manner. I had gone through Evangelism Explosion, the door to door evangelism approach founded by James D Kennedy. I was proficient at knocking on doors and asking: "If you were to die tonight, heaven forbid, do you know for sure, beyond a shadow of a doubt, that you would go to heaven or would you say that is something that you are still working on?" But at the mall, there were no doors to knock on and I didn't just want to walk up to a person and ask that question because it sounded so brassy and "in your face" at the mall. Just like this pastor in the introduction, I wanted to witness, but I didn't know what to say. I was stuck. So in the food court I prayed:

"Father, You are the One that wanted me to come here. I want to witness, but what do I say? How do I transition a conversation from a secular everyday conversation onto the gospel track?"

The following pages contain the revelations or ideas that God gave me to help Christians segue conversations and it all started at Subway.

Section 1

Compassion, Courage, Subway and Testimonies

CHAPTER ONE

It All Started at
the Mall with Subway

A T the mall in the food court, God answered my prayer which was, "God, I want to witness, but what do I say?". I saw the Subway sign and God revealed to me my first icebreaker revelation: *"This **subway** reminds me of how Jesus is the **way** and He was the perfect **sub** for my sins when He died in my place on the cross."*

I was so excited at this wonderful new icebreaker. Now I call them "object evangelism icebreakers." I used it that day at the mall, but the Subway employee at the counter was already a Christian. However later at another Subway restaurant, I used this object evangelism icebreaker again with another employee. The young man had just gotten his tongue pierced that day. I don't know if that had anything to do with it, but he was open to listen to me share. After I said the icebreaker, we talked a bit more and then he repeated a salvation prayer after me and gave his heart to the Lord! I was amazed at how easy it was! I had a small follow up book in my car called "This New Life." I gave it to him and encouraged him to read the Bible and find a church. This was the start of a brand new beginning for me in witnessing to the lost! I was so excited because it was so easy!

Jesus Used Object Evangelism Icebreakers

After this testimony at subway, I read Matthew chapter 13. It was here that the Lord gave me a revelation about how Jesus used objects in His surroundings whenever He taught about the Kingdom of heaven. In short, He used object evangelism icebreakers!

- In Matthew 13:1–23 Jesus taught about the parable of the sower to teach the four ways people hear and apply the Gospel to their lives. Seed sown by the wayside is misunderstood; seed sown on stony paces is received with joy, but people fall away when persecution arises; seed sown by the thorns is choked by the cares of the world and deceitfulness of riches, making it unfruitful and finally the seed sown on good ground is when people understand the Gospel and it produces a harvest, some hundred-fold, some sixty, some thirty.
- In Matthew 13:24 Jesus said, "The Kingdom of heaven is like a man who sowed good seed in his field; but while men slept, his enemy came and sowed weeds among the wheat and went his way." In this parable, He used weeds to describe wicked people who wilted or were useless because of their unbelief of Him. He used wheat to describe born again believers that grew up spiritually healthy and lived for Him.
- In Matthew 13:31 Jesus said, "the Kingdom of Heaven is like a mustard seed, which a man took and sowed in his field, which indeed is the least of all the seeds; but when it is grown it is greater than the herbs and becomes a tree." Jesus relates the Kingdom of Heaven to a mustard seed, that when planted in people's hearts, yields a great harvest of eternal life in heaven.

- In Matthew 13:33 Jesus said, "the Kingdom of Heaven is like leaven, which a woman took and hid in three measures of meal till it was all leavened." Leaven is like the quickening of the Holy Spirit that spreads and releases His power to heal, to deliver, and convict of sin to bring salvation.

- In Matthew 13: 44 Jesus said, "the Kingdom of Heaven is like treasure hidden in a field, which a man found and hid; and for the joy over it he goes and sells all that he has and buys that field." Jesus was relating to them how precious and valuable salvation is and it will require us to give our whole hearts to Him.

- Matthew 13:45 Jesus said, "Again the Kingdom of Heaven is like a merchant looking for fine pearls, who, when he had found one of great price, went and sold all that he had and bought it." Jesus teaches to his disciples that they must "sell out and live for Him.

Actually Matthew 13:34 sums it up by saying: "Jesus spoke to the multitudes in parables. Without a parable He did not speak to them."

As I read through Matthew 13, I realized that these parables can be used as "object evangelism icebreakers" to help transition conversations onto the Gospel track. So how much more should we use parables to witness to the lost to explain the Gospel today?

Jesus spoke of the future or the coming Kingdom, so He said, "the Kingdom of God is like…"

Today, since Jesus Christ has already gone to the cross and died and rose from the dead, we can use the past tense when referring to the Gospel and say: "That_____(object) reminds me of _____ (some aspect of the Gospel)."

Then you simply explain what aspect of the Kingdom of God you are referring to and continue on and start witnessing!

The Best Thing about It

The best thing about object evangelism icebreakers is if the unbeliever is cold or not open to the Gospel at that time, the object is still there to remind them of what you said about the Gospel in reference to that object. That means the Holy Spirit can rewind and play back again all the words that you said that relate to that object and the Gospel at a later time, like the next day or when they are going through a real crisis where their heart is more tender and receptive to receive Jesus as Lord. That could be why Jesus Christ Himself used parables because He said in Matthew 13:13, "seeing they do not see, and hearing they do not hear, nor do they understand" which sadly fulfilled the prophecy Isaiah uttered in Isaiah 6:9–10: And He said, "Go, and tell this people: 'Keep on hearing, but do not understand; Keep on seeing, but do not perceive.' "Make the heart of this people dull, And their ears heavy, And shut their eyes; Lest they see with their eyes, And hear with their ears, And understand with their heart, And return and be healed."

Sadly, there are many people like that today. We need to pray for the lost, for their hearts to "see, hear and understand" God's forgiveness and love and Jesus' saving blood.

The Transition Can Be the Hardest Thing!

Going back to the introduction, I wish I had been in that hospital room when that pastor was witnessing to Frank.   I can empathize with this pastor. I remember how I felt at the Mall with no words to say because I did not know how to transition a conversation onto the Gospel track. The Lord showed me back in 2003 that the hardest part about witnessing is just getting started. It's the transition. If you do not know how to transition, then you will not be witnessing at all. If I were in that hospital room that day, I think would have said to Frank:

"Yes, I like football too. You know that exuberant joy you feel when the Redskins score a touchdown?   I believe that is the same joy that God feels when a person prays to receive Jesus Christ as their Lord and Savior. And then that same joy will become yours when you make peace with God and have that assurance that you are going to heaven...Do you have that assurance, Frank, that you are going to heaven?"   Or I could have said: "That's wonderful your grandson is so good at baseball. I'm glad that the three strikes and you're out rule only applies to baseball. God is much more merciful than that. It says in 1 John 1:9 that when you confess your sins, God is faithful and just to forgive you of all of your sins, not just three, and to cleanse you from all unrighteousness, so Frank, are you in or are you out? Would you like to make it in to heaven?"

Or the pastor could have said: "Home plate reminds me of heaven because that will be my home for all eternity because I received Jesus as my Lord and Savior…have you ever done that, Frank?"

Answering the problematic question: **"I want to witness, but what do I say"** is what this book is all about. In the following pages, you will find over 400 ways to transition or to segue a conversation into the Gospel! You just take an object in your environment and relate it to the Gospel in some way and then, voila! You are on the Gospel track.

Back in 2006, I wanted to publish all of these God–given ideas into a book, but I ran into a lot of obstacles. I was greatly discouraged and was going to quit. The PGA Tournament was coming to Tulsa. God prompted me to put my ideas about how to witness on the golf course in a small yellow tract. I gave out over 120 "golf tracts" at a Fellowship of Christian Athletes dinner.

This tract contained icebreakers to train Christian golfers how to transition conversations onto the Gospel track on the golf course. So after the first golf tract, then God told me to turn *my whole book* into tracts. I was not willing at first. It took 6 months.

I told a fellow prayer partner Jerry Nelsestuen: "These are not regular tracts, but they are teaching tools or a training tool in a tract format."

He replied, so it is like a *"train tract."*

That name stuck and I decided to call my tracts **"train tracts."** After that the Lord told me to build a website. That arduous laborious frustrating task took nine months, but finally in 2009 **www.traintracts.com** was born. Over the past three years, many people have used them to transition conversations onto the Gospel track and many have been saved. Now in this wonderful book, all fifty five train tracts are here in one unique volume. There is an index at the back to help you find just the right object you want to use to transition the conversation onto the Gospel track, so that the unbeliever will have an opportunity to hear the Gospel truth.

For example, at the Mall the Lord gave me these object evangelism icebreakers:

- This **candle** reminds me of Jesus Christ who is the Light of the world.

- This **cell phone** reminds me that I need to call on God.

- As I get this **manicure** and watch you as you file and shape my nails, it reminds me of a Bible scripture that says when you believe in the Lord, He will make the crooked places straight and the rough places smooth in your life. (Isaiah 40:4)

- As I get my **hair colored** to take away all the undesirable gray, it reminds me of my Lord Jesus who died on the cross take away all my undesirable sins.

- This **mirror** reminds me that Jesus Christ is the mirror image of the invisible God. He was God in the flesh and He came to earth to show us what God is like in heaven.

- This **blouse** that is so glittery and shiny reminds me of the garment of praise that God will give me instead a spirit of heaviness or sorrow. (Isaiah 61:3).

- This soft **teddy bear** is so comforting. It reminds me of John 14: 6 which says, "I will ask the Father and He will give you another Comforter to be with you forever."

- These **Hero**–Action Figures remind me of Jesus Christ, who is my super hero. He punched the devil out of the way when He went to the cross and saved me from hell.

- This **water** reminds me of the Living Water who is Jesus Christ. Whoever drinks that water will never thirst again.

- This **wrench** reminds me of how if I trust God, He can turn things around in my life if I just turn my life over to Him. He knows what to do. Romans 8:28.

- This **matchbox car** reminds me of how important it is to run my race for Jesus or do my God-given purpose because it will impact others for all eternity. Jeremiah 29:11, Hebrews 12:1-2

The Vision of the Ocean of Salvation

I never had an experience like this pastor did that shook me up to convict me to share my faith, but I knew I was guilty of being in the 95% bracket. God did show me a vision during church one day to convict me. I was a member of a spirit–filled church that prayed in tongues and loved to praise and worship God and they prophesied a lot, but they did not have a heart for evangelism nor missions at that time. One day I saw this vision of an ocean. It represented salvation. I was looking at the vision from the viewpoint of a bystander on the sidelines. There were many Christians out in the deep parts, floating, swimming and having a lot of fun, dancing in the spirit and praying in tongues and praying for Revival. The irony of it is, from my perspective in this vision, they were not doing anything for Revival to come to pass, except praying. Then I saw a bunch of unsaved people who were on the shore of the beach wanting to come in and get saved. They were longing to come in, but they did not know how because they were unsure or afraid of the water. They wanted someone to help them in, but the other experienced swimmers were out in the deep and were too consumed with themselves to even see the ones on the shore. As I saw

> Hey! You Christians out in the deep – There are lost ones on the shore that want to come in and get saved! Go get them!

this whole scene I yelled at the ones out in the deep:

The ones in the deep did not respond. Either they could not hear me or they did not want to hear me. I was grieved that the ones wanting to be saved remained on the shore. I felt the grieving of the heart of God. I felt His sorrow, His sadness and His broken heart.

Before I had this vision, I did witness to the lost, but it was not that much. I only did it once in a while. I really concentrated more on prophesying and had read 25 different books on the subject. In 1997 God graced me with a prophetic gift where He sings encouraging, comforting and accurate prophetic words through me over people, as the spirit leads. I am just the water hose or the vessel He flows through (so I wrote chapter 18). But after this vision the Lord chastened me saying that He wanted me to concentrate much more on evangelism because He told me:

> "Susan, people can get to heaven without a prophetic word, but they cannot get to heaven unless they are born again."

That thought riveted me. He did tell me that I can use my prophetic anointing to get people saved and I have done that as He gives me words of knowledge for them. But the Lord told me that thinking that you really need a prophetic word or a special leading from the Lord to witness to someone can also "box you in" because that only happens as God wills. But the Bible says to, "Go into all the world and preach the Gospel." So you do not need "a special leading" from the Lord to do whatever the Bible already says to do, which is to witness to the lost and fulfill the Great Commission.

Another lie that God showed me that keeps Christians from witnessing is that evangelism is a gift that only certain Christians have, but the Bible says we are all called to be ministers of reconciliation. All Christians are called to witness to the lost and if we don't, I believe we will be judged.

God said to Ezekiel in Ezekiel 3:16–21: "Son of man, I have made you a watchman for the house of Israel; therefore hear a word from My mouth, and give them warning from Me: When I say to the wicked,

'You shall surely die,' and you give him no warning, nor speak to warn the wicked from his wicked way, to save his life, that same wicked man shall die in his iniquity; but his blood I will require at your hand. Yet, if you warn the wicked, and he does not turn from his wickedness, nor from his wicked way, he shall die in his iniquity; but you have delivered your soul. Again, when a righteous man turns from his righteousness and commits iniquity, and I lay a stumbling block before him, he shall die; because you did not give him warning, he shall die in his sin, and his righteousness which he has done shall not be remembered; but his blood I will require at your hand. Nevertheless if you warn the righteous man that the righteous should not sin, and he does not sin, he shall surely live because he took warning; also you will have delivered your soul."

We Must Live Right AND Speak Words of Truth

Some Christians avoid witnessing by adhering to what Francis of Assisi is said to have said, "Preach the gospel at all times; when necessary, use words." The truth is no biography written within the first 200 years of his death contains this saying nor anything close to it. When Francis did itinerant ministry in the villages, he sometimes preached five times a day! Secondly, that saying is not even Biblical. Of course, we need to live right before people AND at the same time, we need to speak words of truth in love into people's lives and share the Gospel with them. Just living right before them is not enough. The Sadducees and Pharisees lived right before the people and kept the Law and totally missed Jesus as their Messiah and what salvation was all about. I know many Hindus who work at hotels and they are very hospitable nice people who seem to "live right," but their god will not lead them to eternal life in heaven. I know many Muslims who work at gas stations and they are nice and pleasant people as well, but Muhammad or Allah will not lead them to eternal life in heaven. Remember that God does not look at the outer appearance. He looks on the heart. We are saved by grace through faith in Christ, not by our good works. So words must be spoken and the truth of the Gospel must be explained to them to help them understand that Jesus Christ is the Savior of the world.

The Gospel is Simple

- God created us. He loves us and wants to be with us.
- God has a wonderful plan and a purpose for our lives (Jer. 29:11).
- But our sins have separated us from God like a wall between us. Romans 3:23 says, "for all have sinned and fall short of the glory of God." Romans 6:23 says, "For the wages for sin is death."
- Since God created us, this wall grieves Him because He loves us and wants to fellowship with us and be with us. Leviticus 17:11 says, "for it is the blood that makes atonement for the soul."
- **The Solution**: God sent His Son Jesus Christ who paid the penalty when He willingly shed Hi s holy sinless blood and died on the cross for our sins. He was the sacrificial Lamb of God. Then on the third day, God raised Jesus up from the dead. Now He's alive! He is seated at the right hand of God.

Note: Many think that their good works will save them, but Ephesians 2:8-9 says, "For by grace you have been saved through faith, and that not of yourselves; it is the gift of God, not of works, lest anyone should boast."

Your works are not enough to meet God's standard of perfection. God's standard is the Ten Commandments and total obedience to His Word. We all sin and fall short of that. But whoever believes and prays to receive Jesus Christ as their Lord and Savior will become righteous or "right with God" and will be reconciled with Him again and thus, will receive eternal life in heaven.

After that prayer, God will move on their hearts to do good works for Him, like it says in Ephesians 2:10: "For we are His workmanship created in Jesus Christ for good works,, which God prepared beforehand that we should walk in them."

When a person becomes born again, then the love of God in their heart will motivate them to do good works and for the right reason. The love of Christ will compel them.

Be More Than Tolerant. Love Your Enemies

We all know that Jesus is coming soon to take His Church or His Bride up to heaven with Him or all those that believe in Him. We need to witness to the lost now more than ever, especially in this day and age where there is such pressure to "be tolerant." The Bible does not say to be tolerant. It says to love our enemies. If we really love our enemies, we will be more than tolerant. We will love them and we will jump over our fears and share the Gospel of Jesus Christ with them. God's love casts out all fear (1 Peter 4:18). When we know by revelation how much Jesus Christ loves us, then we will not have any fear. The Bible says that the love of Christ should compel us to witness. (Luke 14:23). In John 14:21 says, *"He who has My commandments and keeps them, He is the one who loves Me."*

Jesus' final commandment to us was the Great Commission to: *"Go into all the world and preach the Gospel."*

So many Christians are afraid to share their faith, but Jesus explicitly said to not be afraid to His disciples in Matthew 10:28: "Do not be afraid of those who kill the body, but cannot kill the soul. Rather be afraid of the One who can destroy both soul and body in hell."

In Matthew 10:32–33 Jesus says, "Whoever disowns me before men, I will disown him before my Father in heaven."

In this day and age, there are so many rules and regulations about where you can share the Gospel and where you cannot. I think that the devil puts these doubts in our hearts and minds to make us fearful to prevent us from stepping out and sharing the Gospel in an environment or in a situation where we really could share the Gospel and it is legal. So if you doubt, I say go ahead and do it. Share the Gospel. Throw caution to the wind! If it is not permissible, they will let you know. But until then, be loving, kind and compassionate and respectfully share the Gospel wherever and whenever you can. All Christians must do this because Jesus is coming soon.

We do not know exactly when Jesus is coming. The Bible says in Matthew 24:46, "But of that day and hour no one knows," But we know He is coming back a lot sooner NOW than He was before in Bible days. Jesus answered the disciples' question: What will be the sign of Your coming, and of the end of the age?" in Matthew 24:4-14:

Jesus answered and said to them: "Take heed that no one deceives you. For many will come in My name, saying, 'I am the Christ,' and will deceive many. And you will hear of wars and rumors of wars. See that you are not troubled; for all these things must come to pass, but the end is not yet. For nation will rise against nation, and kingdom against kingdom. And there will be famines, pestilences, and earthquakes in various places. All these are the beginning of sorrows. "Then they will deliver you up to tribulation and kill you, and you will be hated by all nations for My name's sake. And then many will be offended, will betray one another, and will hate one another. Then many false prophets will rise up and deceive many. And because lawlessness will abound, the love of many will grow cold. But he who endures to the end shall be saved. And this gospel of the kingdom will be preached in all the world as a witness to all the nations, and then the end will come.

When you watch the News, you will see that every single thing that Jesus mentions is now going on in the world today. The signs are all there. Jesus could come at any time. NOW is the time to witness to the lost. There is no time to waste

CHAPTER TWO

Creating Compassion
to Witness to the Lost

L oving others should be the motivation for witnessing to the lost. I think that some people do not witness to the lost because they do not love themselves, so they cannot really love others. Mark 12:31 says to, "Love your neighbor as yourself." You cannot give away love to others if you don't have it in you. When you become born again, you are adopted by your Heavenly Father who loves you with an everlasting love.

Many people think that God does not love them because of the bad things that have happened to them or because someone grossly mistreated or abused them. That does not mean that God does not love you. Not at all! It just means that someone totally misused their God–given will and disobeyed God and sinned against you. And this grieves God who thinks you are important and valuable and so precious. When you forgive them, you will not let them off the hook, you will just put them on God's hook. Romans 12:19 says that "vengeance is the Lord's and He will repay you." God will turn it around. You can know that God loves you because: He has given you access to His throne (Hebrews 4:16); He is paying attention to you; He calls you His son/daughter (1 John 3:1); He thinks you are the most valuable thing around because He bought you with His blood; God loves you because He created a purpose for your life and a plan to carry it out (Jeremiah 29:11). I love this scripture: Jeremiah 31:3 – "The LORD hath appeared of old unto me, saying, Yea, I have loved thee with an everlasting love: therefore with loving–kindness have I drawn thee." In Romans 5:8, it says, "But God demonstrates His own love toward us, in that while we were still sinners, Christ died for us." That is God's amazing love!

One way to receive God's love is through singing and worshipping God from your heart and then basking in His manifest presence.

In order to receive God's love, Christians need to accept themselves, embrace their personalities and even their imperfections, knowing that although they are not where they need to be or want to be, they are making progress! Jesus died for us because we have imperfections and weaknesses and we don't have to reject ourselves because of them. Do not compare yourself to others either. You just focus on becoming the best "you" that you can be! God wants us to love ourselves and enjoy how He has made us! So first of all, Christians need to love themselves.

For those who love themselves and yet, are still lax about witnessing, I found that reading scriptures about hell that reveal the horrors, the pain and the suffering there will create a deep compassion for Christians to witness to others, no matter how uncomfortable they may feel. You will not want your worst enemy to go to hell. Satan does not want us to know the truth about hell. Fire and brimstone preachers are often criticized, but as I searched the scriptures, Jesus often preached about not going to hell where there is "weeping and gnashing of teeth."

Matthew 13:41 says, "At the end of the age the Son of Man will send out His angels, and they will weed out of his kingdom everything that causes sin and all who do evil. They will throw them into the fiery furnace where there is weeping and gnashing of teeth.

Mark 9:43 -48 says, "If your hand causes you to sin, cut it off. It is better for you to enter into life maimed, rather than having two hands, to go to hell, into the fire that shall never be quenched: where their worm does not die and the fire is not quenched. And if your foot causes you to sin, cut it off. It is better for you to enter life lame, rather than having two feet, to be cast into hell, into the fire that shall never be quenched: where their worm does not die and the fire is not quenched. And if your eye causes you to sin, pluck it out. It is better for you to enter into the kingdom of God with one eye rather than having two eyes, to be cast into hell fire - where their worm does not die and the fire is not quenched."

This is not a literal command to cut off your hand or put out your eye! That was in the days of the law and we are in the age of grace now. Jesus was using this extreme example to compassionately compel people to believe Him and receive Him as their Lord and Savior because He knew the terrible horrors of hell.

What Does "Worm Does Not Die" Mean?

In Isaiah 14: 11, where it describes Lucifer falling from heaven and going to hell, it says: "your pomp is brought down to Sheol (hell), and the sound of your stringed instruments; The maggot is spread under you, **and worms cover you.**"

Another explanation is a man's testimony that Mary Baxter heard when she went to hell from her book, *Divine Revelation of Hell* (Whitaker House). "I desired to drink strong drink and do the things of this world more than obey Your commands. But I wish now I had listened to those you sent to me. Instead, I did evil and would not repent." Great sobs shook his body as he cried out in regret. "For years I have been tormented in this place. I know what I am, and I know I will never get out. I am tormented day and night in these flames **and these worms.** "

So evidently, in hell, worms eat your flesh and they do not die in the flames, so that they can continue to torment you. Now that alone would cause me to get saved in a minute! Can you imagine having worms crawl all over you that never die for all eternity? That would be the most horrible thing in the world and yet it is probably only one of many terrible horrible things that are in the fires of hell. It is so terrible; you would not want your worst enemy to go there.

Forgive Your Offenders or You'll Miss Heaven

In Matthew 18:32 the Master said, "You wicked servant, I canceled all that debt of yours because you begged me to. Shouldn't you have had mercy on your fellow servant just as I had on you?" In anger his master turned him over to the jailers to be tortured, until he should pay back all he owed. This is how my Heavenly Father will treat each of you unless you forgive your brother from your heart.

After the Lord's Prayer, Jesus said in Matthew 6:14, "For if you forgive men their trespasses, your Heavenly Father will also forgive you. But if you do not forgive men their trespasses, neither will your Father forgive your trespasses."

Since God has forgiven us of our sins, we must forgive whoever has sinned against us or our own sins will not be forgiven, and according to this scripture it seems, we will miss heaven.

What the New Testament Says About Hell

- Matthew 23:27 says: "Woe to you, teachers of the law and Pharisees, you hypocrites! You are like whitewashed tombs, which look beautiful on the outside, but on the inside is full of dead man's bones and everything unclean. In the same way, on the outside you appear to people as righteous but on the inside you full of hypocrisy and wickedness."
- In Matthew 23:33 Jesus condemned them: "You snakes! You brood of vipers! How will you escape being condemned to hell?"
- Matthew 25:27-29 says: "Well then, you should have put my money on deposit with the bankers, so that when I returned I

would have received it back with interest. Take the talent from him and give it to the one who has the ten talents. For everyone who has will be given more and he will have abundance. Whoever does not have, even what he has will be taken from him. And throw that worthless servant outside into the darkness, where they will be weeping and gnashing of teeth."

- Matthew 25: 41 says: "Depart from me, you who are cursed, into the eternal fire prepared for the devil and his angels. For I was and you gave me nothing to eat, I was thirsty and you gave me nothing to drink." They also will answer, "Lord, when did we see you hungry or thirsty or a stranger or needing clothes or sick or in prison, and did not help you?" He will reply, "I tell you the truth, whatever you did not do for one of the least of these, you did not do for Me. Then they will go away to eternal punishment, but the righteous to eternal life."

- Luke 16:19 says: "There was a rich man who was dressed in purple and fine linen and lived in luxury every day. At his gate was laid a beggar named Lazarus, covered with sores and longing to eat what fell from the rich man's table. The time came when the beggar died and the angels carried him to Abraham's side. The rich man also died and was buried. In hell where he was in torment, he looked up and saw Abraham far away, with Lazarus by his side. So he called to him, "Father Abraham, have pity on me and send Lazarus to dip the tip of his finger in water and cool my tongue, because I am in agony in this fire." But Abraham replied, "Son, remember that in your lifetime you received your good things, while Lazarus received bad things, but now he is comforted here and you are in agony."

What the Old Testament Says About Hell

- Deuteronomy 32:21–22 says: "They have moved me to jealousy with that which is not God; they have provoked me to anger with their vanities...For a fire is kindled in mine anger, and shall burn unto the lowest hell and shall consume the earth with her increase, and set on fire the foundations of the mountains."

- Psalm 9:17 says: "The wicked shall be turned into hell, and all the nations that forget God."

- Isaiah 5:11,14 says: "Woe unto them that rise up early in the morning, that they may follow strong drink; that continue until night, till wine inflame them! They regard not the work of the Lord. Therefore hell hath enlarged herself, and opened her mouth without measure: and their glory, and their multitude, and their pomp, and he that rejoices, shall descend down into it."

- Isaiah 13:6 says: "Wail, for the day of the Lord is at hand! It will come as destruction from the Almighty. Therefore all hands will be limp, every man's heart will melt, and they will be afraid. Pangs and sorrows will take hold of them; they will be in pain as a woman in childbirth; they will be amazed at one another; their faces will be like flames. Behold, the day of the Lord comes, cruel, with both wrath and fierce anger to lay the land desolate. And He will destroy its sinners from it."

- Isaiah 66:24 says: "And they shall go forth, and look upon the carcasses of the men that have transgressed against me: for their worm shall not die, neither shall their fire be quenched; nor they shall be an abhorring unto all flesh."

What the Bible Says About Hell and Adultery

- Proverbs 5:3–5 says: "for the lips of a strange woman drops as a honeycomb, and her mouth is smoother than oil: But her end is bitter as wormwood, sharp as a two–edged sword. Her feet go down to death; her steps take hold on hell."

- Proverbs 7:27 says: "A woman with the attire of a harlot, her house is the way to hell going down to the chambers of death."

- Proverbs 6:23 says: "Reproofs and instruction are the way of life, to keep you from the evil woman, from the flattering tongue or a seductress. Do not lust after her beauty in your heart, nor let her allure you with her eyelids. For by means of a harlot a man is reduced to a crust of bread; and an adulteress will prey upon his precious life. Can a man take fire to his bosom and not be burned?",,,"Whoever commits adultery with a woman lacks understanding; He who does so destroys his own soul."

- Proverbs 9: 13 – 18 says: "A foolish woman is clamorous: she is simple and knows nothing. Whoso is simple, let him turn in hither (to her house)…She says to him, "stolen waters are sweet, and bread eaten in secret is pleasant." But he knows not that the dead are there; and that her guests are in the depth of hell."

- Proverbs 27:20 says: "Hell and destruction are never full; so the eyes of man are never satisfied.

If They Have Doubts There is a Hell and a Heaven

If you find someone who doubts there is a hell, tell them about the people who have died and gone there and have come back to life to testify about what they saw. They all say the same thing: flames of fire, darkness, torments, horror, screaming and worms that eat their flesh. Since all of their testimonies concur, we know that hell is really there and what they have all said is true. Many have died and gone to heaven as well. These following people all have written books about their experiences in Hell and also in Heaven:

- Bill Wiese wrote his book, *23 Minutes in Hell*. You can buy his book at Barnes and Noble.

- Mary Baxter wrote *Divine Revelation of Hell* and also: *Divine Revelation of Heaven* (both by Whitaker House).

- Kenneth E. Hagin wrote: *I Went to Hell* – He was a church member, but was not saved and went to hell before he got born again and started his ministry. See: www.rhema.org

- Ian McCormack was stung by a jellyfish and went to hell and wrote a book called *Glimpse of Eternity.*

- Dr. Richard Eby wrote his book *Caught Up Into Paradise* after he went to hell in a brush with death. Later this physician tells about how he also went to heaven.

- The book *Heaven Is Beyond Your Wildest Expectations* - compiled by Sid Roth & Lonnie Lane – contains 10 true stories of people who have been to heaven.

- Dr. Gary L Wood wrote *A Place Called Heaven* about his trip to heaven and back when he died in a car wreck.

Ways to Increase Your Compassion for the Lost

Cast your cares upon the Lord, so that when you are standing in line anywhere, whether that is at the gas station or at the grocery store or in line to buy tickets somewhere, you will not be thinking about your own problems. Instead you will be free to think about whether the people in front of you or behind you in line or the checkout person are born again or not.

Think about your own life and how you have suffered. Have you ever been broken hearted or divorced? Ever been in great financial distress? Ever have a mother or father die young? Or ever have a child die? Ever had a problem with alcohol or drugs or suicidal thoughts? You should have compassion for those who are suffering in the same way or in the same areas that you did. So then you can tell them your testimony of how Jesus Christ helped you through it all and delivered you to give them hope. Tell them that God loves them and Jesus can deliver them too. That is not hard to do.

Be sure to leave "margins in your schedule." What I mean is, leave 15–20 minutes early for any appointment that you may have. It gives God time to use you whether you are running an errand, going to the store, a doctor's appointment or wherever. If you make a habit of this, it will give you TIME to witness wherever you go. Most of the time, that is why God cannot use Christians to witness to the lost. They are in too much of a hurry to stop and listen to people. Hurting people need a compassionate ear that will listen to them. Much can be done for the Kingdom of God if Christians will just leave margins in their schedule. I am preaching to myself as well.

It is hard to have compassion for others when you are tired. It is harder to walk in love and forgive and walk in the fruits of the spirit when you are tired as well. So to increase your compassion, make sure that you get enough sleep. Rest is important so you'll have strength to do His will. Remember that God's yoke is easy and His burden is light (Matthew 11:28).

CHAPTER THREE

Creating Courage in
Christians to Witness to the Lost

Our compassion must override our fears of witnessing. We should not take witnessing lightly. It is a matter of eternal life and death. Joel 3:14 says, "Multitudes, multitudes in the valley of decision! For the day of the Lord is near in the valley of decision." That multitude is about four billion people who are still not Christian believers. We have a lot of work to do.

This is no time to fear. Fearing rejection by people and "peer pressure" will keep you from witnessing. But the truth is they themselves will face the ultimate rejection by Almighty God if they do not pray to receive Jesus Christ as their Lord and Savior. Someone must tell them about the Gospel and the Good News. We must stand on the Word when witnessing:

Isaiah 41:10 says: "Fear not, for I am with you; Be not dismayed, for I am your God. I will strengthen you, Yes, I will help you, I will uphold you with My righteous right hand." If you can watch a scary movie, go on a roller coaster or play a violent video game, then you have the courage to witness to the lost. Think about it. You have done other things that are scary. Keep in mind that fear comes from the enemy to keep you from witnessing. The devil wants everyone to go to hell

Men and Women of God, Be Courageous! Be Warriors for God!

Men want to be courageous. They want to be heroes. They want to be warriors fighting for justice to be done. So they often fulfill these competitive desires through playing sports whether that are football, basketball, baseball or soccer, etc. Or they may play the sport vicariously by watching on TV. Men like to watch war, action and adventurous movies because men are called to be warriors. But men (and women) are really called to be warriors for God. They need to know how to war against the principalities, powers and rulers of darkness. The way to spiritually war is to know how to fight against the enemy's lies and use the sword of the spirit or the Word of God to tell people the truth that will set them free.

If you want to be a true warrior for God, then learn how to combat these lies that lost people believe and learn the truth to say and witness to the lost. Snatching someone from the fires of hell is the highest form of warfare that there is. Witnessing to the lost is an adventure. Many times there is drama and there is action. Don't fear witnessing to the lost. When you witness to the lost, it makes God smile. God receives so much JOY when one sinner is saved from hell and you will too.

In 2 Timothy 2:1–4 it says: "You therefore, my son, be strong in the grace that is in Christ Jesus. And the things that you have heard from me among many witnesses, commit these to faithful men who will be able to teach others also. You therefore must endure hardship as a good soldier of Jesus Christ. No one engaged in warfare entangles himself with the affairs of this life, that he may please him who enlisted him as a soldier."

The two main hindrances to witnessing are based on fear. The first hindrance is the fear of talking to people. The second hindrance is the fear of not knowing what to say. After you read this book, you will have the courage to witness. You can renew your mind through reading and memorizing scriptures that will encourage you to overcome your fears as well. You can renew your mind through singing songs that have scriptures in them too. The following scriptures will help you overcome your fears of witnessing and give your courage:

Faith–Filled Courageous Scriptures

- Isaiah 41:10: "Fear not, for I Am with you. Be not dismayed, for I Am your God. I will strengthen you. Yes, I will help you; I will uphold you with My righteous right hand."

- Proverbs 28:1 says: "the righteous are as bold as a lion." It does not say that the extroverts are bold. It says the righteous are bold. We need to stir up this boldness because Jesus is coming soon.

- 2 Timothy 1:7: "For God has not give you a spirit of fear, but of power, love and a sound mind."

- Matthew 10:28: Jesus said to His disciples, "Do not be afraid of those who kill the body, but cannot kill the soul. Rather be afraid of the One who can destroy both soul and body in hell.

- Matthew 10: 32– 33: Jesus says, "Whoever disowns Me before men, I will disown him before my Father in heaven."

- 1 John 4:18: There is no fear in love. But perfect love drives out fear, fear has to do with punishment. The one who fears is not made perfect in love.

- Romans 8:15: For you did not receive a spirit that makes you a slave again to fear, but you received the Spirit of sonship. And by Him we cry, "Abba Father."

- 1 Peter 3:13-14: Who is going to harm you if you are eager to do good? But even if you should suffer for what is right, you are blessed. "Do not fear what they fear; do not be frightened."

- Isaiah 51:7: "Listen to Me, you who know righteousness, you people whose heart is My law; Do not fear the reproach of men. Nor be afraid of their insults."

Psalms & Proverbs That Will Inspire You to Witness

- Psalm 27:1 - The Lord is my light and my salvation. Whom shall I fear?"

- Psalm 56:11 - In God I have put my trust: I will not be afraid what man can do to me."

- Psalm 118:6 - The Lord is on my side; I will not fear. What can man do to me?"

- Proverbs 29:25 - The fear of man brings a snare, but whoso puts his trust in the Lord shall be safe."

- Proverbs 11:25 – A word fitly spoken is like apples of gold in settings of silver.

- Proverbs 11:30 – The fruit of the righteous is a tree of life and He who wins souls is wise.

- Proverbs 14:25 – A true witness delivers souls.

- Proverbs 15:23 – A man has joy by the answer of his mouth. And a word spoken in due season, how good it is!

- Proverbs 15:28 – The heart of the righteous studies how to answer, but the mouth of the wicked pours forth evil.

- Proverbs 16:1 – The preparations of the heart belong to man. But the answer of the tongue is from the Lord.

- Proverbs 24:26 – He who gives a right answer kisses the lips.

CHAPTER FOUR

It Takes Prayer
To Win the Lost

Prayer is needed to win the lost. I have been a partner at Oral Roberts ministries for over twelve years now, so I know that prayer is needed to win the lost because it is a spiritual battle. The Bible says: *"We do not wrestle against flesh and blood, but against principalities, powers and rulers of darkness.* (2 Corinthians 10:3–6). Most Christians have a fear of witnessing to the lost, but 2 Timothy 1:7 says, **"For God has not given us a spirit of fear, but of power, love, and a sound mind."** Since fear is a spirit, it must be bound in the name of Jesus Christ. You must take authority over it.

Pray for Yourself

Say this with authority: **"I bind the spirit of fear over me and I loose upon me a compassion for the lost, a boldness to witness, the power of God, the love of God, and a sound mind in the name of Jesus Christ."**

Now that you are free from fear and spiritually ready to witness, you need to bind the strong man that is coming against the unbeliever. If you know the specific stronghold, then bind it using the name of Jesus Christ.

Pray for the Unbeliever

Say with authority: **"I bind the god of this world that is blinding their eyes to salvation in the name of Jesus Christ."** (2 Corinthians 4:4)

Then pray with authority and confidence: **"I loose upon them revelation that Jesus Christ is the way, the truth and the life and there is no way to heaven, but through Him and I loose revelation about Ephesians 2:8–9 that we are saved from hell by grace though faith in the shed blood of Jesus Christ on the cross at Calvary and not through works, so that no man can boast in the name of Jesus Christ."** Loose upon them **revelation that the salvation is a gift from God bought with the blood of Jesus Christ.**

If you have time, pray the Ephesians prayers over the unbeliever or your unsaved loved ones. (It is good to pray these over yourself as well!) Just insert the unbeliever's name in the blank.

1st Ephesians Prayer from Ephesians 1:17–20:

"Heavenly Father, I pray that You will give _____the spirit of wisdom and revelation in the knowledge of Christ, the eyes of _____'s understanding will be enlightened and that _____will know the hope of His calling, what are the riches of the glory of His inheritance in the saints, and what is the exceeding greatness of His power towards us who believe, according to the working of His mighty power which He worked in Christ when He raised Him from the dead and seated Him at His own right hand in the heavenly places, far above all principality and power and might and dominion, and every name that is named, not only in this age, but also in that which is to come. In Jesus' name, Amen."

2nd Ephesians Prayer from Ephesians 3:16–21:

"Heavenly Father, I pray that You will grant_____ according to the riches of Your glory, to be strengthened with might through His Spirit in the inner man, that Christ may dwell in _____'s heart through faith; that _____being rooted and grounded in love, may be able to comprehend with all the saints what is the width and length and depth and height – *to know the love of Christ* which passes knowledge; that _____ may be filled with all the fullness of God. Now to Him who is able to do exceedingly abundantly above all that we ask or think, according to the power that works in us, to Him be glory in the church by Christ Jesus to all generations, forever and ever in Jesus name I pray, Amen."

Understand Your Authority in Christ

I must emphasize that when you pray, it is vitally important to understand the supreme authority of Jesus Christ. You also must understand that when He rose from the dead and then ascended to heaven, He delegated that same authority to us Christians here on earth. He is the head and we are His body and He has placed all things under His feet and so they are under our feet as well.

Ephesians 2:6 says that, "He has raised us up together and made us sit together in the heavenly places with Christ Jesus."

That means spiritually we are seated together with the same authority as Jesus Christ. We may be here on earth, but Jesus Christ has given us His heavenly authority, or His seat of authority, to use here on earth to continue to do the works of Jesus and to destroy the works of the devil. In John 14:12 Jesus said, "Most assuredly, I say to you, he who believes in Me, the works that I do he will do also, and greater works than these he will do, because I go to My Father."

In Luke 10:19 Jesus said, "Behold, I give you the authority to trample on serpents and scorpions, and over all the power that the enemy possesses, and nothing shall by any means hurt you."

You may wonder, "How in the world do I have the same authority as Jesus Christ?" It is because He has given us His Name to use. This is similar to one having power of attorney.

Jesus said in John 14:12: "Most assuredly I say to you, he who believes in Me, the works that I do he will do also; and greater works than these he will do, because I go to My Father. And whatever you *ask in My name*, that will I do, that My Father may be glorified in the Son. If you ask anything *in My name*, I will do it. If you love Me, keep My commandments."

Colossians 2:15 says, "Having disarmed principalities and powers, He made a public spectacle of them, triumphing over them in it." It is like Jesus took the all the spiritual guns and weapons away the devil and his demons. The devil uses lies as weapons to try and destroy us, but God's truth sets us free.

2 Corinthians 10:4-5 basically says to 'Cast down imaginations" that go against God's Word. Then you imagine the truth in God's Word so you can walk in your God-ordained authority through Christ. For example:

Imagine yourself as a policeman that can give demons tickets for coming against you in the spirit realm. In the name of Jesus Christ, you bind the demons in handcuffs.

Imagine yourself as a soldier in the Army of the Lord. When you bind demonic spirits in the name of Jesus Christ, it is like you are tying them up and holding them hostage. As a soldier, you shoot down the lies of the enemy quoting the Word of God and replace those lies with the truth from God's Word.

Imagine yourself as a teacher. In the name of Jesus Christ you bind the spirits of lawlessness, disrespect and disobedience and loose upon your students obedient hearts that submit to authority and the rules and do their work. When you speak the Word of God or speak out scripture in prayer, your are using your sword of the spirit, and so then angels move and go to work on your behalf.

The Devil's Tactic is Condemnation: "You Did It Wrong!"

After you witness to someone, condemnation is one of the devil's tactics. When they do not get saved, afterwards it seems that you can always think of what you should have said that was better. You need to trust that what you said was the best that you could do under the circumstances of possibly several demonic spirits (for e.g., fear of man, witchcraft, anti–Christ spirits) coming against you to stop you and the truth–filled words from going forth. Just believe that you did the best that you could have done at the time. There is always room for improvement. No one is perfect. You just do the best that you can. That is all that God expects from you. He is pleased that you are trying to witness because 95% of Christians do not do it! Remember that it is the devil that condemns you that you are no good at witnessing! Why does he do this? Because the truth is, you were effective and the truth you were speaking was having an impact and the person is now closer to getting saved than he/she was before. You planted good seeds in their heart for the next Christian to come along and water.

The devil condemns you to discourage you so that you will not witness anymore because he knows you were good. Romans 8:1 says there is therefore "No condemnation for those who are in Christ Jesus." Do not fall for the enemy's lies. If you have just witnessed to someone, then pat yourself on the back and say:

"I did a good job! I did my best! God is pleased that I tried and stepped out in faith to witness him. The Holy Spirit can rewind, edit and play again what I said. So, shut up, devil! You are a defeated foe!"

CHAPTER FIVE

I Want to Witness,
But <u>How</u> Do I Say It?

How you witness, can be even more important than what you say. Of course, I encourage you to use one of the object evangelism icebreakers in the following pages to get you started. If you don't know how to transition or segue the conversation onto the Gospel track, you will not be witnessing at all. So once, you get started and have successfully transitioned the conversation onto the Gospel track, then you must listen to what they say and use wisdom for your next reply. You may have heard it often preached that Christians need to walk in love and walk in the fruits of the spirit. Well, this is doubly important when you are witnessing to unbelievers. Since you are going against an anti–Christ spirit, it can be doubly hard to walk in love. The way you witness, or the tone of voice you use, can be as important as to what you actually say. So when you pick up an object and start talking about how it relates to the Gospel, be sure to be kind and respectful. Use compassionate boldness. Use a loving and gentle tone of voice and be sensitive as to how you speak your words. Your tone of voice can be used by the Lord as well and it can be even more important than the words that you say.

Sometimes the demons in the unbeliever will cause them to say some pretty hateful things, so you have to learn to quickly forgive and respond in a loving tone of voice instead of reacting in an angry way. Just doing this will witness to them because they expect you to react angrily and retaliate back at them or walk angrily away. Remember what Jesus said on the cross:

"Father, forgive them for they know not what they do."

Unbelievers will act like their father, the devil, because he is from the kingdom of darkness. So do not take anything personal. When an unbeliever rejects you, they are not rejecting you, but the spirit of God that resides on the inside of you. They are rejecting the Lord Jesus Christ.

Use the Fruits of the Spirit When Witnessing

Galatians 5:22 says, "But the fruit of the spirit is love, joy, peace, longsuffering, kindness, goodness, faithfulness, gentleness and self-control." Let's look at these more closely.

LOVE -- It is so important to walk in love when you are witnessing to the lost because God is love, so witnessing with the love of God is how you should witness if you want to truly be His Ambassador and represent Him well. The love of God will break down walls around their heart. Also when you witness to the lost, they may not be very kind, so remember Matthew 5:44, which says to "Love your enemies and pray for those who persecute you." They will know we are Christians by our love. "Love is patient, love is kind, it does not envy, it does not boast, it is not proud. It is not rude, it is not self– seeking, it is not easily angered, and it keeps no record of wrongs. Love does not delight in evil, but rejoices with the truth. Love bears all things, believes all things, hopes all things, endures all things. Love never fails. (1 Corinthians 13:4–8)."

JOY (gladness) -- People are attracted to joyful people because they want that same joy in their dull dreary lives. You should try to witness to others with a spirit of joy about you. It says in Romans 14:17 that "the Kingdom of God is righteousness, peace and joy in the Holy Ghost." It says in Proverbs 15:23: "A man finds joy in giving an apt reply and how good is a timely word."

PEACE -- Walking in peace when other unbelievers around you know that you are going through tough trials is a great witness. You can tell them that: "I'm casting my cares upon the Lord because I know He cares for me" (1 Peter 5:7) or "God keeps me in perfect peace because my thoughts are focused on Him and His faithfulness. I trust in Him to work out my troubles." (Isaiah 26:3). They will want that same peace that you have.

LONG SUFFERING   (patience) – Many times you have to be patient with those neighbors that you witness to until they fully commit their lives to Christ to live for Him. Keep praying for them and loving them unconditionally. Remember that many times unbelievers do not have a clue about the love of their Heavenly Father. Many have a lot of pain, disappointments and heartbreak from their past. Many people sin to cover up, soothe or escape their pain and their past. They do not know any other way, but the truth about God's love and His mercy and grace will set them free.

GENTLENESS (kindness) – When witnessing to a person who gets uptight or irritated, it says in Proverbs 15:1 "A gentle answer turns away wrath, but a harsh word stirs up anger." Proverbs 25:15 says, "Through patience a ruler can be persuaded and a gentle tongue can break a bone." Isaiah 40:11 gives a picture of how the Lord Jesus is with his sheep: "He shall gather the lambs in His arm and carry them in his bosom and shall gently lead those that are with young."

GOODNESS (benevolence) -- Bringing food to an unsaved person will speak volumes to them about God's love. People do not care about what you know until they know how much you care. So doing good deeds for unsaved people will do much to spread the Gospel. In Matthew 25:40 Jesus said: "Whatever you did for the least of these brothers of mine, you did for Me."

FAITH (faithfulness) – After you witness to someone, many times you have to have faith that God is working in their hearts even though they may not show it on their faces. Many people wear masks because of pride. They do not want you to know that the words you are saying are cracking open their hardened hearts. Have faith that the Lord is working in their hearts. Stand on Isaiah 55:11: "So shall my word be that goes forth out of my mouth; It shall not return unto me void, but it shall accomplish that which I please and it shall prosper in the thing where to I sent it."

MEEKNESS (gentleness, humility) - Galatians 6:1 says: "Brethren, if a man be overtaken in a fault, ye which are spiritual, restore such a one in the spirit of meekness; considering thyself, lest thou also be tempted." Remember John 15:5 and "Abide in Jesus, the Vine." Be quick to listen and slow to speak (James 1:19). Listen to the Holy Spirit for the words you are to say to each person you witness to because Jesus said in John 15:5, "for without Me you can do nothing."

TEMPERANCE (self–control, self–restraint) -- Sometimes while witnessing, the demons in the unbelievers will try to make you upset and angry so that you will leave them alone and not bother them anymore. If you are called a hypocrite or ugly words are spoken, it is so tempting to want to retaliate. But if you want to be a godly witness, you have to use self–control through humbling yourself and forgiving them. You may have to be silent and say nothing for several seconds to cool down. Then you can walk in love and respond in a loving peaceful way instead of repaying evil for evil. Remember that Romans 12:19–21 says, "Beloved, avenge not yourselves, but rather give place unto wrath: for it is written, "Vengeance is Mine; I will repay," says the Lord. Therefore if your enemy hungers, feed him; if he thirsts, give him drink: for in so doing you shall heap coals of fire on his head (killing him with kindness). Be not overcome with evil, but overcome evil with good."

When Witnessing, Be Quick to Forgive!

When witnessing to an unbeliever, it is important to walk in temperance because they very well may offend you. Like I said earlier, it is so important to be quick to forgive, especially when they say something slanderous or falsely accuse God or your favorite preacher or pastor. If you quickly forgive their slanderous remark, then you can still witness to them and help them see the truth about God's love. As a prayer partner at Oral Roberts Ministries, once in a while, a caller will be offended at something *even before* I get on the phone with them. Perhaps they were offended they had to wait so long for prayer. So when they say something rude to me, I quickly forgive them. Then I am able to be loving and kind and pray an anointed prayer over them in response to their prayer request.

In order to be an effective evangelist for the Lord, you must also learn to quickly forgive. When you forgive, you are not letting them off the hook. You are actually putting them on *God's* hook and allowing God to deal with them instead of you. When you forgive you take the situation **OUT** of your weak hands and you put the situation **IN** God's strong mighty hands and let Him handle it all and right the wrongs that have been done to you.

Remember that vengeance is the Lord's and He will repay (Romans 12:19). Also remember Matthew 6:14: "You must forgive others that sin against you, falsely accuse you or slander you if you want God to forgive you of your own sins."

I know that the truth of the Gospel itself can be an offense to people because they do not want to change or repent of their sins. So do not feel condemned if they get mad or offended at you. If you witness with the love of God, in a gentle tone of voice you may be able to ward off their offense. It depends on the person. Just remember Proverbs 18:19 says that "a brother offended is harder to win than a city," so do your best to present the Gospel in a way that will not offend people. Just do your best. That is all that you can do. Do not be discouraged and stop witnessing because someone got offended. That is what the devil wants you to do – to just quit! So don't quit. Keep on witnessing. Keep on doing good. God will reward you.

"I'm OK. I'm Good."

There are some people you will meet who have no understanding of their sin. They say, "I'm good. I'm OK." But they need to see that they are *guilty* of their sins, so that they will see and understand their desperate need for a Savior.

Many people think they are "good enough" to make it into heaven because they compare their godliness to others around them who have committed gross sin, like murdering someone or robbing a bank, etc. Comparing their lives to other people around them has become "the standard" in their minds and hearts to judge whether they are good enough for heaven or not.

Preach the Law to Reveal Their Sin

Others may believe that their standard is their own self–righteousness. In short, they measure themselves by man's standard. The devil has blinded people's minds as to what is the true standard by which God judges us. The Lord judges us by what the Word of God says.

This is why Ray Comfort says, **"The preaching of the Law is the devil's best kept secret."** The devil knows that if he can keep people from really understanding that **the Law is the true standard that God judges us by**, not other people around us, then the devil can deceive many people who will think they are "good enough" and they will miss heaven. If the person you are witnessing to is burdened by the guilt of his sin, then he doesn't need awakening to his sin. He knows he has committed sin and he needs a Savior.

If the person you are witnessing to has no understanding of their sin, then a wonderful solution is to use the Law to help them see and understand that they have indeed committed sins that will send them to hell and they have need of a Savior who will forgive them of their sins. You may wonder, how do I do that? Well, you just ask them some questions based on the Law from the Ten Commandments.

Using the Ten Commandments

When they say: "Yeah, I'm good enough."

Then ask them: "So what standard are you going by to judge whether you are good enough? The Bible says that God uses the Law as His standard to judge people as to whether they are worthy or not to make it into heaven."

The Ten Commandments as Found in Exodus 20 Are:

1. You shall have no other gods before Me.
2. You shall not make for yourself any carved image.
3. You shall not take the name of the Lord your God in vain. (That means no cursing)
4. Remember the Sabbath day, to keep it holy.
5. Honor your mother and father.
6. You shall not murder.
7. You shall not commit adultery. Tell them Matthew 5:28 Jesus said, "Whoever looks at a woman to lust for her has already committed adultery with her in his heart."
8. You shall not steal.
9. You shall not bear false witness against your neighbor. In other words, don't lie.
10. You shall not covet. (This means to not be jealous or greedy of another's possessions, but you should be content)

It says in James 2:10 "For whoever shall keep the whole law, and yet stumble in one point, he is guilty of all." Ask the person who thinks they are "good" questions based on the 10 Commandments:

- Have you ever stolen anything, like a paperclip or a pen?
- Have you ever told a lie?
- *To men*: Have you ever lusted after a woman?
- Have you ever taken God's name in vain, or have you ever cursed?
- Have you ever dishonored your mother or father?

When they realize they have sinned and must answer "Yes" to at least one of the questions and realize their guilt, then you can tell them that they deserve to go to hell for that because of James 2:10 repeating the scripture again: "For whoever shall keep the whole law, and yet stumble in one point, he is guilty of all."

Watch their expression. Some do not even believe in hell. If that is their response, then read the section: "If They Doubt There is a Hell" on page 21.

Then when they see the reality of hell and that because of their sin, they will go there and when you see the fear in their eyes, tell them about how God loves them. Tell them that God loves us all so much that He sent His Son Jesus who willingly went to the cross and shed His holy blood that paid the price for our sins and reconciled us back to God, so that we could have eternal life in heaven.

Soul Winning Script

There are several methods and techniques to witness to the lost. In 2009 I went to a Rodney Howard–Browne Revival Outreach in Oklahoma City, OK and I learned about his "Soul Winning Script", which is very effective if you are a bold witness. I found that I could use an icebreaker from my book and then use his script afterwards to win the lost. For the script, go to: www.revival.com.

CHAPTER SIX

Testimonies that Show "Yes, It Works!"

People have asked me, but does this work? Yes, of course it works! If you overcome your fears and do say the object evangelism icebreaker to an unbeliever, it will work in transitioning a conversation onto the Gospel track. You **will** segue the conversation. It surely does work.

The following are several testimonies of people who have received Jesus as their Lord and Savior after using one of these object evangelism icebreakers. Keep in mind that some people plant, some water and some reap the harvest. (1 Corinthians 3:6). After using one these object evangelism icebreakers, whether or not the person prays to receive Jesus as their Lord really depends on whether their hearts are ready. Praying beforehand can really help. If you are led by the spirit to say the right thing and answer their questions after you say the initial object evangelism icebreaker, then you will greatly increase the probability of the unbeliever receiving Jesus as their Lord and Savior. The chapter called: "Truth to Say to

13 False Religions" will help you know how to answer many of their questions. Here are several testimonies on the next few pages.

A Teenager Walking Down the Street

One day my husband painted our front door a pretty maroon color. I really liked it. I saw a young man walking slowly down our street and yelled out to him. "My husband just painted our front door! So what do you think?" He walked closer and replied. "It looks nice." Then I said, "But you know, Jesus Christ is the most important DOOR you will ever walk through. Have you ever walked through that door?" DeAndre replied. "I remember you. I knew you were going to say something like that about God. You talked to me about God when I was nine years old when my Dad came over and fixed your ceiling fan." I said, "Oh my gosh! I remember now!" He ashamedly looked down and continued, "But now I'm 17 now and I got in trouble and now I'm on probation Sigh. I guess it is time to turn my life over to Him." Then he prayed a salvation prayer after me and got saved!

A Neighbor in an Idling Sports Car

One sunny day, my husband David cut down a tall tree because its branches were hanging over our roof and its stray branches were still all over the yard. A high school grad named Manny came by in a fancy sports car with the top down his music blaring across the street. He was waiting for his friend. I went over to the idling car and said, "My husband just cut down that tree. Did you know that your life can be cut down - just like that tree - in an instant?" He was sober and sad because a friend of his recently got shot and killed by a policeman when she drove the "get-away car" involved in a robbery. We talked about it. He did not know if the girl was born again or not. Because you never know when your last day on earth will be, I encouraged him to pray with me now. He was ripe and ready. Then he repeated a salvation prayer after me and received Jesus as His Lord and Savior! What a glorious day that was. My husband felt like that saved soul made it all worth the hard work of cutting down that tree!

Wrigley's Customer Service Rep

I called Wrigley's to find out where I could buy those mini life saver rolls for my Halloween tracts because I could not find them in any store. After the customer service lady told me they were discontinued, I asked her: "So is Jesus your life saver?" She replied: "Well, no..." like it had never really occurred to her before. Then I explained to her the Gospel and she prayed a salvation prayer after me and got born again! I think my desire to find that mini lifesavers size was because of her. She was ripe and ready to be saved and God knew she would answer the phone.

My Auto Insurance Agent

One time I went by my auto insurance office to ask my agent named John a question about my policy. Then I asked him if he had life insurance – for all eternity? I told him that was the most important assurance to have – where you will spend eternity. He said he didn't go to church, but he was open to receive Jesus as His Lord. No one had really asked him about it before. So right then and there, he prayed a salvation prayer after me and got gloriously saved! I was so excited! He was on cloud nine that whole day and said, "If I had known how wonderful it feels to be saved, I would have done it a lot sooner." He was 40 years ago.

A Convenience Store Clerk

I witnessed every week to a dark–skinned man who owned a convenience store within the mall who believed that he was already saved though works and had not prayed to receive Christ as His Lord and Savior. Knowing what he thought and since he was a storeowner, I focused on the obvious – buying and selling. I said to him: "The reason why you cannot buy salvation through good works is because people do not have equal abilities to do good works. So that is not fair to achieve salvation through good works. God is fair and He is just. You see, people have different gifts and talents, different levels of intelligence, different levels of athletic ability and come from different socio– economic backgrounds. But no matter what, God knows that everyone has the ability to believe whatever he or she chooses. So when a person chooses to believe in and receive Jesus Christ as their Lord and Savior – that He died on the cross for their sins and rose from the dead – then they shall receive this free gift of eternal life." He was still hesitating, so I went on: "I know that you stumble over the fact that "salvation is free" and that there are no works involved to obtain it, but let me tell you something, After you receive Jesus Christ as your Lord, following Christ and wholeheartedly obeying Him will cost you everything. There are things that He will ask you to give up in order to serve Him." So after planting several seeds, he finally got it and prayed a salvation prayer to ask Jesus Christ to be His Lord and Savior!

Praise God! Hallelujah! Then a few weeks later, his store moved out of the mall and I haven't seen him since.

A 17 Year Old Who Could Not Vote Yet

One time I was campaigning for a man running for Mayor and I was going door–to–door passing out "Get out the Vote" material. I knocked on one door and a young man answered. He said that his parents were not home and he was only 17. Then the spirit of the Lord compelled me to witness to him. So I told him I was taking off "my political hat" and putting on my own personal hat. He understood. Then I told him that God wants him to spend eternity in heaven with Him, but in order to do that, you have to "vote for Jesus" and ask Jesus to come into your heart and be your Lord and Savior. He said he was brought up a Catholic, but had never prayed a salvation prayer and his parents did not go to church. He agreed to pray a salvation prayer with me right there and got saved! His face brightened and he said he felt joy in his heart. I encouraged him to try to go to church with a friend. He said he did have a couple friends that he could go to Youth group with. I was so glad. It is so important to get teenagers in a good Youth Group at church. They need good godly peer pressure in these last days where there is so much evil running rampant in our schools.

My Mortgage Broker

Another time, I was talking on the phone with my mortgage broker and he asked me what I did for a living. When I told him I was a prayer partner, he was amazed that I pray on the phone for a living. (Well, I don't get paid very much!). I could tell he was not saved. Then I told him that the buyer always wants to buy a house in the right location, but the most important thing is to make sure that your home for all eternity is in the right location. He agreed. I explained the Gospel to him and asked him if he would like to pray a salvation prayer after me. After talking with him a little while longer, he agreed. It was a divine appointment. He repeated a salvation prayer after me over the phone. He was 42. I encouraged him to go to church. He said that he would go with his neighbor who was a Christian.

Four Children at the Mall

One time I witnessed to four children, ranging in ages from eight to thirteen. I started off by saying, "Jesus loves the little children. Jesus said, "Let the children come to me, for of such is the Kingdom of God (Matthew 19:14)." I really thought they were Catholic because they told me that they thought that you were saved by works. The grand father, who was watching them while their mother was away shopping, did not speak any English. But the children all did. It was a divine appointment. Then I explained the whole Gospel to them in about ten minutes. They even asked questions and I answered them. Then they all prayed a prayer of salvation after me! Praise God! Hallelujah! I was rejoicing! I gave them little books about their "New Life" in Christ and got their names and address to follow up as well.

A Motorcycle Dirt Bike Racer at Quik Trip

I ministered to a man at a gas station called **Quik Trip.** I told him, "When Jesus comes again; it will be *a quick trip.*" He was convicted of his sins and looked down. He said that he was from Indiana, but he was here in Tulsa for a motorcycle dirt bike race and he knew that he needed divine protection. He ashamedly said that he knew the gospel, but he had never taken the time or made the commitment to ask Jesus Christ to come into his heart. There are so many people who grew up in church and never made a commitment to receive Jesus as Lord. This is why "children's church" or Sunday school is so important. It breaks down the gospel for children so they can understand it. Anyway, this man realized his sin and repented and repeated a salvation prayer after me. He became born again! I was so elated because that night he *finally* received Jesus Christ as his Lord and Savior! I knew that the angels in heaven were rejoicing too.

A Fan of My Alma Mater – UNC

Another guy I witnessed to at this park where I like to go running was wearing a Carolina blue UNC baseball hat. He was seventeen. I said: "I like your hat! I love the University of North Carolina. I graduated from there in 1992. It reminds me of home. I moved to Tulsa in 1993 to go to RHEMA Bible Training College so saying that I moved to Tulsa to go to *Bible School* got me onto the Gospel track. Then I said, "I learned a lot of things at Bible School. One thing I learned is that a lot of people have heard the Gospel and they know it, but they have never prayed to make a commitment to receive Jesus Christ their Lord and really live for Him."

As we talked, I realized that he was one of those! He knew the Gospel, but had never prayed that salvation prayer. So that day, he repeated a prayer after me and got saved! Praise God! Hallelujah! He said he was going to go to church next Sunday. Sharing about how you "kept your faith in college" is a good way to segue.

A Salvation During My Lunch Break

I witnessed to a guy during my thirty minute lunch break. I went around the corner to Quik Trip and popped my hood because my car was running hot. This guy named Jason put some coolant in for me. I was so thankful for this favor and for his kindness. I was in a hurry so I quickly said, *"Thank you so much for doing me this favor and for helping me! You are so nice that I want you to go to heaven! Do you know how much Jesus loves you?* Have you ever prayed and asked him to be your Lord and Savior?" Jason was in his early twenties and he looked like he was saved because he was clean cut, etc, but God looks on the heart. He said he had never really been to church and had never prayed a salvation prayer. I could barely believe it. So I quickly told him the four spiritual laws. He thoughtfully listened like he was hearing them for the first time. Then I asked him if he would like to pray a salvation prayer. He hesitated, but then I said: "Look, I have to go. I am on my lunch break and have to get back, but I believe that this is a divine appointment and I don't know if I will ever see you again. Are you sure you don't want to pray?" He looked around and saw that no one was watching him and then he said, "Sure." He then repeated a salvation prayer after me!! Praise God! Hallelujah! He got saved! Then I encouraged him to go to church on Sunday. "There are churches everywhere in Tulsa," I said. He laughed and said, "Yeah, I know!" Then he smiled and he thanked me. I drove back to work with such *joy* in my heart! You need joy in your life? Go get some people saved! So when anyone does you a favor, you can use this technique for witnessing to the lost!

A Tech Support Rep from the Philippines

When I was building my website, www.traintracts.com, I had to call tech support many times to figure out what to do. One time at the end of my very long phone conversation, I led a tech support guy from the Philippines to the Lord over the phone. I used all kinds of computer terms. I said, "You know when your computer messes up and you don't know what to do, you hit control, alt, delete, right?" He agreed. But what do you do when your life gets messed up? He was silent. I said, "Well, you do about the same thing, but you call upon Jesus Christ and let Him take *control* of your life. He will *alt*er your life and He will *delete* all your sins. Techs call it "rebooting," but we Christians call it, becoming born–again. At one point, he was behind the scenes online on my computer helping me "transfer files" from one folder to another, so as the yellow files flew over from the left to the folder on the right side, I told him: "That is just what it is like when you become born–again. You see, your spirit is then transferred from the Kingdom of darkness into the Kingdom of Light." He really got it then. So after he helped me, I asked him if he wanted to pray a salvation prayer and he agreed and so he prayed a salvation prayer after me over the phone! He was so happy. He even said that they had churches in the Philippines and that he and his wife would start going to one.

A Couple of Teens at the Mall

A couple of teenage guys, Lance and Nicholas, ages 12 and 16, both got born again in front of the GAP clothes store. I said, "You know, that GAP reminds me of the fact that **G**od **A**nswers **P**rayer. Have you ever thought of that? They were dumbfounded. I talked to them a little bit about prayer. Then I asked them if they knew Jesus as their Savior. They got convicted and agreed to pray a prayer to receive Jesus as their Lord. Then when I asked them about it, they also prayed to receive the Baptism of the Holy Spirit. They immediately began talking in tongues. Everything went so smoothly with them. It was so easy. It seemed that I was the divine appointment that their mother was praying for or her answer to prayer. I'm thankful that I was simply obedient.

Some Plant, Some Water God Gives the Increase!

As you read these testimonies, keep in mind that some people plant, some water and some reap the harvest. (1 Corinthians 3:6). Whether the person prays to receive Jesus as their Lord after using one these object evangelism icebreakers really depends on whether their hearts are ready and if you are led by the spirit to say the right thing and answer their questions after you say the initial object evangelism icebreaker. Whatever you do, just keep witnessing and God will give the increase. He is so pleased and full of joy when you witness to the lost. Down deep, you will feel that joy in your spirit.

I know that there will be many testimonies from using the many icebreakers in this book and I would like to hear your testimony! You can e-mail me at: **susan.nazarewicz@gmail.com**

CHAPTER SEVEN

I Want to Witness,
But What Do I Say
Around Entertainment?

Games
Movies
Music
Toys

The hardest part about witnessing is *the transition* from an everyday conversation onto the Gospel track. One way to do it is through relating the Gospel to objects around you like Jesus did many times in Matthew 13. These object evangelism icebreakers will *train* you how to transition conversations onto the Gospel *track*. Jesus is coming soon, so use loving boldness and be compassionate. Then be led by the Spirit using whatever method you choose. You may prophesy or pray for healing or whatever is needed. After the icebreaker there is an invitation to pray a salvation prayer. Then be bold and encourage them to pray that salvation prayer after you.

"I Want to Witness, But What Do I Say Around Games?"

Wrestling – This arm wrestling match reminds me of how the devil wrestled with God and he lost when God used His righteous right arm and raised His Son Jesus Christ up from the dead. Now I have eternal life in heaven...so do you have Jesus?

Chess – As I play this game, it reminds me of how life is like a game of chess. God sees the board from heaven. He moves the ones whose hearts are surrendered to Him in His perfect will and His perfect way. When God moves you, you will always win...so is Jesus Christ the King of your heart?   Matthew 26:39; Philippians 2:13

Crossword Puzzle – Working this puzzle it reminds me of how Jesus Christ died on the **cross** for all my mistakes and He is also the **Word** of God.   John 1:1

Darts – Playing darts reminds me of the fiery darts or lies that the devil throws at me. So I get him back by quoting the truth from God's Word and then I score a bulls–eye.   John 8:32

Hand Held Video Game – In this game the overall theme is fighting against good and evil. But in reality, the "fight for life" is all about believing lies or believing the truth. Jesus Christ is the truth and there is nothing "relative" about that. He is the way, the truth and the life and there is no way to heaven, but through Him (John 14:6). Many unbelievers believe the lie that there is no hell– so they can commit all the sin that they want with no fear of punishment. Then when they die, they will find out they were very wrong and will suffer in hot fiery flames for all eternity. They will lose for all eternity. God wants you to win the game of life and make it to heaven...Would you like to pray?

Hide –N–Seek – Hide and Seek reminds me of how God stopped hiding and revealed Himself when Jesus came to earth. His goal was to seek and save the lost. So have you allowed God to find you? Or are you still hiding? We can pray right now and then you will find Him and have eternal life.   Luke 19:10

Leap Frog – I like this game because it reminds me of how we Christians must run our race and leap over the devil's obstacles if we are going to win for God.   Hebrews 12:1-2

Matchbox Car – This car reminds me of Hebrews 12:1. "Run the race set before you". God has a race for every person to run and to win! The goal is to finish with joy like Paul who said, "I have finished the race, I have kept the faith."   2 Timothy 4:7

Puzzle – As I put this puzzle together, it reminds me of how life is like a puzzle. There are so many things that we do not understand, so it is hard to put the pieces together. But God sees the whole picture. When we receive Jesus as our Lord and trust in Him, He will lead us by His Spirit and He will help us put all the pieces of our lives together for His glory. Is Jesus your Lord and Savior?
                    Ephesians 2:10; Proverbs 3:5-6

Wii – Playing with this wii reminds me of how Christians are called to use the sword of the spirit, which is the Word of God, to cut down every lie of the enemy. When I quote God's truth I always win.   2 Corinthians 10:3–5

Salvation Prayer: "Heavenly Father, I believe that Your Son Jesus Christ died on the cross for my sins and rose from the dead. I repent of my sins. Jesus, I ask You to forgive me and come into my heart and be my Lord and Savior. Fill me with the Holy Spirit. Thank You for saving me from hell and giving me eternal life in heaven, in Jesus' name I pray, Amen."

I Want to Witness, But What Do I Say at the Movies?"

Now you can simply say, "As we go to this movie, it reminds me of what happened in July 2012 in Aurora, CO in that movie theatre where those 12 people were shot and killed by that crazy guy. If that happened here, would you make it to heaven?"

And then listen to what they say. Also there are so many good Christian movies out right now, so the movie itself preaches the Gospel in some way. When you go with an unbelieving friend to a movie that does **not** have a Christian theme, **if you listen to the Holy Spirit,** I believe He will still give you a creative way to witness to your unbelieving friend. As you watch the movie, the plot, the characters, ask God for wisdom and then you can say something like this:

"When this actor/actress said _____it reminded me of something that Jesus would say...."

"In the scene when that actor/actress did this or that... it reminded of something that Jesus Christ would do..."

"When I saw that scene, it reminded me of this _____ aspect of the Gospel...."

Candy – This candy reminds me of how sweet it is to trust in Jesus, The Bible says in Psalm 34:8 – "Oh taste and see that the Lord is good; Blessed is the man who trusts in Him." When I prayed to receive Jesus as my Lord, I received eternal life in heaven. Jesus is the sweet Savior of my soul. Have you ever put your trust in Jesus?

Popcorn – This delicious popcorn starts out as useless popcorn kernels. The kernels are usually kept in a bag away from the light, which reminds me of unbelievers living in the kingdom of darkness, but when the light and truth and love of Jesus come upon them, *the fire of God touches them* and there is a POP of revelation in the spirit! Their hearts pop and *change* as they pray to receive Jesus Christ as Lord and Savior. In that salvation prayer, they pop right on over into the Kingdom of God and become light and fluffy and white as new. It is a delicious transformation! So are you like a useless kernel or are you like white popcorn? Would you like to pray to receive Jesus as your Savior and have eternal life in heaven?

Soda Pop – When I get a soda from the soda fountain and the foam rises to the top, it reminds me of how important it is to be filled with the spirit. If you are not careful, sometimes the fizz overflows! And yet that is how God wants us to be in our spirit - overflowing with His love and joy and peace, so that we can be good to others and have the strength to fulfill His will for our lives.   Jude 20, Ephesians 5:18

Ticket – When I give my ticket to the movie attendant, I gain entrance to see the movie that I want to see. It reminds me of salvation through Jesus Christ which is my ticket to heaven. That is the place I want to see and be for all eternity. The best part is – it is a free gift...Jesus loves you so much. Have you ever received His free gift of eternal life in heaven? Then pray this prayer after me.

Waiting in Line – This line is taking forever. It reminds me of eternity, which is a very long time to be spent in the wrong place....Do you know where you will spend eternity?

Movie Scene – When I watched that terrible scene unfold where that man totally sinned against God, I thought about my own life and how I have sinned too. I am not perfect. But when I asked God to forgive me for my sins, He forgave me and threw my bad scene in the "sea of forgetfulness" and blotted it out!   So have your bad scenes been deleted?   Isaiah 43:25, 1 John 1:9, Micah 7:19

Salvation Prayer: "Heavenly Father, I believe that Your Son Jesus Christ died on the cross for my sins and rose from the dead. I repent of my sins. Jesus, I ask You to forgive me and come into my heart and be my Lord and Savior.   Fill me with the Holy Spirit. Thank You for saving me from hell and giving me eternal life in heaven, in Jesus' name I pray, Amen.

"I Want to Witness, But What Do I Say Around Music?"

Chord – Those three notes played together make one beautiful sound, one harmonious sound in one accord. It reminds me of the Trinity – Father, Son and Holy Ghost….So are you in one accord with Him? Have you prayed to receive Jesus as your Lord? Philippians 2:2

Drums or Bongos – It is easy to move to the beat of the drum. The beat of that drum sounds like a heartbeat and God is the One that created us and caused our hearts to beat…I know that God's heartbeat is for souls or for people to receive Jesus as their Lord, so they will have eternal life in heaven. Is your heart beating with God? Would you like to pray to receive Jesus as Lord?

Guitar – This guitar reminds me of people who ask for something with no strings attached. Some people say that they believe in God, but don't believe in His Son. I guess they don't want any strings attached, but without those "strings," that is without believing in Jesus as your Lord, you will not receive eternal life. Jesus is like the strings that form a bridge over the hole of the guitar. He is the bridge between God and man that reconciles us to God so that we can have eternal life…. Is Jesus your Lord?   John 5:23

Keyboards – All these keys remind me of the many false religions out there. Some people think that there are multiple ways to get to heaven, but I know, for sure the truth: Jesus Christ is the key to eternal life (hit middle C) and there is no way to heaven but through Him. He is the way, the truth and the life…. Have you received Jesus as your Lord?   John 14:6

Musical Harmony – In the beginning there was so much musical harmony, but then pride and sin entered causing disharmony, which separated God from man and His music. This made God sad. So He sent His only begotten Son Jesus Christ who shed His blood and died on the cross for our sins and rose from the dead. So those who pray to receive Jesus as their Conductor or Lord of their lives are "in tune" with God once again and the music is played into perfect harmony. Are you in tune with God?

Out of Tune or Off–Key – That "out of tune instrument" reminds me of someone who needs to be tuned into Jesus so that they can be saved from hell and be in perfect harmony with Him in heaven for all eternity.

Radio – The many channels to listen to represent the many voices that are in the world. Only the voice of God can really bring salvation and healing into our lives. The voice of God is loving and comforting. It's encouraging and edifying. He is the good Shepherd and His voice lines up with the Word. The devil's voice is condemning and mean and makes you feel like a failure. His voice fills you with fear, doubt and unbelief. He is a liar. God's voice is the channel that we should be tuned into. When you receive Jesus as your Lord, then you become born–again and your spirit becomes tuned into God's frequency to hear His voice in your spirit or in your heart. Would you like to pray to receive Jesus as your Lord so you can hear His voice?   John 10:4–5

Trumpet – That trumpet reminds me of what musical instrument God will use to sound the alarm when Jesus comes again. Matthew 24:31 says, "He will send His angels with a great sound of a trumpet, and they will gather together His elect from the four winds, from one end of heaven to the other."….So when Jesus comes again, are you ready to go up with Him? You do not want to be left behind. Is Jesus your Lord and Savior?

Salvation Prayer: "Heavenly Father, I believe that Your Son Jesus Christ died on the cross for my sins and rose from the dead. I repent of my sins. Jesus, I ask You to forgive me and come into my heart and be my Lord and Savior. Fill me with the Holy Spirit. Thank You for saving me from hell and giving me eternal life in heaven, in Jesus' name I pray, Amen."

"I Want to Witness, But What Do I Say Around Toys?"

Baby Doll – I love and take care of my baby doll like my Mommy takes care of me. But my Mom says that *God* takes care of her. Now I know how much God loves me. He loves me like I love my baby doll…so do you know how much God loves you?   Romans 5: 8

Blocks (or **Legos**) – As I build with these blocks, it reminds me of how I like to build myself in the Spirit through praying in the Holy Ghost, also called praying in tongues…Do you have your prayer language?   Jude 20

Blowing Bubbles – As I blow these bubbles into the air (or with gum), it reminds me of how Jesus first breathed His breath of life into His disciples when He prayed, "Receive now the Holy Ghost." Since they believed in Jesus as their Lord, they became born– again and received eternal life in heaven.   John 20:22

Deflated Balloon – This deflated balloon reminds me of people who do not know Jesus Christ as their Lord and Savior. They have no life. But when you become born again, the Holy Spirit will come into your life and He will *fill you up* with His love, His peace and His joy…so have you ever asked Jesus to fill you up with His saving love?

Hero Action Figures – These action figures that do such heroic things remind me of Jesus Christ, who is my superhero. He died on the cross for my sins and then He rose from the dead. Since I believe and prayed to receive Him as Lord, He saved me from hell. Now I have eternal life in heaven…so have you prayed to receive Jesus as your super hero?   Matthew 28:7, 1 John 4:4

Matchbox Car – This car reminds me of Hebrews 12:1. "Run the race set before you." God has a unique race, which is His plan and His purpose, for every person to run and to finish and win! " But to run and win for all eternity, you must be born again   2 Tim 4:7

Modeling Clay or **Play Doh–** As I mold and shape this clay, it reminds me of how God formed man from the dust of the ground and how God created me in His image.   Genesis 1:27

Teddy Bear -- This teddy bear that is so soft and warm and comforting reminds me of the Holy Spirit when I feel His gentle touch and His loving comfort come upon me. John 14:6 says that the Holy Spirit is the Comforter who will be with me forever because I prayed to receive Jesus Christ as my Lord and Savior...So is the Holy Spirit your Comforter?   Isaiah 40:1–2; Isaiah 66:13; James 4:7; Psalm. 94:19

Transformer – This Optimus Prime (or any kind) reminds me of the Word of God, which has the power to transform my whole life so that I can walk in God's perfect will, do His plan and fulfill His purpose that He has specifically designed for my life – Romans 12:1-2.

Yo–Yo – As I watch the yo-yo go up and down, it reminds me of people who are up and happy and others are down and sad. Since I received Jesus Christ as my Lord, I am up and happy now because I have eternal life in heaven ...so are you up or down? Would you like to pray to receive Jesus as your Lord?

Salvation Prayer: "Heavenly Father, I believe that Your Son Jesus Christ died on the cross for my sins and rose from the dead. I repent of my sins. Jesus, I ask You to forgive me and come into my heart and be my Lord and Savior. Fill me with the Holy Spirit. Thank You for saving me from hell and giving me eternal life in heaven, in Jesus' name I pray, Amen."

.

CHAPTER EIGHT

I Want to Witness, But What Do I Say About Financial Affairs?

Bank

Casino

Real Estate

Stock Market

T he hardest part about witnessing is *the transition* from an everyday conversation onto the Gospel track. One way to do it is through relating the Gospel to objects around you like Jesus did many times in Matthew 13. These object evangelism icebreakers will *train* you how to transition conversations onto the Gospel *track*. Jesus is coming soon, so use loving boldness and be compassionate. Then be led by the Spirit using whatever method you choose. You may prophesy or pray for healing or whatever is needed. After the icebreaker there is an invitation to pray a salvation prayer. Then be bold and encourage them to pray that salvation prayer after you.

"I Want to Witness, But What Do I Say, at a Bank?"

At Drive Thru – Shy people can put a Gospel tract in the vacuum tube when you send it back.

Balance – (to the bank teller)I know my bank balance is kind of low, but that is because I have chosen to "lay up treasure in heaven" by giving to my church and to missionaries to preach the Gospel to the world. It says in the Bible, where your treasure is, there your heart will be also."

Matthew 6:20-21

Bank Account – Everyone opens up bank accounts, but the most important thing to open up is your heart and pray for Jesus come in to be your Lord. Then you will have heaven's treasures for eternity…so do you want to pray?

Check out with Credit Card – Do I swipe the card or use the chip now? Is the amount correct? What is my pin #? Do I want any cash back? Do I want to donate any amount to the march of dimes? All of these questions I have to answer just to check out and buy my stuff. Sigh. And they do not even ask the most important question of all – Are you born again? (Watch the checker's response) and be led

Heads or Tails – This coin toss reminds me of the fact that the Bible says: "I am the head and not the tail (Deuteronomy 28:44)." *If it lands on tails* – The Bible also says: "The last shall be first and the first shall be last" (Matthew 20:16). So either way, I win. Are you are the winning side? Have you ever asked Jesus to be your Lord?

Interest – This interest is so high, but at least I know that *God* is interested in me and He loves me because He sent His Son Jesus Christ to pay the debt for my sins (interest and all) so that I could be spiritually "debt–free" and have the increase of eternal life in heaven. God is not looking at people's balances, He is looking at their heart…Have you ever received Jesus as your Lord?   Matthew 6:33

Investment – Do you have any investments? Well, Jesus is an investment that never loses interest. You can always put your stock in Him for eternal life.   Matthew 6:33

One Dollar Bill – When you look at the back of the one–dollar bill, have you ever noticed that pyramid with the eye on it? I am not afraid of that little eye because *I trust in God.* I know that He is the One who is watching over me, the One who made the sky and all of our eyes and He is called the El Shaddai – the God who is more than enough –a lot more than this one–dollar bill…Have you put your trust in Jesus Christ as your Lord?   Isaiah 9:6–7.

Penny – I'll give you a penny for your thoughts. Do you know what I am thinking? I am thinking about how much Jesus loves you and that He has a plan and a purpose for your life. Did you know that? …so have you ever received Him to be your Lord and Savior?

Savings Account – All Christians should have a "savings account" which is a record of the number of people they have prayed with to be saved. Do you have a savings account? To open one up, first you have to open your heart and pray to receive Jesus as your Lord…. so would you like to pray?   Romans 10:13

Salvation Prayer: "Heavenly Father, I believe that Your Son Jesus Christ died on the cross for my sins and rose from the dead. I repent of my sins. Jesus, I ask You to forgive me and come into my heart and be my Lord and Savior. Fill me with the Holy Spirit. Thank You for saving me from hell and giving me eternal life in heaven, in Jesus' name I pray, Amen."

"I Want to Witness, But What Do I Say at a Casino?"

Dice – As the dice is being rolled, it reminds of "casting lots" which is the term they used for rolling the dice in the Bible. In Psalm 22:18 there is a prophecy about the Messiah: "They divide My garments among them, and for my clothing they cast lots." In John 19:23–24 its fulfillment is recorded: "The soldiers said among themselves: 'Let us not tear it (Jesus' seamless robe), but cast lots for it, whose it shall be.'" That is just one of over 300 Old Testament prophecies that were fulfilled by Jesus Christ, so I know that Jesus Christ is the Messiah. So I received Him as my Lord and Savior. He is coming back again soon for His Church to take us all up to heaven. Time is short….Would you like to pray to receive Jesus as your Lord?

Full House – As I lay down this full house, it reminds me of what God wants up in heaven – a full house. Jesus said in John 14:2: "In my Father's House are many mansions…I go to prepare a place for you." If a person wants to be a member of the Father's House, first they have to pray to receive Jesus Christ as their Lord…. Would you like to pray to be in the Father's house for all eternity?

Hope of Winning it Big – Many people put their hope in gambling to win it big, but if you put your hope in Jesus, you will have the riches of heaven for all eternity.   Matthew 6:19-20; Matthew 6:33

King of Hearts or **Royal Flush–** This King of Hearts card reminds me of who is really the King over my heart. My King is Jesus Christ. I know that He is the One that really loves me, so I put my trust in Him and allow Him reign my heart because His way and His plan for my life is always the best. Would you like to make Him the King of your heart too? Then you will surely win the game of life:

which is really eternal life in heaven.   Psalm 97:1; Isaiah 52:7

Lottery Ticket – I know a sure bet. If you want to go to heaven when you die, a sure bet is receiving Jesus Christ as your Lord and Savior. There is no gambling and you will definitely go to heaven. Going to heaven when you die is as glorious as winning the lottery. Would you like to pray now to receive Jesus as your Lord?

Odds – (*Use Yeshua for a Jewish person*) When I think about odds, I think about the incredible odds of how over 300 prophecies about the Messiah in the Old Testament were completely fulfilled by Yeshua (Jesus Christ) in the New Testament. The odds of *just eight* prophecies being predicted and fulfilled is one in 10^{17} power. The odds of more than *three hundred* prophecies being fulfilled are mind–boggling. I know that Yeshua (Jesus Christ) truly is the Messiah, so I received Him as my Savior. I know He is coming back again for His Church to take them all up to heaven and time is short. So would you like to pray to receive Jesus as your Lord and Savior today? Matthew 2:23; Luke 18:31; Acts 3:18–26

Poker Chips – When the chips are down, look to Jesus Christ and He will lift you up. Put your hope in Him.   Matthew 6:33

Three of a Kind – Three of a Kind reminds me of the Trinity, you know – Father, Son and Holy Ghost. They are three in One. God sent His Son Jesus Christ to save us from our sins. When we pray to receive Him as Lord, the Holy Ghost comes into our hearts, so that is the Trinity...so are you born again?

Salvation Prayer: "Father, I believe that Your Son Jesus Christ died on the cross for my sins and rose from the dead. I repent of my sins. Jesus, I ask You to forgive me and come into my heart and be my Lord and Savior. Fill me with the Holy Spirit. Thank You for saving me from hell and giving me eternal life in heaven, in Jesus' name I pray, A–men.

"I Want to Witness, But What Do I Say About Real Estate?

Disclosure Statement – As the seller, I hate disclosing the things that are wrong with my house because I am afraid that the buyer will not want to buy it. I am so thankful that Jesus Christ shed His blood and paid the price for the wrong things I've done through His death on the cross and bought the imperfect ME with His blood. Have you ever asked God to forgive you for your sins and be your Lord and Savior?   1 John 1:9

Earnest Money – This earnest money (a deposit that is paid in advance when buying a house) reminds me of the Holy Spirit within me Who acts as a deposit that dwells in me on earth.…. When it is my time to die, I will receive all the fullness of the Spirit of God in heaven and my mansion as well.   Ephesians 1:14

House Door – As we stand here by this door, it reminds me of what Jesus said in John 10:9. He said, "I Am the door; Anyone who enters in through Me will be saved." Jesus Christ is the most important door you will ever walk through because it leads to eternal life in heaven. He loves you.   Have you ever opened up the door of your heart to ask Him to come in to be your Lord?

Investment Property – Jesus is an investment that never loses interest. Are you born again? Are you sold out to Him? Matthew 6:20

Key – Do you have your key to eternal life? Jesus Christ is the key that opens the door so you can receive eternal life in heaven.
                                                                John 10:9

Location – I know you want a house that is in the right location. I understand. I like living close to work too. But I am most concerned about where I will live for all eternity. So I received Jesus Christ as my

Lord and Savior. Now I know that I will live in the right location, which is heaven for all eternity. Do you know which location you will spend eternity?   John 10:28

Mansion – I know that most people would love to live in a mansion. The problem is, they cannot afford it, so this verse in John 14:2 comforts me. Jesus said, "In my Father's house are many mansions: if it were not so, I would have told you. I go and prepare a place for you." The only way to get your mansion in heaven is to believe and pray to receive Jesus Christ as your Lord and Savior.... Have you ever prayed that salvation prayer?

Mortgage – I sure wish the mortgage company was like Jesus Christ. When I received Him as my Lord, He forgave my debt of sin. Now I am free and clear. He paid my debt with His blood.

Pre–Qualified – Getting pre–qualified to own a home reminds me of the fact that I am pre–qualified for heaven as well. Because I prayed to receive Jesus Christ as my Lord and Savior, I am now pre–qualified to live in heaven for all eternity... So are you pre–qualified for heaven?

Price –This price reminds me of the price that was paid for me so that I could have eternal life. Jesus shed His blood for me on the cross, which is worth more than all the gold in the world. That's the price He paid for me, so that salvation would be a free gift.... Would you like to pray to receive the free gift of eternal life?   1 Peter 1:19

Salvation Prayer: "Heavenly Father, I believe that Your Son Jesus Christ died on the cross for my sins and rose from the dead. I repent of my sins. Jesus, I ask You to forgive me and come into my heart and be my Lord and Savior. Fill me with the Holy Spirit. Thank You for saving me from hell and giving me eternal life in heaven, in Jesus' name I pray, Amen."

"I Want to Witness, But What Do I Say Around the Stock Market?"

Candlestick Charting – I like to use candlestick charting because the white and the black candles help me see where the market is going more easily. The candles remind me of how Jesus Christ is the light of the world. He is the fire that burns in my heart.... So is He burning in your heart?

Chart – The wavy erratic red line on the Dow reminds me an EKG heart monitor. If the Dow shows huge losses, it can cause investors to have a heart attack. This is why every investor should pray to receive Jesus Christ as their Lord. Then they will have *hope* that if they lose it all, they will still have eternal life in heaven.

Down Trend or Huge Losses -- In the same way that it is hard to tell when the market will fall, it is hard to know when your last day on earth will be. So I received Jesus as my Lord and Savior. When I suffer a huge loss, at least I know I have not lost everything. I am not going to hell. I'm going to heaven. ..So where are you going?

Exchange – All the wisest investors know that the most lucrative exchange was when Jesus Christ gave His blood and *died* on the cross for the sins of the world *in exchange for* a multitude of *new births* into the Kingdom of God. I cashed in on that exchange when I prayed to receive Jesus as my Lord and Savior. Now I have eternal life in heaven, which is the best rate of return filled with eternal treasures.

Investment – Jesus is an investment that never loses interest. You really must put your stock in Him for eternal life.   Matthew 6:20-21

Options – There are so many ways to exercise an option. It reminds me of all the different theories people have on how to get to heaven. But the Bible says in John 14:6 that Jesus Christ is the way, the truth and the life and there is no other way, or *no other option to heaven, but through Him.* So would you like to exercise this option? It's really the only way to go. Let's pray.

Stock Tip – Want a good stock tip? I invest in this stock that has yielded me a higher rate of return than any other stock. It's called the KGJC stock – the Kingdom of God through Jesus Christ. When I prayed to give my heart to Jesus, I received eternal life in heaven. And when I invest in my church and into missionary works, then I will reap an eternal treasure in priceless souls...Would you like this stock? It's free. All you have to do is believe in Jesus as your Lord and pray a salvation prayer. Let's pray.

Stop Loss – When I put a stop loss order in, it reminds me of how thankful I am for Jesus Christ. When I prayed a salvation prayer to receive Jesus as my Lord and Savior, that prayer *stopped the loss* for all eternity. Now I am going to heaven and not hell.... So have you ever put an *eternal* stop loss order in? We can right now. Just pray this salvation prayer.

Up Trend – So are you looking for a stock with a good **up** trend? I know of an amazing stock that has no risk. It always goes up and my profits are huge. So do you want to know about it? Well, years ago I put my stock in Jesus Christ when I prayed to receive Him as my Lord and Savior. I invested my heart into God's kingdom. I am so thankful to know that however this market goes, I will be going up for all eternity. So, how about you?

Salvation Prayer: "Heavenly Father, I believe that Your Son Jesus Christ died on the cross for my sins and rose from the dead. I repent of my sins. Jesus, I ask You to forgive me and come into my heart and be my Lord and Savior. Fill me with the Holy Spirit. Thank You for saving me from hell and giving me eternal life in heaven, in the name of Jesus Christ I pray, Amen.

CHAPTER NINE

"I Want to Witness, But What Do I Say Around Food?"

Coffee
Kitchen
Restaurant
Bar

The hardest part about witnessing is *the transition* from an everyday conversation onto the Gospel track. One way to do it is through relating the Gospel to objects around you like Jesus did many times in Matthew 13. These object evangelism icebreakers will *train* you how to transition conversations onto the Gospel *track*. Jesus is coming soon, so use loving boldness and be compassionate. Then be led by the Spirit using whatever method you choose. You may prophesy or pray for healing or whatever is needed. After the icebreaker there is an invitation to pray a salvation prayer. Then be bold and encourage them to pray that salvation prayer after you

"I Want to Witness, But What Do I Say Around Coffee?"

Making Coffee – The ingredients to make coffee remind me of how a person can receive eternal life. God made man from the dust of the ground. (Psalm 103:14), so that dust reminds me of coffee grinds. And to make coffee, you need a coffee maker and that reminds me of God, who is the *Maker* of heaven and earth. Then you need water to pour into it and water reminds me of Jesus Christ, who died on the cross for my sins, because He referred to Himself as *The Living Water* in John 7:38. To become a Christian, a person (the dust) must repent of their sins and pray to receive Jesus Christ as their Lord. With this decision, the Coffee Maker is turned "on" and the Living Water pours over the dust of their hearts making them new creations in Christ, just like fresh brewed coffee.   2 Cor. 5:17

Sugar – This sugar reminds me of how sweet it is to trust in Jesus. The Bible says in Psalm 34:8, "Oh taste and see that the Lord is good; blessed is the man who trusts in Him." I'm so thankful He loves me…Have you ever put your trust in Jesus?

Cream – As I put this white cream into my coffee, it reminds me of a scripture in the Bible (Isaiah 1:18) that says that God will make my sins as white as snow….All of us have sinned. Our black sin separates us from God, but when a person receives Jesus Christ as their Savior, their sins are paid for through Jesus Christ's shed blood on the cross. Then, in God's eyes, the new believer becomes white as cream and will have eternal life in heaven.

French Vanilla Creamer – I only know one phrase in French, but I sure do like this French Vanilla creamer. The only phrase I know is: *"Jesus Tem"* (*sounds like:* "Juhzee Tem") which means: *Jesus loves you.* Do you know how much Jesus loves you?…Have you ever prayed to receive Him as Lord?

Lukewarm – I hate lukewarm coffee. God did not really like it either. The Bible says in Revelation 3:16: "So then, because you are lukewarm and neither hot nor cold, I will spew you out of my mouth." He was talking about lukewarm Christians. They are the ones that never witness to anyone about the love of Jesus Christ. I am not one of them....Do you know how much Jesus loves you? Have you ever prayed to receive Him as your Lord and Savior?

Pour – As I pour this coffee, it reminds me of how God will pour out his blessings upon us. There are so many Bible promises that we can have if we will simply pray and speak the Word and believe God for them to come to pass.   Mark 11:23-24

Stir – As I stir this coffee, it reminds me of how God can turn things around when I put my trust in Him. Deuteronomy 5:23 says, "The LORD your God turned the curse into a blessing." So He can turn any of my mistakes into a miracle! Have you ever turned your life over to Jesus Christ and prayed to receive Him as your Lord and Savior?

Coffee – The black color of coffee sometimes reminds me of sin, but it says in Romans 14:17 that the Kingdom of God *is not meat and drink*, but righteousness, peace and joy in the Holy Ghost. God is not looking at my coffee. He is looking at my heart to see if I am born again or not....so are you born again?

Salvation Prayer: "Heavenly Father, I believe that Your Son Jesus Christ died on the cross for my sins and rose from the dead. I repent of my sins. Jesus, I ask You to forgive me and come into my heart and be my Lord and Savior.   Fill me with the Holy Spirit. Thank You for saving me from hell and giving me eternal life in heaven, in Jesus' name I pray, Amen."

"I Want to Witness, But What Do I Say in the Kitchen?"

Burnt Toast – This toast is burned. It reminds me of something that they would eat in hell. That's why I received Jesus Christ as my Lord – to be saved from hell. I'm so glad that I did because life with Jesus is so much better than before. I now have more love, joy, peace and His newfound purpose for my life...Have you ever prayed to receive Jesus as your Lord? If you pray with me, I will be so happy that I will make us some more toast!

Egg – As I crack open this egg, it reminds me that I need to crack open my Bible today and read it. I know that the best nourishment that I can ever receive is from the Word of God.... So have you ever prayed to receive Jesus Christ as your Lord and Savior? 1Timothy 4:6

Grilling Meat – As I grill (cook or serve) this meat, it reminds me of John 4:34 when Jesus said: "My meat is to do the will of Him who sent Me, and to finish His work." As I finish this work grilling (or cooking in the kitchen), I know that it is God's will for all men to be saved from the hot coals and flames of hell. And you can be saved through surrendering your life to Jesus Christ through praying to receive Him as your Lord and Savior...So would you like to pray?

Ice – Water – Steam -- As I fill my glass with *ice* and watch the *steam* come off the coffee that I made with *water*, it reminds me of the trinity: Father, Son and Holy Ghost. They are all God manifested in three different forms...So is Jesus in your heart?

Knife – This sharp knife reminds me of the sword of the spirit in the Bible. Hebrews 4:12 says: "the Word of God is quick and powerful and sharper than any two–edged sword." Christians use the sword of the spirit to cut down the *lies* of the enemy that lead to destruction. The truth from God's word will set you free. The truth is God loves you and He has a plan and a purpose for your life. What lies do you think the devil is telling you? .... Would like to pray to receive Jesus as your Lord? Then you'll know the truth.

Oven Mitt – As I take this dish out of the oven, this oven mitt reminds me of Jesus Christ. You see, the mitt saves my hands from being burned. And Jesus Christ saves me from being burned in hell for all eternity. Would you like to be saved as well? Then pray this salvation prayer after me.   John 3:16

Perished Fruit – This fruit has perished. I hate to waste food, but this scripture encourages me in John 3:16 which says, "God so loved the world, that He gave His only begotten son, that whosoever believes in Him, shall *not perish,* but shall have ever lasting life." I am so glad that I will not perish like this fruit because I received Jesus as my Lord. Have you ever done that? If not, you can pray a salvation prayer after me.   2 Peter 3:9

Spatula – I use this spatula with hamburgers and pancakes because if I don't turn them over, they will burn on one side. It reminds me of the time that I *turned my life over* to Jesus Christ. I thank God that I will not be burned on the wrong side of eternity because I now have eternal life in heaven.

Spoon – As I use this big spoon to stir up these ingredients, it reminds me that "all things work together for good for those who love God and are called according to His purpose."   Romans 8:28

Salvation Prayer: "Heavenly Father, I believe that Your Son Jesus Christ died on the cross for my sins and rose from the dead. I repent of my sins. Jesus, I ask You to forgive me and come into my heart and be my Lord and Savior. Fill me with the Holy Spirit. Thank You for saving me from hell and giving me eternal life in heaven, in Jesus' name I pray, Amen."

"I Want to Witness, But What Do I Say at a Restaurant?"

Bread – This bread reminds me of what Jesus said in Matthew 4:4, "Man shall not live by bread alone, but by every word that proceeds from the mouth of God." He said that because Jesus Christ is the Word of God and so when we read it, then we are being spiritually fed. This is why Jesus says: "I Am the Bread of Life. He who comes to Me will never go hungry (John 6:35)." ...so are you hungry for God?

Door – As I pause here by this door, it reminds me of what Jesus said in John 10:9: "I Am the Door; anyone who enters in through Me will be saved." Jesus is the most important door you'll ever walk through...Have you ever opened the door of your heart to let Jesus Christ come in and be your Lord and Savior?

Fish – Eating this fish reminds me of what Jesus said: "Come, and I will make you fishers of men (Matthew 4:19)." Do you know how much Jesus loves you? ...Is He your Lord?

Salt & Pepper Shakers – These salt and pepper shakers remind me of the Kingdom of Light (salt) the Kingdom of Darkness (pepper). The Bible says in Matthew 24:29–31 that when Jesus comes again, the sun and the moon will be darkened, the stars will fall and the powers of the heavens *shall be shaken* just like these salt and pepper shakers. Then Jesus Christ will come again in the clouds, the angels will gather all the Christians together and take them up to heaven. Those who refused to receive Jesus as their Lord will be left behind. Jesus is coming soon. Have you prayed to receive Him as your Lord and Savior yet?

Hamburger/Steak -- This meat reminds me of what Jesus said: "My meat is to do the will of my Father (John 4:34)."... First of all, God's will is for you to be saved.

Knife – This sharp knife reminds me of Hebrews 4:12, which says:

"the Word of God is quick and powerful and sharper than any two–edged sword." It cuts away the devil's lies. The truth is Jesus Christ is the only way to heaven.... Is He your Lord?

Server/waiter – Thank you! Your excellent service reminds me of Jesus Christ. He came to earth to **serve us** through multiplying the loaves and fishes, turning the water into wine. Then He shed His blood and died on the cross for our sins so that we could be reconciled to God and receive eternal life. Have you ever received Jesus as your Lord? (*Please tip well.*)

Spoon – As I use this spoon to stir up these ingredients, it reminds me that "all things work together for good for those who love God and are called according to His purpose."   Romans 8:28

Sugar – This sugar reminds me of how sweet it is to trust in Jesus. Taste and see that the Lord is good (Psalm 34: 8). Do you know how much Jesus loves you? Do you trust in Him?

Water with Lemon – Many do not understand the Baptism of Holy Spirit. Just imagine that the **water** is the Holy Spirit and the **lemon** is you. First, you pray and ask God to fill you and then He baptizes you in the Holy Spirit: (*Flip & dunk the lemon in the water with your spoon*). You see, the lemon is baptized by the Holy Spirit and is filled to overflowing. Then the Holy Spirit will give you your prayer language (utterance). You cooperate with Him by boldly moving your tongue and lips. It helps to relax because you receive with **your spirit,** not your mind...So would you like to pray today to receive the Baptism of the Holy Spirit?   Acts 1:8; 19:6; 1 Corinthians 14:22

Salvation Prayer: "Heavenly Father, I believe that Your Son Jesus Christ died on the cross for my sins and rose from the dead. I repent of my sins. Jesus, I ask You to forgive me and come into my heart and be my Lord and Savior. Fill me with the Holy Spirit. Thank You for saving me from hell and for giving me eternal life in heaven, in the name of Jesus Christ I pray, Amen.

"I Want to Witness, But What Do I Say at a Bar?"

Backslider – So you say you are a backslider, huh? Well, you can always *slide back* and rededicate your life to the Lord.

Beer – Do you want better grades? Do you want to be wiser? Then you need to stop drinking this beer (budweiser). You won't become any wiser drinking beer and that is the truth.

Bloody Mary – This drink reminds me of the blood of Jesus Christ. With His blood He paid for our sins on the cross so that we could be reconciled to God and saved from going to hell, so this blood's for you.

Cheers! - (*Clink glasses*) That reminds me of what Jesus said in Matthew 16:33: "Be of good *cheer*, I have overcome the world." So are you cheerful because of Jesus or because of this drink? If you want to quit drinking, He will help you overcome and then joy of the Lord will be your strength.   Nehemiah 8:10

Cigarette Pack – (*When the smoker hits the cigarette pack against the palm of his hand*) When you did that, it reminded me of the hammer that drove the nails into Jesus' hands. He died on that cross because He loves you…So have you ever prayed to receive Jesus as your Lord and Savior?   John 20:26–27.

Cigarette Ashes – As I look at those cigarette ashes, it reminds me of something comforting that God said – that He will give us "beauty for *ashes*, the oil of joy for mourning and a garment of praise for the spirit of heaviness. Do you know how much God loves you?   Isaiah 61:3

Cigarette Butt – That cigarette butt reminds me of all the people that say: "I am going to get saved and live for God, **BUT** I want to party a little more first…" **But** one never knows when their last day on earth will be. A person could, heaven forbid, die suddenly in car wreck. Those that intended to get saved, *but* never did will end up in hell. *Today* is the day of salvation. Would you like to pray and receive Jesus Christ as your Lord?   Luke 16:19:31

Drunk – Have you ever been drunk in the spirit? Ephesians 5:18 says, "Do not be drunk with win wherein it is excess, but be filled with the spirit through singing with songs and hymns and spiritual songs making melody in your heart to the Lord." Getting drunk in the spirit and laughing in the spirit is really what God wants us to do.

Light Beer – That light beer reminds me of the Light of the world that fills me up with love and joy and peace. His name is Jesus Christ. There is no high like the Most High.   John 8:12.

Lukewarm – *When a friend(s) asks you to go to a bar.* Well, I hate it when my drink becomes lukewarm. God doesn't like lukewarm either. Revelation 3:15 says: "Because you are lukewarm, and neither hot nor cold, I will spew you out of my mouth." So as a Christian, I do not want to go because I'd be lukewarm, but we can somewhere else *(and name a better place!)*

Liquor – This used to be my favorite liquor, but then I found a new Comforter. When I prayed to receive Jesus as my Lord and Savior, I found *THE Comforter* who is the Holy Spirit. Now he lives down *south* in my soul. Ephesians 5:18 says "to not be drunk, but *be filled* with the Spirit through singing spiritual songs making melody in your heart to the Lord. Psalm 16:11 says that "in God's Presence is fullness of joy."

Salvation Prayer: "Heavenly Father, I believe that Your Son Jesus Christ died on the cross for my sins and rose from the dead. I repent of my sins. Jesus, I ask you to forgive me and come into my heart and be my Lord and Savior. Fill me with the Holy Spirit. Thank you for saving me from hell and giving me eternal life in heaven, in Jesus' name I pray, Amen."

CHAPTER TEN

I Want to Witness, But What Do I Say Around Healthcare?

Dentist
Hospital
Suicidal Person

The hardest part about witnessing is *the transition* from an everyday conversation onto the Gospel track. One way to do it is through relating the Gospel to objects around you like Jesus did many times in Matthew 13. These object evangelism icebreakers will **train** you how to transition conversations onto the Gospel **track.** Jesus is coming soon, so use loving boldness and be compassionate. Then be led by the Spirit using whatever method. You may prophesy or pray for healing or whatever is needed. To help pull them in after the "..." there is an invitation to be saved. Then be bold and encourage them to pray after you a salvation prayer.

"I Want to Witness, But What Do I Say at the Dentist?"

Anesthesia –While the dentist is putting on my crown, I am so thankful that I will be crowned with anesthesia, so I won't feel the pain. That anesthesia reminds me of Psalm 103:4, which says: "God will crown you with *loving kindness and tender mercies.*" Our sins separate us from God, so God sent His Son Jesus Christ into the world. He became the sacrificial lamb of God Who shed His blood on the cross and paid the price for our sins so that we could be forgiven and reconciled with God so that we would not feel the pain and suffering of hell and have eternal life in heaven. ...Have you ever received Jesus Christ as your Lord?

Crown – I am not very excited about getting this crown put on, but what comforts me is thinking about how thankful I am that I am a Christian. When I get to heaven, I will receive a *crown* of righteousness, which is my reward for receiving Jesus as my Lord... Is Jesus your Lord?

Filling – As I am waiting to get a cavity filled I am not excited, but I am thankful that I am *spirit–filled.*... Since I received the Baptism of the Holy Spirit, I pray in tongues God's perfect will for my life. God downloads His prayers into my spirit and I pray them out so that His perfect will can be done on earth. At times, He fills me with His Peace that really helps me, especially right now...Have you ever been filled with the Spirit? Ephesians 5:18

Teeth– As I sit here and wait for the dentist, I will tell you the truth, I am not excited. Going to the dentist is my least favorite thing to do, but since I am a Christian I know that at least I will go to heaven when I die. The Bible says that those who do not know Jesus as Savior will go to hell where there is "weeping and gnashing of *teeth*" for all eternity (Matthew 22:13). They gnash and grind their teeth because the pain and suffering is so tormenting there. I thank God

I'm going to heaven! How about you? Have you ever prayed to receive Jesus as your Savior?

Toothpaste – As I use this toothpaste, it makes my teeth white. That reminds me of what God does to my sins when I ask Him to forgive me for my sins and cleanse me from all unrighteousness - He makes my sins whiter than snow! Jesus can make your sins white too! You just pray and ask Him to be your Lord and Savior   Isaiah 1:18

Toothpick – As I use this wooden toothpick to get this food that is bothering me out of my teeth, it reminds me of the wooden cross that Jesus died on that gets the sin that is bothering God out of my heart.... Have you ever prayed to receive Jesus Christ as your Lord and Savior?   1 John 1:9

Floss or Flosser – As I use this floss to get the food out between my teeth, sometimes my gums bleed, but it reminds me of how Jesus Christ stood in between God and man to reconcile them to God through His shed blood on the cross that paid the price for my sins so I could go to heaven, where I will have perfect teeth!....Have you ever prayed to receive Jesus as your Lord?

X–ray– As I look at that x–ray that shows the inside of my teeth, it reminds me of the fact that God can see the inside of my heart. He knows every thought that I think (Psalm 139:2) and He still loves me. I am so thankful that God loves me. Since God loves me even when I mess up, it makes me want to love Him and please Him and serve Him all the more...Have you ever received Jesus Christ as your Lord and Savior?

Salvation Prayer: "Heavenly Father, I believe that Your Son Jesus Christ died on the cross for my sins and rose from the dead. I repent of my sins. Jesus, I ask you to forgive me and come into my heart and be my Lord and Savior. Fill me with the Holy Spirit. Thank you for saving me from hell and giving me eternal life in heaven, in Jesus' name I pray, Amen."

"I Want to Witness, But What Do I Say at the Hospital?"

Blood Donor – A blood donor saved my life. Jesus Christ gave His blood for me on the cross for my sins. Since I prayed to receive Him as my Lord, now I have eternal life.

Crutch – That crutch reminds me of prideful people that say that religion is just a crutch for the weak who have low self–esteem. The truth is they cannot save themselves through their own works. Proverbs 16:18 says, "pride goes before a fall (into hell)," But those who humble themselves and by grace through faith receive Jesus as their Lord will have eternal life. They will walk with the Lord (with no crutches) for all eternity.

Doctor – That doctor reminds me a little bit of the Great Physician, who is Jesus Christ. Psalm 103:3 says, "Praise the Lord...and forget not all His benefits, who forgives all your sins and heals all your diseases." So I am not depending on doctors to heal me. I am depending on the Lord. ...Would you like to receive Jesus as your Lord and Savior or prayer for healing? Let's pray.

EMSA logo – That logo of the serpent on a pole is from the Bible in Numbers 21:5–9. The Israelites in the wilderness got discouraged and sinfully spoke against God and Moses. So the Lord sent fiery serpents that bit the people and many died. Then they repented for their sins. The Lord told Moses to make a bronze serpent and lift it up on a pole and when those who are bitten look upon it, they will live. This foreshadowed Jesus Christ when He was lifted up on the cross. Whoever looks to Jesus and receives Him as Savior shall not die, but have eternal life in heaven forever.

Medicine – This medicine reminds me of Proverbs 17:22: "A merry heart does good like a medicine." The Joy of the Lord is my strength (Nehemiah 8:10)." Psalm 16:11 says, "In God's Presence is fullness of joy." When I praise and worship God I often feel His presence. So let's sing: "I Am the God that healeth thee. I Am the Lord your healer…"

Red Cross – After Jesus Christ died on it, it *was* a red cross. It was a bloody mess. He bore our sins in His own body on the cross and "by whose stripes, you were healed" (1 Peter 2:24)…. Would you like prayer for salvation or for divine healing?

Stethoscope – A doctor uses a stethoscope to listen to one's heart to see if it is beating right, but I listen to a person while they *talk* to see if their heart is beating right with God. A heart that beats right with God is one that believes in God's Son, Jesus Christ, and has received Him as their Lord. John 3:16 says, "God so loved the world that He gave His only begotten Son and whoever believes in Him shall not perish, but have everlasting life." Would you like to have prayer for salvation or healing?   Matthew 12:34

Waiting Room – It is taking so long here in the waiting room, it reminds me of eternity. Eternity goes on forever. It is a very long time to be spent in the wrong place…Do you know where you will spend eternity? Have you ever asked Jesus to be your Lord?

Salvation Prayer: "Heavenly Father, I believe that Your Son Jesus Christ died on the cross for my sins and rose from the dead. I repent of my sins. Jesus, I ask You to forgive me and come into my heart and be my Lord and Savior. Fill me with the Holy Spirit. Thank You for saving me from hell and giving me eternal life in heaven, in Jesus' name I pray, Amen."

"I Want to Witness, But What Do I Say to a Suicidal Person?"

God loves you and He wants you to live. Your life is a gift from God. He gave it to you and He wants you to keep it. You may feel so crushed from your circumstances, but God can make all things new. Isaiah 43:18–19 "Remember not the former things nor consider the things of old. Behold I will do a new thing...I will even make a way in the wilderness and rivers in the desert." *God has a plan and a purpose for your life.* Jeremiah 29:11 says: "I know the thoughts and the plans that I have for you. They are good and not for evil, to give you a future and a hope." *Life is like a puzzle.* God can see the whole picture from His view, but you can only see a few puzzle pieces. Trust in God to put all the pieces together in His way and in His timing. *What you are going through is temporary.*

Don't Be Mad at God. God is on your side. Be mad at the devil that influences people's sinful acts, to reject you and abuse you and hurt you. This is not God's will. The devil is a liar who will cause people to sin against you and then tell you that it was *God's fault or His will* to build a wall between you. But Jesus says in John 10:10: "The thief (the devil) comes not, but for to steal, to kill, and to destroy. I Am come that they might have life and have it more abundantly." So bad things come from the devil and good things come from God. Do not get it mixed up. God is a good God.

Remember that God gave everyone a free will because love is not truly love unless it is *freely* given. God wanted His creation to freely love Him. Robots have no choice, so they can't give true love. God knew that giving His creation a free will was a risk, but He also knew it was the only way to reach out to people with His love. Many times people do not receive Jesus as Lord and instead they use their free will to sin against God and others. This grieves God. He is angry with those who mistreat His children and desires to bring justice.

Forgive those who have hurt you. Now that is not letting them off the hook. It is putting them on God's hook. It is taking your hands off the situation and allowing God's hands to intervene and fight for you. After you forgive, then stand on Romans 12:19: "'Vengeance is Mine, I will repay,' says the Lord." Unforgiveness is sin and it builds a wall between you and God (Matthew 6:14). When you forgive those who have hurt you and trust the Lord, He will right the wrongs that have been done to you and turn things around (Mark 11:25). God will bless you with hope in His Presence, His comfort, love, peace and joy as you sing and worship Him. Forgiving others sets you free.

You are not a failure. Because God is God, He can make plan B even better than what plan A ever would have been. God never fails. Romans 8:28 says: "All things work together for good for those who love God and are called according to His purpose. Give God time to move on your behalf. Be patient (Ecclesiastes 3:11). Life is like a movie. Trust in God's love to bring your happy ending.

Choose to Live for the Lord. Friends come and go, divorce happens, parents and children can prematurely die, so we cannot live for them. *Our true purpose is to live for the Lord.* God needs you! The harvest is plenteous and the laborers are few. Living for the Lord means finding and fulfilling your God–given purpose, loving people, walking in the fruits of the spirit, witnessing to the lost, and giving to or going on mission trips. Living for the Lord is overcoming evil with good. It is turning people who are heading for hell around towards God's love and eternal life in heaven.

Salvation Prayer: "Heavenly Father, I believe that Your Son Jesus Christ died on the cross for my sins and rose from the dead. I repent of my sinful suicidal thoughts. Jesus, I ask You to forgive me and come into my heart and be my Lord and Savior. Fill me with the Holy Spirit. Thank You for saving me from hell and giving me eternal life in heaven, in Jesus' name I pray, Amen."

CHAPTER ELEVEN

I Want to Witness, But What Do I Say Around Holidays And Special Times?

Christmas
Fourth of July
Easter
Funeral
Wedding

The hardest part about witnessing is *the transition* from an everyday conversation onto the Gospel track. One way to do it is through relating the Gospel to objects around you like Jesus did many times in Matthew 13. These object evangelism icebreakers will *train* you how to transition conversations onto the Gospel *track*. Jesus is coming soon, so use loving boldness and be compassionate. Then be led by the Spirit using whatever method you choose. You may prophesy or pray for healing or whatever is needed. After the icebreaker there is an invitation to pray a salvation prayer. Then be bold and encourage them to pray that salvation prayer after you.

"I Want to Witness, But What Do I Say Around Christmas?"

Candy Cane – The maker of the candy cane invented it in order to share the Gospel message. When you turn it upside down, the shape is in the shape of a "J" which stands for Jesus Christ. When you turn it right side up, you see the Shepherd's crook because the Lord is our Shepherd watching over us. The candy is rock hard and God is the solid rock upon which we can stand. The candy is white just like God's holiness and purity. And lastly, the candy canes' red stripes represent the 39 blood stripes across Jesus' back caused by the Roman soldiers' whip lashing and by those red stripes we are healed.… So have you ever asked Jesus Christ to be your Lord and Savior?
Psalm 23:1; Psalm 62:5; Psalm 18:2; 1 Peter 2:24

Angel – My favorite angel is the one in Luke 2:10 that said to the shepherds: "Fear not, for behold, I bring you good tidings of great joy which shall be to all people. For unto you is born this day in the city of David, a Savior, which is Christ the Lord.".… So have you ever received Jesus as your Lord? Psalm 91:11; Psalm 34:7

Christmas Tree – This tree reminds me of how Jesus Christ was born, so that He would die for our sins on the tree, in the form of a cross. 1 Peter 2:24 says that He died so that we "may *live* for righteousness." The Christmas tree is really an evergreen tree. "Ever" represents *eternity* and "green" represents *growth*. So the evergreen tree reminds me of the fact that Jesus Christ is still alive today for all *eternity* in heaven. And whosoever believes that Jesus Christ shed His blood and died on the tree (cross) for our sins and rose again and then prays to receive Him as their Lord and Savior shall have eternal life. Then as they read the Word and go to church, they will continue *growing* like this evergreen tree in their relationship with Him. …Have you ever prayed to receive Jesus as your Savior?

Gift – Jesus Christ is God's loving gift to whosoever chooses to believe in and receive His Son Jesus Christ as their Lord and Savior...Have you prayed to receive God's gift of eternal life? Christmas is the best time to receive Him. John 3:16

Manger Scene – Isn't that manger scene beautiful? Jesus is the King of Kings and could have been born in a palace. But instead, God chose for Him the path of humility, lowliness and poverty to identify with the poorest and weakest among us. The manger is where the holiest of lambs, who were destined for sacrifice on the altar, were born. So Jesus, the holiest sacrifice, was born in the same place. Do you know the Christmas message? Let me tell you about it.   Luke 1- 2.

Reindeer – The reindeer reminds me of how glad I am that Jesus Christ *reigns* as the Lord over my life and how *dear* He is to me. He is the lover of my soul...Have you ever prayed to receive Jesus as your Lord and Savior?

Santa Claus – He reminds me of Jesus Christ. If Jesus were here on earth, He would give children gifts just like Santa does because Jesus is loving, kind and giving. Actually Jesus Christ *is* the Christmas gift. God gave His Son Jesus Christ, Who was born and later died on the cross shedding His blood for our sins so that we could have reconciliation or peace with God and eternal life in heaven. You receive this gift by believing and receiving Jesus Christ as your Lord. Would you like to pray?   1 John 4:7–10; Isaiah 11:1–7

Salvation Prayer: "Heavenly Father, I believe that Your Son Jesus Christ died on the cross for my sins and rose from the dead. I repent of my sins. Jesus, I ask You to forgive me and come into my heart and be my Lord and Savior. Fill me with the Holy Spirit. Thank You for saving me from hell and giving me eternal life in heaven, in Jesus' name I pray, Amen."

"I Want to Witness, But What Do I Say Around the Fourth of July?"

American flag – The flag represents our nation that is under God. The **white stripes** represent God's holiness and purity. When the soldiers whipped Jesus Christ, the 39 lashes wrought **red stripes** of blood all over His back. It says in Isaiah 53:4–5 that by His stripes, we were saved and healed. In Genesis 22:17 God promised Abraham, "I will surely bless you and make your descendants as numerous as the **stars** in the sky…" America has the most Christians in the world, so it is fitting that we have so many stars on our flag and that the background of the stars is **blue**, the color of our heavenly skies…. So are you a Christian? Is Jesus your Lord?

Fireworks – As I watch those beautiful and spectacular fireworks being shot into the air, it reminds me of the glory of God. Psalm 72:19 says, "The whole earth shall be filled with His glory." It also reminds me of how Christians need the **fire** of God to do the **works** that God has called us to do…So do you have that fire? Have you prayed to receive Jesus as your Lord?

Freedom – Freedom reminds me of what Jesus Christ did for me. He died on the cross and paid the price for my sins, so that I could be reconciled to God. I now have the freedom to live by His Spirit instead of being bound to the Old Covenant laws. I am free from all the bondage of sin and the false religions that separated me from God. In Christ Jesus, I am free! So are you free? John 8:32

Independence Day – One of the reasons why the US fought to gain independence from England is to have freedom of religion. So while the United States has freedom to be independent from England, God still wants us Christians to be dependent on the power of the Holy Spirit. As He abides in us, we must obey God and abide in Him...Do you have that dependence upon the Lord?

Soldier – I'm proud of you and I appreciate you for going to fight for our country. I believe that in fighting for our country, you are really fighting for us to help keep our religious freedom to worship the Lord. The Bible says in 2 Timothy 2:3 to "Endure hardness, as a good soldier of Jesus Christ." So many people know about God, but they have never personally prayed to receive Jesus Christ as their Lord and Savior. Before you go, I want you to be sure of your salvation...C'mon, let's pray.

Uniform – Seeing that soldier in uniform reminds me of how we Christians need to put on the whole armor of God everyday to stand against the evil in this world. Ephesians 6:14 describes the armor as: the belt of truth, the breastplate of righteousness, feet fitted and ready with the Gospel of peace, the shield of faith, the helmet of salvation, and the sword of the spirit, which is the Word of God. As soldiers of the Lord, we need to pray daily for those around us. The most important prayer is the "Prayer of Salvation.".... Have you ever prayed to ask Jesus Christ to be your Savior?

Tombstone - From looking at this memorial tombstone, I believe that this soldier was born again. It reminds me of Matthew 27:52-53 "The tombs were opened, and many bodies of the saints who had fallen asleep were raised; and coming out of the tombs after His resurrection. They entered the holy city and appeared to many." That was then, but I know that this soldier, along with all the other Christians, will also be raised up at the rapture when Jesus comes again. So will you be going up in the rapture? Are you born again?   1 Corinthians 15:52

Salvation Prayer: "Heavenly Father, I believe that Your Son Jesus Christ died on the cross for my sins and rose from the dead. I repent of my sins. Jesus, I ask You to forgive me and come into my heart and be my Lord and Savior. Fill me with the Holy Spirit. Thank You for saving me from hell and giving me eternal life in heaven, in Jesus' name I pray, Amen."

I Want to Witness, But What Do I Say at Easter?"

Easter is really a pagan holiday with Easter eggs and bunnies and such. And yet, church tradition uses this time to also celebrate the resurrection of Jesus Christ. The pagan Easter objects can be creatively used to remind people about Jesus and what His true gospel message is really all about. The Apostle Paul declared, "Christ died for our sins, He was buried, and that He rose again the third day according to the scriptures" (1 Corinthians 15:3-4). After He rose from the dead, Jesus appeared to many people over a span of forty days before He ascended to heaven, to sit at the right hand of God.

Easter Egg Hunt – This Easter egg hunt reminds me of Jesus and what He said in Luke 19:10 "for the Son of Man has come *to seek and to save that which* was lost." Lost people are so much more important than lost eggs… Have you found Jesus? Is He in your heart?

Empty Plastic Easter Egg – This empty egg reminds me of Jesus Christ's empty tomb. On Easter morning, God resurrected Jesus from the dead and the tomb became empty and now He is alive in heaven. Since I am born again, Jesus is alive in my heart as well… Is He alive in your heart? I would glad to pray a salvation prayer with you.

Easter Basket ‑This Easter basket reminds me of the big large covered basket that was used to save the Apostle Paul's life. It says in Acts 9:23-25: *Now after many days were past, the Jews plotted to kill him. But their plot became known to Saul (aka Paul). And they watched the gates day and night, to kill him. Then the disciples took him by night and let him down through the wall in a large basket."* I am so thankful for that basket because it saved Paul's life! He escaped and later wrote two thirds of the New Testament! He was the Apostle to the Gentiles, who are not Jewish, but people like you and me.

Chocolate Bunny - This chocolate reminds me of how *sweet* it is to trust in Jesus. The Bible says in Psalm 34:8: "Oh taste and see that the Lord is good; blessed is the man who trusts in Him." I'm so thankful He loves me… Have you ever put your trust in Jesus?

Easter Grass - As I look at the green grass, it reminds me of this scripture in Isaiah 40:8: "The grass withers, the flowers fade, but the Word of our God will stand forever." I am so thankful that the Word of God never changes. He is the same yesterday, today and forever. Praying to receive Jesus Christ as your Lord will give you new life just like fresh green grass…Would you like to pray to receive Jesus as your Lord?

April Showers Bring May Flowers

Rain – As I watch that rain come down, it reminds me of how thankful I am that the Lord reigns in my life. I received Jesus Christ as my Lord and Savior and now He rules and *reigns* in my heart all day long. He knows everything about everyone and His way is the best way. Does Jesus reign in your heart?   Psalm 93:1; Isaiah 55:10

Lilies – Lilies remind me of that verse in Song of Solomon 2:1 that says that Jesus Christ is *the lily of the valley*. He is the bright spot during the trials and tribulations of life when we feel so down, like we are in a valley. Lilies also surround the altar at church to celebrate the Resurrection of Jesus Christ….Have you ever prayed to receive Jesus Christ as your Lord and Savior?

Salvation Prayer: "Heavenly Father, I believe that Your Son Jesus Christ died on the cross for my sins and rose from the dead. I repent of my sins. Jesus, I ask You to forgive me and come into my heart and be my Lord and Savior. Fill me with the Holy Spirit. Thank You for saving me from hell and giving me eternal life in heaven, in Jesus' name I pray, Amen"

"I Want to Witness, But What Do I Say at a Funeral?

Brother/Sister died – Jesus said in Matthew 12:50: "Whosoever shall do the will of my Father which is in heaven, the same is my brother and sister and mother." The first step to doing God's will is to receive Jesus Christ as your Lord. Then He will be like a brother to you and will also bless you with brothers and sisters in Christ.

Coffin – As I look at this coffin, it represents closure –that this person is no longer a part of my life. But I know that when one door closes, another door opens. And out of death comes new life, new hope and new vision. When God gives us vision, He wants us to write it down and run with it. This new life begins with Jesus Christ…Have you ever received Him as your Lord?

Father died – I know that you will miss your father, but if you ask Jesus Christ to be your Lord, then God will become your Heavenly Father and He will adopt you (Romans 8:15). And Psalm 27:10 says, "When my father and my mother forsake me, then the Lord will take me up."….Would you like to pray to be adopted into God's family and receive God as your Heavenly Father? He will surely carry you.

Flowers – You will go through a season of grieving, but remember that God is with you. As you look at these beautiful flowers remember Isaiah 61:3: God will give you "beauty for ashes, the oil of joy for mourning and the garment of praise for the spirit of heaviness." His love will comfort you and God makes all things new…Have you ever received Jesus as the lover of your soul?

Husband died – I know you are sad and you miss him, but God has not abandoned you. The Bible says in Isaiah 54:5: "Do not fear for Your Maker is your husband, the Lord of hosts is His name." Would you like to pray to receive Jesus as your Lord and also *as Your husband* today? Also read Isaiah 41:10

Inheritance – The Bible says in 1 Peter 1: 3–4 that because of Christ's resurrection from the dead, we have *an inheritance* that is incorruptible and reserved in heaven for all eternity for those who believe in Him...So do you have that eternal inheritance?

Mother died – I know you miss your mother, but God will be with you. He will comfort you like your mother did. Isaiah 66:13 says, "As one whom his mother comforts, so will I comfort you. In John 14:16 Jesus said, "I will pray to the Father, and He shall give you another Comforter, that He may abide with you forever." Have you ever prayed to receive Jesus as your Lord and your Comforter?

Tissues – Here, have a tissue. The Bible says in Matthew 5:4, "Blessed are they that mourn, for they shall be comforted." God will comfort you during this time. Don't be mad at Him for allowing your loved one to die. There are many things that we just do not understand. So just trust in Him and receive His love. He wants you to know the height and the depth and the width and the length of the love that He has for you....Have you ever received the Lover of your soul to be your Lord? Ephesians 3:17–18.

The Will – If the will was not clearly written up, a lot of people contest it. The devil loves to stir up strife and division as families fight over the will. We must remember that the most important thing is for the family to forgive, walk in love and be in **God's** perfect will.

Salvation Prayer: "Heavenly Father, I believe that Your Son Jesus Christ died on the cross for my sins and rose from the dead. I repent of my sins. Jesus, I ask You to forgive me and come into my heart and be my Lord and Savior. Fill me with the Holy Spirit. Thank You for saving me from hell and giving me eternal life in heaven, in Jesus' name I pray, Amen."

"I Want to Witness, But What Do I Say at a Wedding?"

Candles – Those candles remind me of what Jesus said in John 8:12, "I Am the light of the world. He who follows Me shall not walk in darkness, but have the light of life." I prayed to receive Jesus as my Lord, so now I am in the Kingdom of Light with eternal life in heaven. Would you like to pray for His light to come into your heart so that you can have eternal life as well?

Lilies – Those lilies remind me of how Jesus Christ is *the lily of the valley* and He is the resurrection in my life as well...Have you ever made Him your Lord and Savior?   Song of Solomon 2:1

Ring – I know that the ring is the symbol of the marriage covenant to our spouse: "to be faithful forsaking all others, to love and to cherish, for better or for worse, for richer or for poorer, in sickness and in health until death do you part." The engagement ring reminds me the covenant I have with God, like a gold ring around my heart, because I prayed to receive Jesus Christ as my Lord...So are you in covenant with God for all eternity?

Hebrews 8:6–10

Roses – The pretty roses remind me of Jesus Christ, who is *the Rose of Sharon* in Song of Solomon 2:1. He blooms in the hearts of those who love Him...So does the love of God bloom in your heart?

Wedding Reception – This wedding reception reminds me of the Marriage Supper of the Lamb that will soon take place up in heaven. The Lamb of God is Jesus Christ, also known as the Bridegroom who will come again to get His Bride, who is the Church (or those who are saved/born–again.). So after the church is raptured to heaven, there will be a great feast called the Marriage Supper of the Lamb. I know I will be there because I prayed to receive Jesus as my

Lord...So will you be there? Would you like to receive Jesus as your Lord?   Revelation 21 and 22:17

White Wedding Dress – That white wedding dress reminds me of how the Bride of Christ will be when Jesus Christ comes again for her. It says in Ephesians 5:27 that we will be "without spot or wrinkle, holy and without blemish." That all means we will be free from sin and spiritually washed clean on the inside. To be a part of the church at all, which shall be the Bride of Christ; first you need to receive Jesus Christ as your Lord and Savior. Then by His loving grace and mercy, He will help you get the spots and the wrinkles out as He pours His love into your heart you when you pray and read His Word…. If Jesus were to come back today, would you be ready to be His Bride? Would you like to pray right now to receive Him as your Lord and Savior?

Wedding Gift – This wedding gift reminds me of the best gift of all – eternal life. Since I have received Jesus Christ as my Lord and Savior, I know that I will have eternal life in heaven. Now that is a gift that keeps on giving! Jesus Christ is God's gift for all eternity to whosoever chooses to believe in and receive His Son Jesus Christ as their Lord and Savior…Do you know how much He loves you? Would you like to pray to receive the gift of eternal life? Then you will be able to take part in the Marriage Supper of the Lamb in heaven.   Ephesians 2:8–9

Salvation Prayer: "Heavenly Father, I believe that Your Son Jesus Christ died on the cross for my sins and rose from the dead. I repent of my sins. Jesus, I ask You to forgive me and come into my heart and be my Lord and Savior. Fill me with the Holy Spirit. Thank You for saving me from hell and giving me eternal life in heaven, in Jesus' name I pray, Amen.

CHAPTER TWELVE

I Want to Witness, But What Do I Say Around the Great Outdoors?"

**Beach, Camping,
Dogs & Cats,
Farm, Fishing, Flowers,
Park, Swimming Pool
Weather and Zoo**

The hardest part about witnessing is *the transition* from an everyday conversation onto the Gospel track. One way to do it is through relating the Gospel to objects around you like Jesus did many times in Matthew 13. These object evangelism icebreakers will *train* you how to transition conversations onto the Gospel *track*. Jesus is coming soon, so use loving boldness and be compassionate. Then be led by the Spirit using whatever method you choose. You may prophesy or pray for healing or whatever is needed. After the icebreaker there is an invitation to pray a salvation prayer. Then be bold and encourage them to pray that salvation prayer after you.

"I Want to Witness, But What Do I Say at the Beach?"

Anchor for Boat – This anchor reminds me of Jesus Christ because He is the same yesterday, today and forever. He never moves. He always loves me and will never leave me nor forsake me. This gives me great hope, which is like an anchor for my soul. Have you ever asked Jesus Christ to your Lord?

Hebrews 6:19, 13:8; Isaiah 41:10

Boat - That boat reminds me of Jesus and His 12 disciples that were in the boat with Him, but these days many people are rebellious and are not in the same boat with Jesus. Are you in His boat?

Lifeguard – As I look at that lifeguard watching over me, it reminds me of the One that is really my lifeguard. His name is Jesus Christ. He protects me and keeps me from going under (into hell) so I shall be safe in heaven for all eternity....Have you ever made Jesus Christ your lifeguard?   Isaiah 62:6; Psalm 121:3–5

Ocean – The ocean is so vast. It reminds me of Psalm 93:4 "Mightier than the thunder of the great waters and mightier than the breakers of the sea, the Lord on high is mighty." As I look upon the waves, I know that only God could have created the ocean. If He created that, then I know He created everything else too, including me. So I received Jesus as my Lord because I know that He really loves me...Do you know how much Jesus loves you?

Sailing – As I look at those sailboats propelled by the wind, it reminds me of how believers are led by the Spirit of God. As a Christian surrenders their will to Father God, then with the wind of the Holy Spirit, God can gently lead their lives in whatever direction He wants them to go. I know that God loves me, so I chose to receive Him as my Lord. His way is always the best way. Have you ever made Jesus Christ your Lord?   John 3:8; Romans 10:9–10

Sand – Some people are so depressed. They think that no one cares about them. But it says in Psalm 139:17–18: "How precious also are thy thoughts unto me, O God! How great is the sum of them! If I should count them, they are more in number than the *sand.*" So I know that God thinks about you a lot too! He loves you so much…Would you like to receive Jesus as your Lord?

Sunburn – If you are a Christian, then at least this burn will be temporary, but all those that have *not* received Jesus Christ as their Lord and Savior will burn for all eternity. But don't worry because God loves you and receiving Jesus Christ as your Lord, will save you from burning in hell…. So would you like to pray after me a salvation prayer?

Sunglasses – I like to get the rose-colored lenses because it reminds me of my righteousness with God. Jesus Christ paid the price for the sins of the world. So since I received Jesus as my Lord, God does not see my sins anymore. It is like God sees me now through rose-colored glasses that are stained rose by the blood of His Son Jesus Christ. He loves us so much. Would you like to receive Jesus as your Lord and Savior?

Suntan Oil – This suntan oil reminds me of the Holy Spirit. When a person asks Jesus Christ to come into their heart, the Holy Spirit, also called "the oil of joy," comes into their heart to abide and gives them eternal life too. God will fill us with His joy and peace as we trust in Him…Would you like to have this oil of joy?

Isaiah 61:3

Salvation Prayer: "Heavenly Father, I believe that Your Son Jesus Christ died on the cross for my sins and rose from the dead. I repent of my sins. Jesus, I ask You to forgive me and come into my heart and be my Lord and Savior. Fill me with the Holy Spirit. Thank You for saving me from hell and giving me eternal life in heaven, in Jesus' name I pray, Amen.

"I Want to Witness, But What Do I Say When Camping?

Birds – When I am poor and needy, the birds remind me of God's love for me. Matthew 6:26 says: "They (the birds) do not sow or reap or store away in barns, and yet your Heavenly Father feeds them. Are you not much more valuable than they?"...Do you know how much Jesus loves you too? Have you made Him your Lord?

Camping – When I think about bears or snakes around here, it reminds me of Psalm 34:7 that says, "The angel of the Lord *encamps* around those that fear Him and delivers them." So God's divine protection is only for those who fear Him or know Jesus as Lord...So is Jesus your Lord? If not, let's pray right now before it gets dark.

Grass or Flowers – These wilted flowers remind me of Isaiah 40:8: "The grass withers, the flowers fade, but the Word of our God will stand forever." Circumstances and people change, but God never changes. The best change of all is receiving Jesus as your Lord and Savior... Have you ever made that change?

Fire – The campfire reminds me of Acts 2:2: "Suddenly a sound from heaven came as of a mighty rushing wind and there appeared to them cloven tongues like as of *fire* and it sat upon each of them and they were all filled with the Holy Ghost and began to speak with other tongues as the Spirit gave them utterance." Would any one like prayer to receive your prayer language?

Firefly – That firefly reminds me of Christians who "shine their light" for Jesus through witnessing and doing good works...So have you become born again yet, so you can be a firefly for Jesus?

Mountain – That mountain, it reminds me of the heart-breaking trials that people experience in their lives, but God's love is so great, He can lift you up over any problem in your life. In God's eyes, the biggest mountain was mankind's sin that separated us all from God, but God removed this mountain when He sent Son Jesus Christ who shed His blood and died on the cross for our sins so that we could have eternal life...So is Jesus your Lord?   Mark 11:23

River – That River reminds me of getting filled with the spirit: "out of your belly will flow *rivers* of living water." I remember the first time I prayed in tongues... Have you ever been baptized in the Holy Spirit?   John 7:38

Rock – This rock reminds me of Psalm 18:2: "The Lord is *my Rock*, my fortress, my strength, in Whom I will trust." ... So have you ever made Jesus your Rock?

Stream – This stream here reminds me of the "live stream" on the internet. So many churches now have their Sunday morning church services live streamed on their website...Have you ever watched a live stream?   Hebrews 10:25?

Tent – This tent reminds me of how Abraham lived in tents for years as he walked by faith with God, which really pleased God, so he became the father of many nations (Genesis 17:5)...So have you ever put your faith in God?

Wilderness – As I walk through this wilderness, it reminds me of John the Baptist who cried out in the wilderness before Jesus Christ came: "Prepare the way of the Lord; make His paths straight and the rough places smooth." I know that Jesus is coming again...If He should come today would you be ready to meet Him?   Isaiah 40:5

Salvation Prayer: "Heavenly Father, I believe that Your Son Jesus Christ died on the cross for my sins and rose from the dead. I repent of my sins. Jesus, I ask You to forgive me and come into my heart and be my Lord and Savior. Fill me with the Holy Spirit. Thank You for saving me from hell and giving me eternal life in heaven, in Jesus' name I pray, Amen."

"I Want to Witness, But What Do I Say Around Dogs & Cats?"

Cat's Fur – It is so comforting to pet the soft fur of my cat. It reminds me of the Holy Spirit whose manifest presence is my true Comforter from the pain and sorrow in life. When I praise and worship the Lord, His presence comes full of love and peace and joy. So do you have that comfort in your life? Have you ever prayed to receive Jesus Christ as your Lord and Savior?

Ephesians 5:18; John 14:16

Cat Nursing Kittens – As I watch that cat nurse her kittens it reminds me of El Shaddai which is a name for God meaning "The many breasted One" to signify that God's provision never runs dry.   1 Peter 2:2 says, "As newborn babes, desire the pure milk of the word, that you may grow thereby,"....So is Jesus your Lord?

Philippians 4:19; Matthew 6:33

Cat and Mouse – Did you hear the joke about how the cat ate the mouse? The cat's owner was so upset! She could not answer her e–mails that day. She had to buy a new *computer* mouse! (*Laugh*) I am so thankful that prayer does not work like e–mail. Because I received Jesus as my Lord, I have a connection with God *by His Spirit* and that is better than any wireless connection could ever be. God always hears my prayers. . So are you connected to God?

Dog Poop – When I clean up this dog poop, it reminds me of how thankful I am that God cleaned up the messes that I made in my life.   When I received Jesus Christ as my Lord, His shed blood on the cross cleansed me and reconciled me back to God. Now I have a relationship with God and eternal life in heaven! And now when I mess up, I remember 1 John 1:9 and ask the Lord to forgive me. He is faithful and just to do that and I continue to walk with Him...so do you have a born again relationship with God?   John 1:9

Dog Tugs on Leash – When I walk my dog, sometimes he tugs and pulls away from me to go where he wants to go, so I have to pull him back. It reminds me of how Jesus is my Lord and so the Holy Spirit pulls me back when I am tempted to sin or rebel and go my own way. Have you ever felt God's pull on your heart to pray to receive Jesus as Lord and Savior?   1 Corinthians 10:13

Dog Collar – If your dog's collar is too tight, it can suffocate the dog. If you have it too loose, then you dog can easily slip out of it and run away, leaving you with just your leash in hand! When I became born again, by the power of the Holy Spirit, I am thankful that God put a collar on me (or a yoke, the Bible calls it) and His collar or His yoke is easy and light, so it makes for a pleasant walk with my Lord.   Matthew 11:28-30

Tail Wagging – I know my dog is happy and excited when he/she wags its tail. That tail wagging reminds me of how God feels when one sinner repents and receives Jesus as their Lord. He is so joyful because He knows that because of that one right decision that He will spend eternity with them!   Luke 15:7

Walking your Dog – Since I am his master, my dog goes wherever I lead him on /her leash. And since I am a Christian, I go wherever the Lord leads me to go by His Spirit. So He walks me! Today He led me to walk my dog down this street so that I would run into you. So you must be someone special. Do you know how much Jesus loves you? Have you ever prayed to receive Jesus as your Lord?   Romans 8:14

Salvation Prayer: "Heavenly Father, I believe that Your Son Jesus Christ died on the cross for my sins and rose from the dead. I repent of my sins. Jesus, I ask You to forgive me and come into my heart and be my Lord and Savior. Fill me with the Holy Spirit. Thank You for saving me from hell and giving me eternal life in heaven, in Jesus' name I pray, Amen."

"I Want to Witness, But What Do I Say on a Farm?"

Barn – This barn reminds me of the barn in Matthew 13:30. In this parable, the barn means Heaven. At harvest time, the wheat will be gathered up into the barn and the weeds (the sinners) will be burned in hell. Harvest time is when Jesus Christ comes again and He tells the angels to reap those who received Jesus as Lord (the wheat) and take them up into His barn. Harvest time is coming soon...So are you a weed or wheat? Do you want to receive Jesus as Lord?

Cowboy – The Bible says that Jesus Christ is coming back on a white horse.... He is coming back for His Bride, which is the whole Body of Christ all over the world, to take us all to heaven with Him. Since Jesus is coming back on a horse, He must be a cowboy at heart. You probably have a lot in common with Him.... So is Jesus your Lord and Savior?

Green Pasture – As I look out upon that beautiful green pasture, it reminds me of Psalm 23, "the Lord is My Shepherd, I shall not want. He makes me lie down in *green pastures*. He leads me beside the still waters" ...Have you ever received Jesus Christ as Savior and your Good Shepherd?

Harvest – As I look upon these fields, it reminds me of the Good News of God's harvest field. But *the bad news is* if you sin (like a weed), you will be separated from God because God is holy and perfect and will not allow sin to come into His heaven where He dwells. We all have all sinned. No one is perfect. Only God is. So if we are separated from God, then we will all go to hell – a place of torment, pain and suffering. Reconciliation with God is only possible if your sins are forgiven. There is no forgiveness of sins without the shedding of blood. So in the Old Testament only the priests (wheat) shed the blood of perfect lambs and sacrificed them on the altar to atone for the Israelite's sins. Back then, only Moses and the priests had a relationship with God. But God wants a relationship with everyone (lots of wheat!). The Good News is God sent His Son Jesus Christ to be the "Lamb of God" for the world. He sacrificed His blood on the cross for our sins and God raised Him from the dead, so that all that believe in Jesus could be forgiven, reconciled to God and reap the harvest of heaven. Have you received Jesus as your Lord?

Horse – That beautiful horse reminds me of the fact that Jesus Christ is coming back again on a white horse (Revelation 19:11). He is coming back for His Bride, whom are all the Christians, to catch us all up to heaven with Him. They call it the rapture. Those who have not received Jesus as Lord will be left behind…If Jesus came back today on that white horse would you be ready?

Seed – As I look at this seed, it reminds me of John 12:24 "Unless a grain of wheat falls into the ground and dies, it remains alone; but if it dies, it produces much grain." God gave His Son Jesus Christ as a seed for the whole world. He willingly died on the cross for our sins so that those who believe in Him could be reconciled to God and become His sons and daughters whom He could love and cherish for all eternity…. Have you received Jesus as your Lord?

Salvation Prayer: "Heavenly Father, I believe that Your Son Jesus Christ died on the cross for my sins and rose from the dead. I repent of my sins. Jesus, I ask You to forgive me and come into my heart and be my Lord and Savior. Fill me with the Holy Spirit. Thank You for saving me from hell and giving me eternal life in heaven, in Jesus' name I pray, Amen."

✝

"I Want to Witness, But What Do I Say When Fishing?"

Bait – This bait reminds me of the bait of satan, which is offense. Offense keeps many people out of church. Pastors and church members are not perfect. They are just forgiven. Unless your sins are forgiven, you won't make it into heaven. When you pray to receive Jesus as Lord, your sins will be forgiven…. When you forgive others, Romans 12:19 says that vengeance is the Lord's and He will repay you. Would you like to pray to receive Jesus as your Lord? Matthew 6:14

Fisherman – Being out here fishing reminds me of what Jesus said to His disciples in Matthew 4: 19: "Come, I will make you fishers of men." It says in Proverbs 11:30 that "he who wins souls is wise." I asked Jesus Christ to be my Lord and I committed my life to be a fisher of men. Do you know how much Jesus loves you? Is Jesus your Lord? John 3:16

Lake – I love to go fishing in lakes, but there is one lake that I want to avoid and that is the lake of fire. That is the punishment for people who will not receive Jesus as Lord…but do you know how much Jesus loves you? He wants you to spend eternity with Him

Net – This fishing net reminds me of what it says in Matthew 13:47. Jesus said that the Kingdom of Heaven is like a *net* that was let down into the lake and caught all kinds of fish. The *good fish* were collected in baskets and the *bad fish* were thrown away. He explained that this is how it will be at the end of the age. The angels will come and separate the wicked from the righteous. They will throw the wicked into the fiery furnace, where there will be weeping and gnashing of teeth. But the good fish will be saved. I know I am a good fish because I have accepted Jesus as my Lord. Are you a good fish? Would you like to pray to receive Jesus Christ as your Lord and Savior?

Rod and Reel – As I go fishing with my rod and reel it reminds me of what it says in Psalm 23:4: "Yea, though I walk through the valley of the shadow of death, I will fear no evil; for You are with me: Your rod and Your staff; [or *Your rod and Your reel!*] They comfort me." It is a comfort knowing that Jesus is my Shepherd and my Lord… Is He your Shepherd and your Lord?

Tug on the Line – Fishing is so relaxing. You just sit and wait until you get a bite. So I take the time to quietly pray and then listen to God. Many times He will tug on my heart and then I will catch an exciting fresh revelation about Him that I never knew before. It is the same excitement I feel when a fish is tugging on my line…I believe God is tugging at your heart right now…Will you let Him catch you and pray to receive Jesus as Lord?

Worm – This bait reminds me of the many times that Jesus referred to worms and He was not fishing. In Mark 9:44 Jesus describes hell as where: "their worm does not die and the fire is not quenched." There is so much fire in hell, I know that the worms should burn to death, but they never die. That is so gross! I'm so glad that I received Jesus as my Lord. I'm saved from hell …So is Jesus your Lord? Are you saved?

Salvation Prayer: "Heavenly Father, I believe that Your Son Jesus Christ died on the cross for my sins and rose from the dead. I repent of my sins. Jesus, I ask You to forgive me and come into my heart and be my Lord and Savior. Fill me with the Holy Spirit. Thank You for saving me from hell and giving me eternal life in heaven, in Jesus' name I pray, Amen."

"I Want to Witness, But What Do I Say with Flowers?"

Brown–Eyed Susan – This flower reminds me of my friend Susan who has brown eyes and often asks people: *"Do you know how much Jesus loves you?"* She witnesses to the lost a lot and has a website called: www.iwanttowitness.com. Have you ever received Jesus as your Lord?

Clover –This clover reminds me of the Trinity – Father, Son and Holy Spirit. Many people take a lot of time to try and find a four leaf clover to get lucky, but I feel like I am already lucky and blessed because I prayed to receive Jesus as my Savior and now I have eternal life in heaven.   Matthew 28:19

Dogwood Tree Flowers – I heard that the dogwood tree was once firm and strong, like an oak tree, so it was chosen to be the wood for Jesus' cross where He died. The dogwood was greatly distressed for being used for such a cruel purpose. So Jesus had mercy on the dogwood tree and said: "Because of your pity for My suffering, never again shall you grow large enough to be used as a cross. Now your blossoms shall bloom in the shape of a cross. In the center of the outer edge of each petal there will be nail prints - brown with rust and stained with red. In the center will be a crown of thorns."...Have you ever prayed to receive Jesus as your Lord? Matthew 27:29

Lily – Oh how I love lilies. Lilies remind me of that verse in Song of Solomon 2:1 that says that Jesus Christ is *the lily of the valley*. He is the bright spot during the trials of life when we feel like we are in a valley. Lilies also surround the altar at church during Easter to celebrate the Resurrection of Jesus Christ. Have you ever prayed to receive Jesus Christ as your Lord and Savior?

Impatiens – As I look at these flowers, it reminds me to not be impatient because God is so very patient with us. He is patiently waiting for multitudes of people to receive Jesus Christ as their Lord and bloom into Christians.

Poinsettias – I love these pretty poinsettia plants that are used to decorate the altars at church during Christmas time. The red and white ones are so pretty. Do you ever see them there at church? Do you go to a church? Would you like to come to mine?

Roses – I love roses because they remind me of Jesus. In the Bible in Song of Solomon 2:1 He is described, as the *Rose of Sharon* Jesus Christ is the lovely rose between the ugly thorns of sin, sickness and sorrow. Our sins separate us from God, but when Jesus Christ died on the cross; His blood paid the price for our sins and reconciled us to God. When we pray to receive Him as Lord and Savior, we become His born–again children like these smaller tea roses... Have you received Jesus as your Lord and Savior?

Wilted Flowers – As I watch these flowers wilt in this vase, Isaiah 40:8 comforts me: "The grass withers, the flowers fade, but the Word of our God will stand forever." With so many things changing all the time, I am so thankful that the Word of God never changes. He is the same yesterday, today and forever.... So do you need a change? Would you like to pray and receive Jesus Christ as your Lord and Savior?   Isaiah 40:8

Salvation Prayer: "Heavenly Father, I believe that Your Son Jesus Christ died on the cross for my sins and rose from the dead. I repent of my sins. Jesus, I ask You to forgive me and come into my heart and be my Lord and Savior. Fill me with the Holy Spirit. Thank You for saving me from hell and giving me eternal life in heaven, in Jesus' name I pray, Amen."

I Want to Witness, But What Do I Say
at a Park?"

Birds – When I am feeling down, it comforts me to look at the birds. Matthew 6:26 says: "Look at the birds of the air; they do not sow or reap…and yet your Heavenly Father feeds them. Are you not much more valuable than they?" I know I am. God is My Provider and My Salvation through His Son Jesus and so I shall trust in Him…. Have you ever put your trust in Him? Would you like to pray?

Fountain – The flowing water from this fountain reminds me of how Jesus Christ is the Living Water that floods my soul with His wonderful love, joy and peace. He is the fountain of eternal life (Psalm 36:9)… Do you have this fountain of life flowing in you? Would you like to pray?

Grass – As I look at the grass that is kind of brown, it reminds me of this scripture in Isaiah 40:8 "The grass withers, the flowers fade, but the Word of our God will stand forever." I am so thankful that the Word of God never changes. He is the same yesterday, today and forever. Are you feeling a little brown like this grass? Praying to receive Jesus Christ as your Lord will give you new life just like fresh green grass – Would you like to pray?

Merry--Go–Round – This reminds me of Proverbs 17:22: "A merry heart does good like a medicine." Receiving Jesus as your Lord will cause you to be merry with His joy and you will have eternal life…Would you like to pray?

Park Bench – Sitting here reminds me that Jesus Christ is seated too at the right hand of the Father, waiting until time for Him to come again to get His Bride, who is the Church. When He comes again will you be ready? Would you like to pray?

Seesaw – When it comes to serving God, some people are up and down just like this seesaw. When they are around their church friends, they act like a Christian and live for God. But when they are around unbelievers they blend right in with the crowd and act like them too. But I'm not afraid of what others think. I only care about what God thinks and so I always live for God and do not seesaw. Do you know how much Jesus loves you? So is He your Lord?

Slide – As I get on the slide, I am glad that I am sliding forward. I would not want to *backslide* because then I might go to hell. Do you know how much Jesus loves you? Is He your Lord?

Swing – I hate to spoil your fun for how high you can swing, but the truth is: You cannot get to heaven on that swing, but only through praying to receive Jesus as your Lord. Then your spirit will be swinging with Him...So would you like to pray?

Tree – That tree reminds me of what the Bible says about trees. Christians are called: "trees of righteousness." We are supposed to be rooted and grounded in the Word of God. Then, just like a tree grows, we will spiritually grow and bear good fruit. In order to be a tree of righteousness, you need to receive Jesus Christ as your Lord and Savior. Isaiah 61:3; Ephesians 3:17–18

Trashcan – This trashcan reminds me of the devil and how he is always talking trash to people to make them feel like they are not going to make it in life. Well, he is a liar. The Bible says, "I can do all things through Christ who strengthens me."   Philippians 4:13

Salvation Prayer: "Heavenly Father, I believe that Your Son Jesus Christ died on the cross for my sins and rose from the dead. I repent of my sins. Jesus, I ask You to forgive me and come into my heart and be my Lord and Savior. Fill me with the Holy Spirit. Thank You for saving me from hell and giving me eternal life in heaven, in Jesus' name I pray, Amen."

"I Want to Witness, But What Do I Say at a Swimming Pool?"

Lifeguard – As I look at that lifeguard watching over me, it reminds me of the One that is really my lifeguard...He is Jesus Christ, my Lord and Savior. He guards me from any attacks of the enemy because He loves me. He keeps me from going under (you know, <u>way</u> down under to hell) and He keeps me safe for all eternity.... Have you made Jesus your lifeguard?

Suntan Oil – This suntan oil reminds me of how God comforts those who grieve. Isaiah 61:3 says God gives them "the *oil of joy* for mourning and a garment of praise for the spirit of heaviness." When a person asks Jesus Christ to be their Lord, then the Holy Spirit, who is that oil of joy, comes into their heart...Would you like to pray to receive that oil of joy right now?

Ointment for Burns – I'll bet that sunburn really hurts. I have some ointment that will take away the sting. Here, put some of this on. This ointment reminds me of Song of Solomon 1:2: "Your name is ointment poured forth." Jesus Christ is that name. He is the Savior and the Healer. Is Jesus your Lord? Can I pray for your sunburn to be healed?

Sunglasses – When I buy sun– glasses, I get the rose–colored lenses because it reminds me of my righteousness. Since I received Jesus as my Lord, God does not see my sins, but He sees me through rose–colored glasses that are stained rose by the blood of His Son Jesus Christ. I'm so thankful that God loves me. He loves you too...Do you want to receive Jesus as your Lord?

Butterfly – As I watch that swimmer swim the butterfly, it reminds me of how the caterpillar goes into his cocoon and then in God's timing comes out as a butterfly, like a new creature. Have you ever become a new creature in Christ Jesus through praying to receive Jesus as Lord? 2 Corinthians 5:17

Backstroke – Watching the backstroke reminds me of sinners that are backwards in their believing as atheists or agnostics. It also reminds me of Christians who are *backslidden* because of ungodly peer pressure, false religions, alcohol, drugs, pre–marital sex or homosexuality, which are all forbidden in the Bible. Jesus is coming soon, so I pray when they do hit the wall, that they will do a flip–turn in their hearts and repent and rededicate their lives to God once again…So are you doing the backstroke?…Would you like to pray with me to rededicate your life to the Lord?

Pool Water – As I look at the pool water, it reminds me of the Baptism of Holy Spirit. Imagine that the **water** is the Holy Spirit. First, you pray and ask God for the Baptism of the Holy Spirit. Then He gives it to you. (*Then jump into the water submerging your head as well*). In the same way the water went over my head, the Holy Spirit fills me to overflowing. Then the Holy Spirit gives me my prayer language (utterance). I cooperate with Him by boldly moving my tongue and lips. I learned to relax and not think too much because you receive with **your spirit,** not your mind. Your utterance may sound strange, but it is a heavenly prayer language and God understands you. If it is His will, God will give you the interpretation. So would you like to pray to receive the Baptism of the Holy Spirit? We can pray right now.

Salvation Prayer: "Heavenly Father, I believe that Your Son Jesus Christ died on the cross for my sins and rose from the dead. I repent of my sins. Jesus, I ask You to forgive me and come into my heart and be my Lord and Savior. Fill me with the Holy Spirit. Thank You for saving me from hell and giving me eternal life in heaven, in Jesus' name I pray, Amen."

"I Want to Witness, But What Do I Say About the Weather?"

Bright Morning Star – As I look at that bright morning star I am reminded of a scripture in Revelation 22:16 where Jesus said, "I Am the bright and morning star." He is the most famous star Who shines bright in my heart. Do you know how much Jesus loves you? Would you like to receive Him as Lord, so He can shine in your heart?

Cloudy Day – Those clouds remind me of how Jesus Christ will come again. The Bible says the Son of Man will come back in a **cloud** with power and great glory. Since Jesus is my Lord and Savior, when He comes again in the clouds, He will take me up with Him to heaven, but those who do not know Jesus as their Lord and Savior will be left behind. So are you ready to meet Jesus if He were to come in the clouds today?   Luke 21:27

Hot Day – It is so hot out today! It makes me thankful that Jesus is my Lord and Savior and I will not be spending eternity in the hot fires of hell. Heaven will have perfect weather. Do you know where you will spend eternity?

Lightning – Wow! Look at that lightning. That reminds me of Matthew 24:27: "For as lightning that comes from the east and flashes to the west, so also will be the coming of the Son of Man be." When Jesus comes again, I will be so happy, but many will mourn because then they will finally realize that Jesus really is the Son of God, the Savior of the world, and they were deceived and are too late to get their hearts right with God.... But you don't have to mourn. You can pray with me receive Jesus right now.

Rain – As I watch that rain come down, it reminds me of how thankful I am that the Lord reigns in my life...I received Jesus Christ as my Lord and Savior and now He rules and *reigns* in my heart all day. He knows everything about everyone and His way is the best way. Does Jesus reign in your heart? Psalm 93:1; Isaiah 55:10

Snow – This snow is so holy looking. It reminds me of Isaiah 1:18 when the Lord said, "Though your sins be as scarlet, they shall be as white as snow." When a person receives Jesus Christ as their Lord, then their sins are washed away and in God's eyes, they become holy again, like white as snow...Would you like to pray to receive Him as your Lord and Savior and receive eternal life in heaven?

Sunny Day – I am so thankful for the sun that gives me light to see, but I am more thankful for the Son of God, who loves me and gives light and life for all eternity.... In Revelation 1:16 when John saw the Lord, he said, "His face was like the sun shining in all of its brilliance."... Have you ever prayed to receive Jesus as your Lord?

Windy Day – This wind reminds me what happened on the Day of Pentecost..."And suddenly there came from heaven, as of a rushing *mighty wind*, and it filled the whole house where they were sitting. And there appeared to them cloven tongues as of fire... and they were all filled with the Holy Ghost as the Spirit gave them utterance. Have you ever received the Baptism of the Holy Spirit and prayed in tongues? Acts 2:2–2

Salvation Prayer: "Heavenly Father, I believe that Your Son Jesus Christ died on the cross for my sins and rose from the dead. I repent of my sins. Jesus, I ask You to forgive me and come into my heart and be my Lord and Savior. Fill me with the Holy Spirit. Thank You for saving me from hell and giving me eternal life in heaven, in Jesus' name I pray, Amen."

†   †   †

"I Want to Witness, But What Do I Say at a Zoo?"

Calf – That calf reminds me of when the Israelites sinned against God by worshipping a golden calf. The Lord was so angry and jealous that He wanted to destroy them, but Moses interceded and prayed, so God relented (Exodus. 32:14). Many people worship idols today (too much sports or TV), but if you give your heart to God as your first love, you will have eternal life…. Would you like to pray?

Camel – As I look at that camel it reminds me of what Jesus said, "It is easier for a camel to go through a needle's eye, than for a rich man to enter the kingdom of God." I guess that is because they trust in their wealth instead of trusting in Jesus to be saved. So have you ever prayed to receive Him as your Lord? Luke 18:24–25

Deer – As I look at that deer, it reminds me of that Psalm 42:1 "As the deer pants for the water brooks, so pants my soul for You, O God."…I love the Lord and I long to be with Him just like that deer pants for the water because I know that He loves me and He is so faithful. He will never let you down. He loves you too…. Do you know Him as your Lord?

Dove – That dove reminds me of when the Holy Ghost descended like a dove upon Jesus, and voice from heaven said, "Thou art my beloved Son; in thee I Am well pleased."…So is Jesus your Lord? **Lamb** – As I look at that cute lamb, it reminds me of what John the Baptist said about Jesus Christ in John 1:36: "Behold the Lamb of God!"…So is He in your heart?

Lion – Seeing that lion reminds me of what the Bible says in Proverbs 28:1 that the righteous are as bold as a lion. The spirit of God on the inside of Christians gives us the power and the authority through our Lord Jesus Christ to command demons and darkness to leave us alone. Would you like to have that same power? It all begins with receiving Jesus as your Lord and Savior.... Would you like to pray? Luke 10: 19

Trashcan – This trashcan reminds me of the devil and how he is always talking trash to people to make them feel like they are not going to make it in life. Well, he is a liar. The Bible says, "I can do all things through Christ who strengthens me." Philippians 4:13

Zebra – Seeing those stripes on that zebra's back reminds me of the red stripes of blood on Jesus' back after the Roman soldiers whipped Him. It says in 1 Peter 2:24 that "By His stripes we were healed." And because Jesus died on the cross for our sins, those who believe and receive Him as Lord and Savior shall be saved from hell and will go to heaven. ...So are you going to heaven?

Zoo – I love going to the zoo. It reminds me of Noah's ark. I am so thankful for Noah because if it weren't for him, we would not have this zoo here today because we would have no animals at all. But Noah obeyed God. He built the ark and put all of the animals and his family on it so that they would survive the massive flood that God brought upon the earth to judge it for man's sin. It is so important to obey God and walk in His will. God's will is for all people to receive Jesus Christ as their Lord and Savior so that they can go to heaven. . Is Jesus Christ your Lord and Savior? Would you like to pray to receive Him as your Savior? Genesis 9:11–15

Salvation Prayer: "Heavenly Father, I believe that Your Son Jesus Christ died on the cross for my sins and rose from the dead. I repent of my sins. Jesus, I ask You to forgive me and come into my heart and be my Lord and Savior. Fill me with the Holy Spirit. Thank You for saving me from hell and giving me eternal life in heaven, in Jesus' name I pray, Amen."

CHAPTER THIRTEEN

"I Want to Witness, But What Do I Say When Shopping or Doing Errands?"

**Beauty Salon, Bookstore
Grocery Store, Hardware Store
Laundromat, Mall
Post Office**

The hardest part about witnessing is *the transition* from an everyday conversation onto the Gospel track. One way to do it is through relating the Gospel to objects around you like Jesus did many times in Matthew 13. These object evangelism icebreakers will **train** you how to transition conversations onto the Gospel **track.** Jesus is coming soon, so use loving boldness and be compassionate. Then be led by the Spirit using whatever method. You may prophesy or pray for healing for whatever is needed. After the icebreaker, there is an invitation to help reel them into salvation. Then be bold and encourage them to pray a salvation prayer after you.

I Want to Witness, But What Do I Say at a Beauty Salon?"

Brush or Comb – As I pull this comb through my tangled hair, it reminds me of how God can make every crooked place straight and take the tangles out of my life if I just put my trust in Him and let Him be in control. Have you ever asked Jesus to come into your heart to take control of your life?   Proverbs 3:6

Fingernail Polish – As you apply that **red** polish to cover my nails, it reminds me of the blood of Jesus Christ that covers my sins. (Romans 4:7). I'm thankful He loves me. I know that in a week or so, this nail polish will fade and chip away, but God will never leave me. His love never fades nor chips away. His love never fails. Jesus loves you too...Would you like to receive Him as your Lord? Hebrews 13:5; 1 Corinthians 13:8

Hair Colored – I like to get my hair colored because it takes away all the undesirable gray. It reminds me of Jesus Christ who died on the cross to take away all my undesirable sins. He removed them with His shed blood so that I could be reconciled to God and receive eternal life in heaven... Would you like to receive Jesus Christ as your Lord?   Romans 4:7; John 3:16

Haircut – Getting these dead ends cut off reminds me of all those that are cut off from God because they will not believe and pray to receive Jesus Christ as their Lord and Savior. So if they die before they pray, they will be cut off from Him for all eternity and go to hell. It is a tragic thing to be cut off from God. I made Jesus my Lord and Savior...so is He your Lord? John 15:6

Make Over – I love the new look that I get with this new makeup. It reminds me of the "new spiritual look" that I got on the inside when I became a born again believer. I became a new creature in Christ Jesus with the old passing away and a new Christ–centered outlook coming forth in my life. It was the best make over I ever had. Would you like this eternal make over? 2 Corinthians 5:17

Manicure – As I watch you file and shape my nails, it reminds me of a scripture that says when you believe in the Lord, He will make the crooked places straight and the rough places smooth in your life…Do you know how much Jesus loves you? Have you ever prayed to receive Jesus as your Lord? Isaiah 40:4

Mirror – Mirrors remind me of the truth that Jesus Christ is the mirror image of the invisible God. Jesus came to earth to show us what God is like in heaven. As a person reads the Bible that tells about all that Jesus did while here on earth, then they will come to know what God in heaven is like because God and Jesus Christ are one or mirror images of each other. Have you received Jesus as your Lord?

Pedicure – Watching you wash and pedicure my feet reminds me of when Jesus Christ washed the disciples' feet. He was so humble and kind, just like you are. I am thankful to have someone pedicure my ugly feet, but Isaiah 52:7 says: "Oh how beautiful are the feet of those that bring Good News"… Do you know how much God loves you? He has a plan and a purpose for your life. Would you like to pray to receive Him as your Lord and Savior?

Salvation Prayer: "Heavenly Father, I believe that Your Son Jesus Christ died on the cross for my sins and rose from the dead. I repent of my sins. Jesus, I ask You to forgive me and come into my heart and be my Lord and Savior. Fill me with the Holy Spirit. Thank You for saving me from hell and giving me eternal life in heaven, in Jesus' name I pray, Amen."

I Want to Witness, But What Do I Say at the Bookstore?"

Best Selling Book – You know what book for centuries has been the best–selling book? It's the Bible. It has the power to save even the worst sinner from their sin and set them free! There is love, joy, peace, healing, deliverance, your identity and the meaning of your life. It is all in this one supernatural book, but in order to truly understand it, you need to pray to receive Jesus as your Savior...Would you like to pray?

Bookmark – I put this in the place where I stopped reading so that I can find my place again. In the same way, I thank God that He helps me find *my place in this world* as I pray and read His Word. I press on towards *the mark* that He has called me to do...Have you ever called on Jesus as your Lord? Philippians 3:14

Bookworm – Are you a bookworm? I am. If you're a true bookworm, you'd rather spend Friday nights on the couch with a book than out at a party. You know, intellectually, the best book I ever read was the Bible. I read all the Gospels and realized that they could not be "made up stories," but that it was all true, so I did the intelligent thing and prayed to receive Jesus as my Lord....Have you ever done that?

Knowledge – As I look at all these books, it blows my mind how much knowledge there is to take in and yet God knows it all. He is omniscient – all knowing. He knows who is born–again and He knows who is not ...So which one are you?

Book of Life – Have you ever read **the Lamb's Book of Life?** My name is published in there because I prayed to receive Jesus Christ as my Lord and now have eternal life. It is like heaven's reservation book...Would you like to pray to make a reservation for heaven? Revelation 21:27

My Favorite Author – is the One who is the *author* and the finisher of my faith. .Hebrews 12:2 says, "looking unto Jesus, *the author and finisher of our faith*, who for the joy set before Him endured the cross." Jesus had joy in enduring the cross because He knew that His great pain would result in a great gain of souls into His Kingdom…Do you know how much He loves you?

Pages – All these pages remind me of the pages of my life and each page has a specific memory – some good and some bad. It's amazing that God knows every single page of my life. He knows every mistake I ever made and He still loves me. So I prayed to receive Him as my Lord and Savior. Have you ever done that?

Thick Book – When I think about how long it would take me to read this thick book, it reminds me of eternity. Our life here on earth is like the first one or two pages, but eternity is like the whole rest of the book. That is *a long time* to be spent in the wrong place…. Do you know how much Jesus loves you? Have you ever prayed to receive Him as your Lord and Savior?

What Would God Read? As I browse and think about what book I want to read, sometimes I wonder what God would read? I think that He reads people minds. I know that He wants every unbeliever to know how much He loves him or her and if they believe in Jesus, then He will give them eternal life. Life here on earth can be miserable, but Jesus died so that we could have eternal life in heaven and that is just so wonderful…. Don't you agree?

Salvation Prayer: "Heavenly Father, I believe that Your Son Jesus Christ died on the cross for my sins and rose from the dead. I repent of my sins. Jesus, I ask You to forgive me and come into my heart and be my Lord and Savior. Fill me with the Holy Spirit. Thank You for saving me from hell and giving me eternal life in heaven, in Jesus' name I pray, Amen."

"I Want to Witness, But What Do I Say at the Grocery Store?"

Bread – As I buy this bread, it reminds me of what Jesus said: "I Am the Bread of Life. He who comes to Me will never go hungry..." (John 6:35). This *wonder bread* must have been the kind that Jesus used when God multiplied the five loaves so that the 5,000 could eat. According to John 6:11, that was a sign and a <u>wonder</u>! ...So are you hungry for God? Have you ever received Jesus as your Savior?

Bleach – This bleach reminds me of something that can get your clothes even whiter than that bleach. His name is Jesus Christ...In Isaiah 1:18 the Lord says, "Though your sins be as scarlet, they shall be as white as snow." ...Have you ever prayed to receive Jesus as your Savior? Would you like to pray now?

Deli Meat – This meat reminds me of something that Jesus said: "My meat is to do the will of my Father"...It is always important to do God's will. The first thing that God wants us to do is to believe in His Son Jesus Christ and receive Him as Lord and Savior and then you will have eternal life...Would you like to pray? John 4:34

Fruit – This fruit reminds me of the nine fruits of the spirit: love, joy, peace, patience, kindness, goodness, faithfulness, gentleness and self-control. This fruit here nourishes your body, but the "fruit of the spirit" is so healthy because it nourishes your relationships with family and friends. But you cannot truly have spiritual fruit without first receiving Jesus as your Lord....Would you like to pray? Galatians 5:22

Healthy Food - I see that you are buying healthy food. It is good to eat healthy. It will probably help you live longer. But I don't know if that really matters much because I know that Jesus is coming soon. When He comes, He'll take all the born again Christians up to heaven with Him for all eternity...So are you going up? Are you saved? If not, I can pray with you so that you will not be left behind. Romans 14:17

Hollywood Tabloids – I think that these actors and actresses are more famous for their own personal trials than for the movies they star in. I believe the most famous person is Jesus Christ who went through His own personal trial when He went to the cross and died and rose again. His death reconciled me to God and gave me eternal life, so He is my star. It says in Revelation 22:16 that Jesus is "the bright and morning star." My goal in life is to make Jesus Christ famous...So have you ever prayed to receive Him as your Lord and Savior?

Ketchup or Salsa – This ketchup reminds me of the blood of Jesus Christ. His blood is what separates Christianity from every other religion.... Many people do not realize that without the shedding of blood, there is no forgiveness of sins. The payment for sin is death. Jesus' blood was holy and pure because His blood was from God. When Jesus Christ shed His blood and died on the cross, He became the ultimate sacrifice for the sins of the world. He is also called the "Lamb of God." With His blood, Jesus paid the price for our sins. Those who pray to receive Him as their Lord and Savior shall be saved from hell and shall receive eternal life in heaven...Would you like to pray now? Hebrews 9:22; John 3:16; 1 Peter 1:19

Waiting in Line – Seems like this line is taking so long, it reminds me of eternity waiting in this line. Actually, eternity lasts forever. It is a very long time to be spent in the wrong place...Do you know where you will spend eternity? ...Have you ever received Jesus as your Lord?

Salvation Prayer: "Heavenly Father, I believe that Your Son Jesus Christ died on the cross for my sins and rose from the dead. I repent of my sins. Jesus, I ask You to forgive me and come into my heart and be my Lord and Savior. Fill me with the Holy Spirit. Thank You for saving me from hell and giving me eternal life in heaven, in Jesus' name I pray, Amen."

"I Want to Witness, But What Do I Say at a Hardware Store?"

Electric saw – That saw reminds me of the grace of God. It is so much easier than a hand saw. It is the Holy Spirit that convicts me to cut off every branch or sinful thing in me that bears no fruit...So is Jesus your Lord?

Home Improvement – Taking my family to church every Sunday is the best "home improvement" that I ever made. As we all learn to forgive each other, embrace Christ's love and the joy and peace of God, my home life has greatly improved...Does your family go to church?

Ladder – That ladder reminds me of Jacob's ladder in the Bible when the angels went up and down on it. But you know, you can't get to heaven through a ladder. You can only get there through receiving Jesus Christ as Lord...So have you prayed to receive Him as your Lord?

Nails – When I look at those nails, it reminds me of how painful it must have been for Jesus Christ having those nails hammered into His hands and feet on the cross. He went through so much pain and suffering in shedding His blood for my sins. It makes me want to live a *holy* life that will please my God. Pleasing God all begins with receiving Jesus Christ as your Lord...Would you like pray?   1 Peter 1:19; 1 John 4:8–10

Paint –I like white paint the best. It reminds me of Isaiah 43:25 when God said, "I, even I Am He that blots out your sins for Mine own sake." When I received Jesus Christ as my Savior, it's like He painted a new white coat of paint over my sinful coat so that I could be reconciled to God and have eternal life.

Snake or Auger –This auger that unclogs a toilet reminds me of how forgiving others can unclog a sinful heart and cleanses it so that it can receive God's love and the Living Water of eternal life. Matt. 6:14; John 4:10

To Build, Count the Cost – In order to build anything, you must count the cost. That reminds me of building the Kingdom of God. It may cost you in different ways, but God is so worthy and His rewards and benefits are of eternal value. So have you prayed yet to receive Jesus as your Lord?

Stone – That stone reminds me what Jesus said: "The stone the builders rejected has become the chief cornerstone; This is the Lord's doing, and it is marvelous." It is sad that many Jews rejected Jesus, but those who believe and receive Him as Lord and Savior will have eternal life in heaven. ...Would you like to pray to receive Him now as your Lord? Matthew 21:42; 1 Peter 5:6

Workmanship – Wow! That is beautiful workmanship. You sure do have some talent. It reminds me of Ephesians 2:10 which says that "we are God's own workmanship created in Christ Jesus" to do those good works which God predestined for us to do. Doing something great for God all begins with receiving Jesus as your Lord.... So have you prayed to receive Him as Lord?

Wrench – As I use this wrench, it reminds me of how if I trust God, He can turn things around for me...Have you ever put your trust in the Lord? Would you like to now? Romans 8:28

Salvation Prayer: "Heavenly Father, I believe that Your Son Jesus Christ died on the cross for my sins and rose from the dead. I repent of my sins. Jesus, I ask You to forgive me and come into my heart and be my Lord and Savior. Come fill me with the Holy Spirit. Thank You for saving me from hell and giving me eternal life in heaven, in Jesus' name I pray, Amen."

"I Want to Witness, But What Do I Say at the Laundromat?

This _____ laundry detergent reminds me of...
(insert the name of detergent in the blank with the icebreaker below)

All -- Psalm 34:19 that says, "Many are the afflictions of the righteous, but the Lord delivers them out of them **ALL**" and Jesus also said, "With God, **all** things are possible."...Has God ever delivered you out of an impossible situation?

Cheer -- John 16:33 when Jesus said, "Be of good **cheer.** I have overcome the world."...Have you ever been cheerful because of an answer to prayer?

Gain -- Acts 2:24 which explains that Jesus' pain on the cross was our gain because He paid for our sins with His blood... Have you gained eternal life through praying to receive Jesus as your Lord?

Shout – 1 Thessalonians 4:16 which says, "For the Lord Himself will descend from heaven with a **shout,** with the voice of the archangel and with the trumpet of God, and the dead in Christ will rise first." When Jesus comes again, He will be shouting and the Christians who died will rise **first** and then the Christians who are still alive will go up second...So are you ready for the rapture?

Bleach – As I use this bleach to get the stains out and make it white again, it reminds me of what Jesus does. He forgives me of my stains or sins and makes *me spiritually* white again. Isaiah 1:18 says, "Though your sins be as scarlet, they shall be as white as snow."...Have you ever prayed to receive Jesus as your Lord?

Clothes Hanger – As I put this dress on this hanger to keep it from wrinkling, it reminds me of how Jesus Christ is coming back soon for a church *that is without spot or wrinkle.* The spots and the wrinkles are our sins, but Jesus died on the cross for our sins, so we could be clean and white and right with God...So is your heart clean? Have you prayed to receive Jesus Christ as your Lord and Savior?

Dryer – As I watch those clothes going around in that dryer, it reminds me of how my mind at times can go around and around just trying to figure out an answer to a problem I'm facing. But that is when I need to cast my cares upon the Lord and trust in Him with all my heart and lean not to my own understanding. As I cast my cares, I believe that in God's timing I will know what to do because God will show me.....So is Jesus your Lord?   1 Peter 5:7, Proverbs 3:5–6

Dryer Sheet – That dryer sheet reminds me of Gideon's fleece. In Judges 6:39 Gideon was trying to determine God's will, so he put out *a fleece* and prayed: "Let it now be dry only upon the fleece, and upon all the ground let there be dew." The next morning, it was so! But when you are a Christian, you don't need a fleece. Just read God's Word and listen to Him and you can be led by His Spirit and know what to do...So are you a Christian yet?

Lost Sock – I lost one of my socks. It reminds me of how the Good Shepherd feels when one of His sheep is lost. The Lord is my Shepherd...So have you ever prayed to receive Jesus Christ as your Lord?   John 10:14–16

Whites and Darks – As I sort these white and dark clothes, it reminds me of Matthew 25:31–43. Jesus said He would set the sheep on His right hand, but the goats on the left. The sheep hear His voice and follow Him, so they will inherit eternal life. But the goats will go into the everlasting fire.... So do you think that you are a sheep or a goat? I can pray with you to become a sheep.

Salvation Prayer: "Heavenly Father, I believe that Your Son Jesus Christ died on the cross for my sins and rose from the dead. I repent of my sins. Jesus, I ask You to forgive me and come into my heart and be my Lord and Savior. Come fill me with the Holy Spirit. Thank You for saving me from hell and giving me eternal life in heaven, in Jesus' name I pray, Amen."

"I Want to Witness, But What Do I Say at the Mall?"

Blouse – That blouse is so colorful and shiny. The glitter on it reminds me of a "the garment of praise." In Isaiah 61:3 God said that to console those who mourn, He will give them "beauty for ashes, the oil of joy and *the garment of praise* for the spirit of heaviness." In sad times, I am so thankful for His love. To put on that garment of praise, a person has to receive Jesus as their Lord. Have you ever prayed a salvation prayer?

Candle – This candle reminds me of Jesus Christ, who is the light of the world. He said, "He who follows Me shall not walk in darkness, but have the light of life."...Is the light of Jesus Christ burning in your heart? We can pray right now for His light to be turned on in your heart. John 8:14; 1 John 4:8

Mirror – Mirrors reminds me of the truth that Jesus Christ is the mirror image of the invisible God. Jesus came to earth to show us what God is like in heaven...Have you received Jesus as your Lord?

One Dollar Bill – When you look at the back of the one–dollar bill, have you noticed that pyramid with the eye on it? But I am not afraid of that little eye because I trust in God. I know that He is the One that is watching over me, the One who loves me, the One that made the sky and all of our eyes and He is called the El Shaddai – the one God who is more than enough –a lot more than this one dollar bill...So is Jesus your Lord and Savior?

Perfume – Mmmm. I love the sweet fragrance of Red Door (made by Elizabeth Arden). Doesn't it smell like heaven? It reminds me of the door to heaven, whom I know is Jesus Christ that is stained red by His blood. He is the door that leads to eternal life. Have you ever prayed to ask Jesus to come into your heart?

Piercing – I see that you have a piercing(s). I was wondering, did you get your —— pierced to identify with Christ? Jesus was pierced when He died on the cross for my sins, reconciled me to God and saved me from hell Jesus' piercings saved my life…Have you made Jesus your Lord?

Purse – In my purse I hold precious things that I hold dear like my credit cards, my keys and my make–up. It reminds me of my Bible, which is even more precious to me than my purse, because its pages hold the way to eternal life in heaven, and God's peace, love and joy…So do you hold Jesus in your heart?

Rainbow Colored anything – I like that shirt! Whenever I see rainbow colors, it reminds me of how thankful I am for the rainbow because it is the symbol for the promise to Noah that God will never flood the whole earth again to judge it for man's sin. I'm so thankful because there is so much sin in the world, God could flood this place right now! But I'm not afraid because I prayed to receive Jesus Christ as my Lord and Savior…Have you? Genesis 9:11–15

Teddy Bear – This comforting soft teddy bear reminds me of the Holy Spirit. Jesus said in John 14:6 said: "I will ask the Father and He will give you another Comforter to be with you forever." Do you know how much Jesus loves you? He wants to comfort you. Have you ever prayed to receive Him as your Lord?

Salvation Prayer: "Heavenly Father, I believe that Your Son Jesus Christ died on the cross for my sins and rose from the dead. I repent of my sins. Jesus, I ask You to forgive me and come into my heart and be my Lord and Savior. Fill me with the Holy Spirit. Thank You for saving me from hell and giving me eternal life in heaven, in Jesus' name I pray, Amen."

"I Want to Witness, But What Do I Say at a Post Office?"

Door – As I stand here by this door, it reminds me of what Jesus said in John 10: 9 that He is the door to eternal life…. Have you ever walked through that door? Jesus is the most important door you will ever walk through. Have you made Him your Lord?

E–mail is Faster – This is a long line, but I could not send this by e–mail because of the important papers in here. Did you know that paper is really made out of wood? They take the wood and then grind it to a pulp. Once the wood pulp has been treated, washed, bleached and beaten, it becomes paper. This whole process reminds me of Jesus Christ. He was treated badly and then beaten to a pulp with a whip 39 times, then died on a wooden cross…but now we have eternal life if we believe in Him. And His Gospel is written on this paper – in which they have so much in common because this paper and Jesus Christ went through a very similar process! Isaiah 53:4–5

Love letter – I wish I had a love letter. All I ever get is junk mail or bills. Sigh. I must remember that the Word of God is God's love letter to me telling about how God loves me. "God loved the world so much that He gave His only begotten Son and whoever believes in Him shall not perish, but have everlasting life." Yes, Jesus is the true lover of my soul and is the healer of the broken hearted… Have you ever prayed to receive Jesus as your Lord? John 3:16; 1 John 4:8

Mail Man – The mailman that delivers mail to my door reminds me Jesus Christ, Who is the doorway to heaven. When a person receives Jesus Christ as their Lord and Savior, then the Holy Spirit will "deliver mail" to their heart. As a person reads their Bible, the Holy Spirit sends fresh revelation and inspiration. It is divine mail that helps us fulfill the plan and purpose for our lives with God's love, joy, peace and strength to fulfill it.   Romans 8:32

Package – This package reminds me of the gift. (*What gift?*) The gift that God gave was His Son Jesus Christ. When the Holy Spirit over shadowed Mary, baby Jesus was conceived. So He came special delivery. He was born in a manger and later shed His blood and died for our sins on the cross. Whoever believes in Him will have the gift of eternal life – When they die, they get to unwrap this gift by living in heaven for all eternity…Would you like to pray now to receive Jesus as your Lord? John 3:16; Ephesians 2:8–9.

Special Delivery – This package that is being sent "special delivery" reminds me of how Jesus Christ was born into the earth. He came special delivery. The Holy Spirit overshadowed the Virgin Mary causing her to miraculously conceive Him. He was sent by God to become the Savior of the world. Whoever believes in Jesus shall have eternal life. Luke 1:35

Stamp –A prayer without "in Jesus name" is like a letter with no stamp. It is not going anywhere. Jesus Christ paid the price so that salvation could be delivered to everyone who receives Him as his/ her Savior… Would you like to pray to receive Jesus as your Lord and Savior? 1 Peter 1:18–19

Waiting in Line – This line is taking so long, it reminds me of eternity. Actually, eternity lasts forever. It is a very long time to be spent in the wrong place. Do you know where you will spend eternity? Have you ever received Jesus as your Lord?

Salvation Prayer: "Heavenly Father, I believe that Your Son Jesus Christ died on the cross for my sins and rose from the dead. I repent of my sins. Jesus, I ask You to forgive me and come into my heart and be my Lord and Savior. Fill me with the Holy Spirit. Thank You for saving me from hell and giving me eternal life in heaven, in Jesus' name I pray, Amen."

CHAPTER FOURTEEN

"I Want to Witness, But What Do I Say About Sports?"

Baseball, Basketball
Boxing, Football
Golf, Gym
Hockey, Skiing
Soccer, Tennis

The hardest part about witnessing is *the transition* from an everyday conversation onto the Gospel track. One way to do it is through relating the Gospel to objects around you like Jesus did many times in Matthew 13. These object evangelism icebreakers will **train** you how to transition conversations onto the Gospel **track.** Jesus is coming soon, so use loving boldness and be compassionate. Then be led by the Spirit using whatever method. You may prophesy or pray for healing or whatever else is needed.. After the icebreaker, there is an invitation to help reel them into salvation. Then be bold and ask them to pray a salvation prayer after you.

"I Want to Witness, But What Do I Say About Baseball?"

Baseball – When I think of baseball, it reminds me of the Gospel. It's like an analogy: The pitcher is like the Christian who throws the pitch, which is the Good News of the Gospel. The hitter can accept the Gospel and make a hit **or** he can sadly reject the Gospel and strike out. When the hitter accepts the Gospel, he prays to receive Jesus Christ as His Lord and Savior and he is saved from hell. He makes a hit for heaven. Then he starts running his race for the Lord Jesus around the bases of life until he makes it to home plate, which is heaven where his home will be for all eternity…Have you ever made a hit? So will you make it to home plate or to heaven for all eternity? If not, then we can pray a salvation prayer right now.   Isaiah 55:11

Grass – This green grass I know is probably artificial or it will get brown and wilted–looking after the season. It reminds me of this scripture in Isaiah 40:8: "The grass withers, the flowers fade, but the Word of our God will stand forever." I am so thankful that the Word of God never changes. God is the same yesterday, today and forever. Do you need a change in your life?…Have you ever asked Jesus to be your Lord?   Hebrews 13:8

Home plate – Home plate reminds me of heaven because that will be my home for all eternity because I received Jesus as my Lord and Savior…So is Jesus your Lord?   John 14:2

Home Run – Hit Out of the Park –Wow! It's a home run! He hit that ball farther than the eye can see!! It reminds me of eternity. Eternity is a long time to be spent in the wrong place…So do you know where you will spend eternity? Have you ever prayed to receive Jesus as your Lord and Savior?

Outfield/Infield – The outfield and the infield remind me of the outer court of *God's temple* in the Old Testament and the inner court, which is much closer to God. Within the inner court, behind *the veil,* is the Holy of Holies and this is where God dwelt. Only the priests could go in there But when Jesus Christ shed His blood and died on the cross for our sins, an earthquake *tore the veil in two* (Matthew 27:51). So now born again Christians are the temples of the Holy Spirit and can fellowship with God! Not just the priests, but ALL that receive Jesus as Lord can fellowship with God, who is Love...So are you born again?   1 Corinthians 6:19

Safe – That was a close call, but I am safe! It reminds me of those that wait until they are on their deathbed to receive Jesus as their Lord. That is not wise because you never know when your last day on earth will be....Would you like to pray to receive Jesus as your Lord so that when you die, you will be safe in heaven?

Three Strikes and You're Out – I'm glad that the "three strikes and you're out" rule only applies to baseball. God is much more merciful than that. 1 John 1:9 says that when you confess your sins, God is faithful and just to forgive you of all your sins and cleanse you from all unrighteousness...So is Jesus your Lord?

Umpire – As I watch that umpire call the shots, it reminds me of Jesus Christ on Judgment Day. He will call who is safe in heaven and who is out... Those who receive Jesus as their Lord will be safe in heaven for all eternity...so are you safe?

Salvation Prayer: "Heavenly Father, I believe that Your Son Jesus Christ died on the cross for my sins and rose from the dead. I repent of my sins. Jesus, I ask You to forgive me and come into my heart and be my Lord and Savior. Fill me with the Holy Spirit. Thank You for saving me from hell and giving me eternal life in heaven, in Jesus' name I pray, Amen."

"I Want to Witness, But What Do I Say About Basketball?

Basketball – (watching on TV) Watching a basketball game can be like an emotional roller coaster. Before I became a Christian, I would get so bummed out if my college team lost, like I was a loser. I would even feel depressed about it. But when I became a Christian, I realized that my value and worth is truly based on what Jesus Christ did for me. He loves me so much that He shed His blood and died on the cross for my sins, so that I could have the best victory of all – eternal life in heaven. So in Christ I am always on the winning team. I'm always triumphant because my spirit has been born again into God's Kingdom...Would you like to be on God's winning team for all eternity? (yes) OK, let's pray.

1 John 5:4; 2 Corinthians 2:14

Center – That center that is so big and tall, reminds me of the One who is the center of my life. He is my hero because He saved me from sin and eternal death when He died on the cross for my sins. His name is Jesus Christ...Have you ever met Him?

Cheerleaders – They remind me of the "great cloud of witnesses" in heaven. They are watching and praying as the Christians play out God's game plan for their lives to win the prize of their high calling. God has a game plan for your life too. So would you like to play? Then pray with me to receive Jesus your Lord and Savior. Hebrews 12:1–2; Philippians 3:14

Free Throws – Going to the line to shoot free throws reminds me of the free grace of God.... All of us sin and fall short of God's standard. Even NBA players all miss the basket at one time or another. But salvation is not obtained by works or making baskets. It is a free gift received by grace through faith in the Lord Jesus Christ Would you like to pray to receive Him as your Lord? Ephesians 2:8–9

Net – Whoa! That play was "nothing but net." It reminds me of a fishing net used to catch fish. And the Gospel is also symbolized by a fish because Christians are called to be "fishers of men." So have you ever received Jesus Christ as your Lord? Jesus is coming again soon. You do not want to be left behind. Would you like to pray to receive Jesus as your Lord and Savior?   Matthew 4:19

Point Guard – I like point guards because they remind me of Jesus Christ...From the cross, Jesus points the way to my Heavenly Father so I can have eternal life. Since I received Him as my Lord and Savior, He also guards me from any attacks of the enemy. Then He tells me the plan or the plays for my personal life to serve Him and play for Him, which gives me purpose for my life. ...Have you ever asked Jesus Christ to be your Lord and Savior?
Jeremiah 29:11; Psalm 91

Turnover – *(If it was to your team's advantage)* Did you see that great turnover?! We have the ball now! That play reminds me of how a life can be turned over to God. All you have to do is repent and pray to receive Jesus Christ as your Lord and Savior. Then you will win for all eternity.... So would you like to pray to turn your life over to Jesus Christ?

Salvation Prayer: "Heavenly Father, I believe that Your Son Jesus Christ died on the cross for my sins and rose from the dead. I repent of my sins. Jesus, I ask You to forgive me and come into my heart and be my Lord and Savior. Fill me with the Holy Spirit. Thank You for saving me from hell and giving me eternal life in heaven, in Jesus' name I pray, Amen."

†   †   †

"I Want to Witness, But What Do I Say About Boxing?"

Boxing Match – As I watch those two boxers fight, it reminds me of **"the fight of faith"**, but in that fight, the battle is in my mind. The devil wants me to think his thoughts of doubt and unbelief, of fear and false judgments. But the Bible says to think on God's Word, to believe in faith, forgive those that hurt you and to walk in love. It's called fighting the flesh and allowing the spirit of God to rule and reign…. So have you ever fought in that kind of fight?   1 Timothy 6:12

Bloody Face – As I see that blood it reminds me of Leviticus 17:11 which says, the blood makes atonement for the soul. So Jesus Christ willingly went to the cross and shed His blood to pay the price for our sins so that all who believe could be forgiven and reconciled to God…Do you believe in Jesus?

Boxing Ring – The boxing ring reminds me of the place where I fight off demonic attacks. That's in my prayer closet or the place where I go and pray. It says in 1 Timothy 6:12 that we Christians are called to fight the good fight of faith –against the doubt and unbelief that the devil throws at us…So have you ever stepped into that boxing ring? I mean, have you ever prayed to receive Jesus as your Lord and Savior?

Fight – As I watch those two boxers fight, it reminds me of "the fight of faith", but in that fight, the battle is in **my will.** The devil wants me to rebel and follow his evil will and ways. It may look sweet, sexy and enticing on the surface, but underneath are evil roots of death and destruction. God wants me to obey Him, trust Him and follow His will for my life. It may look uncertain on the surface, but underneath are His everlasting arms, So are you fighting for the devil's will or for God's will for your life? Let's pray.

1 Timothy 6:12

Judge – That judge reminds me of God who is the ultimate Judge. When we pray to receive Jesus as our Lord, God will always rule for us to win eternity in heaven. Have you ever prayed a salvation prayer?

Knockout – Watching that knockout reminds me of when Jesus Christ died on the cross. It looked like He was the one that got knocked out by the devil, but looks can be deceiving. That's why Christians are called to walk by faith and not by sight. Jesus won the victory 3 days later when God raised Him from the dead! Now whoever believes and prays to receive Jesus as their Lord and Savior will have eternal life in heaven.

2 Corinthians 5:7

Punch – As I watch that boxer throw that punch, it reminds me of the power of prayer. Every time I pray and bind the evil powers and rulers of darkness in the name of Jesus Christ, I am throwing a punch at the devil. It defeats him every time, especially when I pray in tongues. So do you pray?

Jude 20

Water – As I drink this refreshing water, it reminds me of the Living Water, who is Jesus Christ. He said in John 4:14 that whoever drinks of Him will never be thirsty again and will have eternal life...So have you ever had the Living Water? You can receive Him through a prayer of salvation.

Salvation Prayer: "Heavenly Father, I believe that Your Son Jesus Christ died on the cross for my sins and rose from the dead. I repent of my sins. Jesus, I ask You to forgive me and come into my heart and be my Lord and Savior. Fill me with the Holy Spirit. Thank You for saving me from hell and giving me eternal life in heaven, in Jesus' name I pray, Amen."

"I Want to Witness, But What Do I Say About Football?"

Conversion – We missed the conversion! Sigh. Oh well, at least I have not missed the most important conversion of all. I made the conversion from the Kingdom of darkness into the Kingdom of God when I received Jesus Christ as my Lord…Have you ever made that conversion? Let's pray.

Cheerleaders – They remind me of the saints up in heaven that are watching and cheering us on down here to run our race for Christ and finish strong so that many will become born again.   Hebrew 12: 1-2

End zone – The "end zone" reminds me of eternity. Since Jesus is my Lord, I know that *in the end of my life*, I will be in heaven's zone…How about you? Which zone will you be in?

Fumbled the Ball – I can't believe he fumbled the ball! Sigh. You know, that reminds me of how God forgives us of all our sins when we fumble the ball in our own lives at work, at school or at home. No one is perfect. God knew that our fumbles in life or our sins would separate us from God, so He sent His Son Jesus Christ who died on the cross for our sins and reconciled us to God so we could go to heaven. So fumbling with Jesus is not so bad, but if you fumble without Jesus, it will be hell…Would you like to pray to receive Jesus as your Lord?   Romans 3:23; 1 John 1:9, Acts 2:38

Goal Posts – As I watch that player try to kick the ball in between those goal posts it reminds me of Matthew 7:13 which says "broad is the way to destruction and narrow is the way which leads to life." When a person prays to receive Jesus Christ as their Lord that means they have chosen the narrow way leading into the heavenly goal of eternal life….Would you like to pray to receive Jesus as your Lord and Savior?

Penalty – That penalty cost us some good field position. It reminds me of the penalty of sin, which is death. When we sin, it costs us from having a good position with God. But Jesus Christ paid the penalty for our sins on the cross so that we could gain back our right position with God and have eternal life…Have you ever prayed to receive Jesus as your Lord and Savior?

Romans 3:23; Romans 6:23

Tackled & Deep Under – As I watch that player get tackled, it reminds me of how our wrong decisions and our sins can make us feel "tackled" just like that football player out there, but when a person repents of their sin and prays to receive Jesus Christ as their Lord, then their sin will be removed off of them and they will be reconciled to God once again. He will come and raise you up and give you eternal life in heaven.   1 John 1:9, Ephesians 2:6

Touchdown – The exuberant joy that I get when my team scores a touchdown I believe is the same joy that God and the angels get when a person receives Jesus Christ as their Lord. The Bible says in Luke 15:10 that there is joy in the presence of the angels of God over one sinner who repents …Have you ever prayed to receive Jesus Christ as your Lord and Savior?

Turnover – *(If it was to your team's advantage)* Did you see that great turnover? We have the ball now! That awesome play reminds me of how a life can be turned over to God. All a person has to do is repent and pray to receive Jesus Christ as their Lord and Savior….Have you turned your life over to Jesus yet?

Romans 2:4

Salvation Prayer: "Heavenly Father, I believe that Your Son Jesus Christ died on the cross for my sins and rose from the dead. I repent of my sins. Jesus, I ask You to forgive me and come into my heart and be my Lord and Savior. Fill me with the Holy Spirit. Thank You for saving me from hell and giving me eternal life in heaven, in Jesus' name I pray, Amen."

"I Want to Witness, But What Do I Say About Golf?"

Bogey – I did not make par. I'm glad that my salvation is not based on my good works or my being perfect. It is a free gift based on grace through faith in the Lord Jesus Christ. That means I can take as many strokes as I want and still win or have eternal life...So is Jesus Christ your Lord and Savior? Ephesians 2: 8–9

Caddy – I'm thankful for my caddy. He reminds me 1 Peter 5:7 – casting all your care upon Him, for He cares for you.

Golf holes – As I think about golf, it reminds me of how a person can receive eternal life. The holes remind me of the holes that were made in Jesus' hands and feet when He was nailed to the cross for our sins so that all that believe in Him could have eternal life. So the **golf ball** reminds me of the unbeliever who has not received Jesus Christ as His Lord and Savior yet. The only way to win the game in golf or the only way to God is through those holes... Do you know how much Jesus loves you? Would you like to pray to receive Him as Lord?

Golf Tee – As I drive (or as I watch him drive) this golf tee in, it reminds me of the nails that were driven into Jesus' hands and feet on the cross. That one act shows how much He truly loves you because He willingly shed His holy blood and died on the cross for the sins of you and me so that those who believe in Him could be reconciled to God and receive eternal life...Have you ever made Jesus Christ your Lord and Savior?

Hole–in–One – A hole–in–one reminds me of the Son of God, Jesus Christ, because He is the **"Holy One"** who is perfect and without sin. So He willingly received the **holes** in his hands and feet when they nailed Him to the cross. He died for our sins, so that those who receive Jesus as Lord could be reconciled to God and have eternal life. So have you ever prayed to receive Jesus as your Lord?

On the Green – I am so happy that the ball made it onto the green! It reminds me of Psalm 23: "The Lord is my Shepherd. I shall not want. He makes me lie down in *green pastures.*" So is Jesus the Savior and the Shepherd of your own life?

Sand Trap – That sand trap reminds me of the traps, you know, those hard places of trials and tribulations that make me think, "God, don't you care about me?" And yet I know the Bible says in Psalm 139:17, "How precious also are Your thoughts to me, O God! How great is the sum of them! If I should count them, they are more in number than the *sand.*" So I know that God does care. I just have to trust in Him and His ability to get me out of those traps. Actually God got us out of the worst trap of all – the trap of hell. John 3:16 says, "God so loved the world that He gave His only begotten Son that whosoever believes in Him shall not perish, but have everlasting life." Would you like to pray to receive Jesus as your Lord?

Scorecard – I used to get really depressed when I lost until I became a Christian. Then I came to realize that my true worth and value is based on the price that was paid for me – the blood of Jesus Christ, which is worth more than all the gold and silver in the world! And having eternal life is the true prize for all eternity, so I am always a winner…Are you a winner? Have you ever won the prize of eternal life in heaven? It is your choice to win or not.

Salvation Prayer: "Heavenly Father, I believe that Your Son Jesus Christ died on the cross for my sins and rose from the dead. I repent of my sins. Jesus, I ask You to forgive me and come into my heart and be my Lord and Savior. Fill me with the Holy Spirit. Thank You for saving me from hell and giving me eternal life in heaven, in Jesus' name I pray, Amen."

"I Want to Witness, But What Do I Say at the Gym?"

Lifting Weights – Lifting this barbell or weight reminds me of how Jesus Christ must have felt in lifting that heavy wooden cross on His back as He walked up to Mount Calvary where they crucified Him, but His pain was my gain. You see, my sins separated me from God. But when Jesus shed His blood and died on the cross for my sins, He lifted the heavy weight of my sins off of me so I could be reconciled to God and receive eternal life. Even though Jesus suffered a lot, He had joy because He knew that if He died, then multitudes of people could **live** or receive eternal life. I am so thankful for what He did on the cross that I prayed to receive Him as my Lord and Savior. ...Have you ever done that?

Running – Running or jogging reminds me of Hebrews 12:1: "Let us run with patience the race that is set before us, looking unto Jesus, the author and the finisher of our faith." God has a race for all of us to run. God has given each person a unique plan and purpose for their lives, but the only way you can begin finding His plan and purpose is through praying to receive Jesus as your Lord and Savior. Would you like to pray?   Jeremiah 29:11

Sit–Ups – Sit–ups remind me of God's resurrection power. God sent His Son Jesus Christ, Who shed His blood and died on the cross for my sins. Then God made Jesus to do the *ultimate sit up*. God raised him up from the dead!   Do you want His resurrection strength in your life? Then pray after me this salvation prayer to receive Jesus as your Lord.   Ephesians 1:20–21

Steroids – You know what is better than even steroids? *God's* strength is even better! Isaiah 10:27 says that "His anointing breaks the yoke." So His anointing breaks the devil's power in our lives as we yield to God's spirit..

Then we become so much stronger in the Lord because His strength overcomes our weaknesses…Best of all, when you give Him your heart, He'll give you eternal life…Would you like to pray to receive Him as your Lord?   Philippines 4:13; Ephesians 6:10

Mat – As I sit on this mat to stretch, it reminds me of the fact that I am really seated in heavenly places with Christ.   Ephesians 2:6

Walking – I like walking because it keeps me fit, but sometimes I get tired. But it says in Isaiah 40:31, "Those that wait upon the Lord shall renew their strength, they shall run and not grow weary and *they shall walk* and not be faint." My relationship with God is also called "my walk with God."…. I used to walk aimlessly through life with no purpose, no direction, no hope and no eternal life. Then I stumbled and fell and realized that I needed a Savior to walk with me through my life. So I received Jesus Christ as my Lord and Savior who died on the cross for my sins. Now I walk with Him and He walks with me and since I walk with God, I have eternal life… How about you? How is your walk? Are you walking with God?

Water – After that hard work out, this water is so refreshing to my body. It reminds me of the living water. Have you ever had any of that water? I am talking about Jesus Christ. In the Bible, it says that He is the Living Water. After I drink this water, I will thirst again, but because I received the Living Water, as my Savior, I will never thirst again because now I have eternal life…So have you received this Living Water? Would you like to pray a salvation prayer?   John 4:14

Salvation Prayer: "Heavenly Father, I believe that Your Son Jesus Christ died on the cross for my sins and rose from the dead. I repent of my sins. Jesus, I ask You to forgive me and come into my heart and be my Lord and Savior. Fill me with the Holy Spirit. Thank You for saving me from hell and giving me eternal life in heaven, in Jesus' name I pray, Amen."

"I Want to Witness, But What Do I Say About Hockey?"

Cross–Checking – In hockey, cross checking is when you drive the shaft into an opposing player and it is a penalty. It reminds me of Jesus Christ. He died on the cross taking our penalties and sins upon Himself so that we could be reconciled to God, forgiven of our sins and receive eternal life in heaven. So let me do a cross check on you: Is Jesus your Lord and Savior? I was just checking.

Goal – In hockey, the main point of the game is to score goals. That reminds me of having goals in life. The most important goal is to believe in and then pray to receive Jesus Christ as your Lord to receive eternal life in heaven. As a Christian, my goal is to know Him and make Him known (Philippines 3:10) so is Jesus your Lord and Savior?

Greatest Hockey Game – The greatest hockey game ever played in the history of hockey I believe was in the 1980 Olympics when the US team beat the undefeated Soviet team. They called that win "The Miracle on Ice" and even made a movie about it. I believe that God helped them win that game. And yet I know that the greatest miracle of all is the Christmas miracle – that God sent His only begotten son Jesus Christ into the world. He healed many and did many miracles and then finally shed His blood on the cross and died for our sins. Whosoever believes in Him and prays to receive Him as their Lord and Savior will receive the miracle of eternal life in heaven...So have you ever received that miracle? If not, I can pray with you right now. Just repeat this salvation prayer after me. John 3:16

Penalty Box – When you sin in hockey, you sit in the penalty box for only two minutes, so it is not so bad. But if you sin and never pray to receive Jesus Christ as your Lord, the penalty is hell and

that lasts for all eternity...So have you ever prayed to receive Jesus
Christ as your Lord and Savior?

Saved – In that 1980 Olympic hockey game, when the Russians
tried to score against the US, the announcer exclaimed over and over
39 times:"**Saved by Craig!**" That great defense by goalie Jim Craig
caused the USA to win the gold medal. It reminds me of what God
yells at the devil when he accuses Christians of sinning, falling short,
and deserving to go to hell. The devil is right. We have all sinned and
fallen short of God's standard, but God loves us and has great mercy!
So for everyone who repents of their sin and has prayed to receive
Jesus Christ as their Lord and Savior, **God defends us** and yells back
at the devil: **"<u>Saved</u> by Jesus Christ!"** And like winning the game of
your life, the believers go *to heaven* for all eternity. It is the most
glorious victorious <u>**save**</u> of all! So are you saved by Jesus Christ?

Violent Sport – I think that hockey is one of the most violent
sports. It reminds me of Matt. 11:12: "The kingdom of God
suffers violence, but the violent take it by force." This means that, like
being a hockey player, because of the persecution and opposition,
becoming a Christian and being a bold witness for Him is not easy. It
takes courage, unwavering faith, determination and endurance, but
the rewards are eternal life in heaven...So have you ever prayed to
receive this heavenly reward?

Salvation Prayer: "Heavenly Father, I believe that Your Son Jesus
Christ died on the cross for my sins and rose from the dead. I
repent of my sins. Jesus, I ask You to forgive me and come into my
heart and be my Lord and Savior. Fill me with the Holy Spirit.
Thank You for saving me from hell and giving me eternal life in
heaven, in Jesus' name I pray, Amen."

†   †   †

I Want to Witness, But What Do I Say When Skiing?"

Crossed Skis – When my skis cross like this, it reminds me of the cross of Jesus Christ. I know that if I don't straighten out my skis, I will fall. And I know that if I don't receive Jesus as my Lord and Savior, I will also fall into a dark eternity suffering without Him. **But I have prayed** to receive Jesus Christ as my Lord and (*now straighten out your skis*) He has truly straightened out my life…So have you ever prayed to receive Jesus as your Lord and Savior?

Gloves – These gloves that protect my hands from the cold remind me of God's divine protection that I am praying for, to surround me with His angels, even as I ski today. Since I prayed to receive Jesus as my Savior, He ultimately protects me from going to hell.   Psalm 91

Mountain – As I look at that mountain, it reminds me of the huge problems or trials that people experience in their lives. They are like mountains. But God's love is so great; He can lift you over or remove any mountain in your life. No problem is too big for Him. The biggest problem was mankind's sin that separated us all from God, but God sent His only begotten Son Jesus Christ into the world who shed His blood and died on the cross for our mountain of sins so that we could have eternal life…That is how much He loves you. So is Jesus your Savior?   Mark 11:23

Ski Boots – When I click my boots into my skis, it reminds me of my relationship with God. John 14:4–5 says: "Abide in Me and I in you…for without Me you can do nothing" and without these skis on, I can do nothing on the slopes…. So have you ever prayed to ask Jesus to abide in you?   John 15:7

Ski Lift – I am so thankful for this ski lift. Can you imagine trying to get up the mountain without it? That would be so much work! So this ski lift reminds me of the grace of God. It is by grace through faith in the Lord Jesus that we receive eternal life in heaven, not by works (Ephesians 2:8–9). Grace is a free gift from God. It's like this ski lift – a free lift to the top for all eternity…. Have you ever received this wonderful grace? Have you ever prayed to receive His Son Jesus Christ as your Lord and Savior?

Ski Jump – I love the thrill of flying through the air doing these ski jumps, but I know I could crash and wipe out or at the worst, even die…and I don't want to jump into eternity without Jesus, so I already prayed to receive Him as my Lord and Savior…So have you ever prayed to ask Jesus to be your Savior?

Ski Poles – These ski poles are so vital when skiing. They remind me of the Good Shepherd's rod and staff in Psalm 23:4 "His rod and staff, they comfort me." Yes, these poles help me stand and they also help me up when I fall. They remind me of the power of the Holy Spirit that gives me the courage **to stand** for God and He also gives me mercy when I slip and **fall** into sin…So have you received Jesus Christ as your Lord and Savior yet?

Snow – This snow is so holy and pure looking. It reminds me of Isaiah 1:18: "though your sins be as scarlet, they shall be white as snow." Our dirty sins separate us from God, but He loves us, so He sent His Son Jesus, who shed His blood on the cross and died for our sins to reconcile us to God so that those who receive Jesus as their Lord and Savior become pure, holy and "white as snow" in God's eyes…Would you like to pray to receive Him as your Lord?

Salvation Prayer: "Heavenly Father, I believe that Your Son Jesus Christ died on the cross for my sins and rose from the dead. I repent of my sins. Jesus, I ask You to forgive me and come into my heart and be my Lord and Savior. Fill me with the Holy Spirit. Thank You for saving me from hell and giving me eternal life in heaven, in Jesus' name I pray, Amen."

'I Want to Witness, But What Do I Say About Soccer?"

Cleats (boots) – I use these cleats because they give me good traction on the field so that I can play hard and run hard against the opposing team. It reminds me of what praying in tongues does for me. It keeps me on track with God and it helps me to pray hard and run hard for Him against the opposing enemy, who is the devil...So have you ever prayed in tongues?

Acts 2:2; Acts 1:8; Jude 20; Hebrews 12:1–2

Free Kick – A free kick reminds me of the Gospel, which is the **free** gift of eternal life. You can get this free gift by believing in Jesus Christ and praying to receive Him as your Savior. ...Have you ever received this free gift? Receiving Jesus as your Savior will kick you into heaven.

Ephesians 2:8, Romans 10: 9.

Goal – As I look at that soccer goal, it reminds me of the goal for my life. As a Christian, my goal is to know Christ and to make Him known...Do you know how much Jesus loves you? Do you know that He has a plan and a purpose for your life? Would you like to pray to receive Jesus as Lord?

Philippines 3:10

Header – At times, I use a header to get the ball down the field in the right direction. A header reminds me of when I read the Word of God, it renews my mind and gets my life headed in the right direction.

Romans 12:1–2; Psalm 119:105

Instep Drive – An accurate instep drive reminds me of how successful my life is when I walk step by step with my Lord and Savior Jesus Christ. The Bible, His Word, is a lamp to my feet and a light to my path He knows the best way to go, not just on this field, but for my whole life.

1 Peter 2:21; Psalm 119:105

Juggling the Ball – When I juggle the ball without using my hands, it reminds me of what my hands are really for. Well, since I am a Christian, I use them to pray and to lay hands on the sick and I lift them up when I sing and worship God. Have you ever prayed to receive Jesus as your Lord and Savior?   1 Timothy 2:8

Marking – Marking the opposing player enables my teammate to get the ball up the field and closer to the goal. As a Christian, that reminds me of how, no matter what denomination, we are all on the same team. The opposing team is the devil. So we all need to pray and guard each other from the devil's schemes, so that we can all fulfill the call of God on our lives.   John 17:11

Referee – The referee that judges all the close calls, reminds me of God who will judge where I will spend eternity. If a person prays a salvation prayer to receive Jesus as their Lord, then they will go to heaven for eternity…Have you ever prayed that salvation prayer?   Isaiah 33:22

Soccer Ball – This black and white soccer ball, that I am trying to control and dribble towards the goal, reminds me of the Bible. The Bible is also black and white. When I read it and believe it and give God control of my life, then I will have the best life and I will win. I know that God loves me. My goal is to trust in Him and let Him take control of my life. Then I will score big for all eternity. I will gain eternal life for me and for many others too.   Proverbs 3:5–6

Salvation Prayer: "Heavenly Father, I believe that Your Son Jesus Christ died on the cross for my sins and rose from the dead. I repent of my sins. Jesus, I ask You to forgive me and come into my heart and be my Lord and Savior. Fill me with the Holy Spirit. Thank You for saving me from hell and giving me eternal life in heaven, in Jesus' name I pray, Amen."

"I Want to Witness, But What Do I Say Around Tennis?"

Fault – When the judge yells **"fault!"** it reminds me of what the devil yells at God when I sin while I am serving God. He is the accuser of the brethren and yells: "It's his **fault!"** God knows that it is the devil that tempted me to sin in the first place, so it is really **his** fault. When I repent and ask God to forgive me for yielding to temptation and sinning, He forgives me and Jesus takes the "fault" or sin on the cross for me. Then I get back on the "court of life" and serve the Lord again ....So have you ever served God? Is He your Lord and your Savior?

Loser – I am sorry that you did not win, but you do not have to be a loser. In 1 John 5:4 it says, "Everyone that is born again overcomes the world. This is the victory that overcomes the world, even our faith." So if you have a relationship with God through His Son Jesus Christ, then you will have the victory for all eternity. You will never be a loser that goes to hell but a winner in heaven who praises God! So are you a winner? If not, let's pray.

2 Corinthians 2:14

Net – The ball went right into the net. Sigh. But that net reminds me of a fisherman's net used to catch fish. Christians are called to be "fishers of men." Do you know how much Jesus loves you? Have you ever prayed to receive Him as your Lord? He is coming soon... Do you want to pray?   Matthew 3:3

Serving the Ball – As I watch him serve that ball, it reminds me of how we should all serve the Lord with passion and aggression. One way to serve Him is to witness to unbelievers and tell them about God's love...So do you know how much God loves you? Have you ever prayed to receive Jesus Christ as your Lord?

Tennis – I always thought that it was kind of funny how they keep score in Tennis. When the score is "30– Love," it really means that it is 30 to zero. I guess they decided to replace the zero with *Love* so that the losing player will not feel so bad. The truth that's so ironic is that the Bible says that *God is Love*. So the score could be: "30 – God." If the score was 30 – God, then it does not matter how many points the other side had, you know that *God's side* will win because He is God! But seriously, the only way to be on God's side for all eternity is praying to receive Jesus Christ as your Lord and Savior….Would you ask Jesus to come into your heart to be on God's side in heaven? Then pray this prayer after me.

Romans 8:31, 37–39; 1 John 4:8

Water – After that workout, I need a drink. This water reminds me of the Living Water. His name is Jesus Christ. His Spirit fills me up to overflowing so that I will never thirst again. Have you ever had any of that Living Water? Would you like to pray to receive Jesus as your Lord and Savior?

John 4:10

Winner – You won! Good job! I'm proud of you. People love to win and I believe that is because <u>God</u> loves to win and we are all created in His image. But do you know what God really wants to win? He wants to win *you*. He loves you so much and so He wants to win you over into His Kingdom. When you pray to receive Jesus Christ as your Lord you will win the reward of heaven for all eternity…So would you like to pray?

Proverbs 11:30

Salvation Prayer: "Heavenly Father, I believe that Your Son Jesus Christ died on the cross for my sins and rose from the dead. I repent of my sins. Jesus, I ask You to forgive me and come into my heart and be my Lord and Savior. Fill me with the Holy Spirit. Thank You for saving me from hell and giving me eternal life in heaven, in Jesus' name I pray, Amen."

CHAPTER FIFTEEN

"I Want to Witness, But What Do I Say Around School & Work?"

Computer
Office
Junior High School
High School or College
Housework

T he hardest part about witnessing is *the transition* from an everyday conversation onto the Gospel track. One way to do it is through relating the Gospel to objects around you like Jesus did many times in Matthew 13. These object evangelism icebreakers will *train* you how to transition conversations onto the Gospel *track.* Jesus is coming soon, so use loving boldness and be compassionate. Then be led by the Spirit using whatever method you choose. You may prophesy or pray for healing or whatever is needed. After the icebreaker there is an invitation to pray a salvation prayer. Then be bold and encourage them to pray that salvation prayer after you.

"I Want to Witness, But What Do I Say Around a Computer?"

Control, Alt, Delete – When your computer messes up and you do not know what to do, you just hit control, alt, and delete then the computer will reboot and you can start over. It is the same way in life. When a person's life gets messed up and they don't know what to do, they can give Jesus Christ control and let Him alter their life and delete all of their sins. It is just like starting over, but Jesus calls it becoming born–again because your spirit is born into the Kingdom of God. Would you like to **start over today and become born again?**

Delete key – I made a mistake. Thank God for the merciful delete key. It reminds me of the blood of Jesus Christ that was shed on the cross, so that my sins could be deleted and I could be reconciled with God to receive eternal life. To activate the delete key, you must repent and ask God to forgive you of your sins and pray to receive Jesus Christ as your Lord and Savior. Would you like to pray?   1 John 1:9

Download – Have you ever downloaded Jesus Christ into your heart? That's what you need. Through praying to receive Jesus as Lord, you can have eternal life.

Explorer – Explorers are always searching for religious artifacts, but when a person discovers that "Jesus is Lord," then they can stop exploring. There is no way to heaven, but through Him…So are you still exploring?   John 14:6

Internet or Online – Getting online reminds me of how an unbeliever can be reconciled to God or born–again. If you imagine the World Wide Web as Father God, then the Internet Service Provider (ISP) is none other than Jesus Christ. Jesus is the way, the truth and the life and there is no way to the Father, or onto the web, but through

Him. So, a born–again Christian is online with God for all eternity...So, are you online? If not, I can help you get connected.

Mouse – As I control this mouse, it reminds me of what "surrender" truly is. Imagine that you are the mouse. True surrender is allowing the hand of God to come upon you to control you and direct your life wherever He wants it to go. It is putting your trust in Him knowing that His way is the best way... Would you like to surrender your life to the Lord? Let's pray.

Password – As I type in my password that gets me into my computer, it reminds me of the password that gets me into heaven.... His name is Jesus Christ. He is The Word and whoever passes through Him will be saved from eternal death and they will receive eternal life...Would you like to pray to receive Jesus as your Lord and Savior?

Save – Saving this document reminds me of how thankful I am that I am saved...I did the smart thing and received Jesus as my Lord and Savior. Now I am saved from going to hell when I die. Matthew 18:11

Yahoo! – That was what I exclaimed when I realized that Jesus Christ died for my sins and took my place on the cross so that I don't have to go to hell! Yahoo! Now I get to go to heaven! Yahoo! Do you want to come with me? Then pray this salvation prayer.

Salvation Prayer: "Heavenly Father, I believe that Your Son Jesus Christ died on the cross for my sins and rose from the dead. I repent of my sins. Jesus, I ask You to forgive me and come into my heart and be my Lord and Savior. Fill me with the Holy Spirit. Thank You for saving me from hell and giving me eternal life in heaven, in Jesus' name I pray, Amen.

"I Want to Witness, But What Do I Say at the Office?"

Cell phone – As I make this call to my friend for advice, I am reminded of my shortcomings that I really need to call on God. He is the One that has the answers and Jesus is a friend that sticks closer than a brother. Those that call upon the Lord shall have eternal life...Have you ever called upon Jesus Christ to be your Lord? Proverbs 18:24; Romans 10:9–10

Copier – As I make this copy, it reminds me of how Christians are called to copy Christ, to follow Him in doing what He says and what He does...Do you know how much He loves you? So have you ever asked Jesus to be your Lord?

Door – As I stand here waiting, I am reminded of what Jesus said in John 10: 9. He said, "I Am the door. If anyone enters by Me, he will be saved." Jesus is the most important door that we could ever walk through because it leads to eternal life in heaven...Have you ever opened the door of your heart to allow Jesus Christ to come in?

Highlighter – As I use this yellow highlighter, it reminds me of the One who is the Most High and is the light of the world. Jesus is the highlighter of my life...Do you know how much He loves you? So is Jesus Christ the highlighter of your life as well? If not, I can pray a salvation prayer with you.

Internet – Getting online reminds me of how an unbeliever can be reconciled to God or born–again. Imagine the World Wide Web as Father God, then the Internet Service Provider (ISP) is none other than Jesus Christ. Jesus is the way, the truth and the life (John 14:6) and there is no way to the Father without Jesus Christ.

When a person receives Jesus as their Lord and Savior, it causes them to be online with God for all eternity…. So are you online with God? If not, I can help you get connected. C'mon, pray with me.

Lamp – That lamp reminds me of Psalm 119:105: "Thy Word is a lamp unto my feet and a light unto my path." All the answers in life can be found in the Word of God. Jesus Christ is the answer. He is the light of the world. So to get the answers that you want, first of all you need to receive Jesus Christ as your Lord and Savior…. Would you like to pray right now?

Pen *(that does not write)* –This pen ran out of ink. It is useless. It reminds me of Christians who do not witness to others about how much God loves them.

Pencil – The lead in this pencil reminds me of how important it is to be led by the spirit of God. He knows exactly where I should go and what I should do with my life. But in order to be led by the spirit, you have to have a relationship with God through His Son Jesus Christ. Then you will have "spiritual ears" to hear what He is saying to your heart …So would you like to pray?

Staple – This staple that looks like a bridge reminds me of Jesus who is the bridge between God and man…so have you ever crossed that bridge? Have you ever asked Jesus to be your Savior?

Salvation Prayer: "Heavenly Father, I believe that Your Son Jesus Christ died on the cross for my sins and rose from the dead. I repent of my sins. Jesus, I ask You to forgive me and come into my heart and be my Lord and Savior. Fill me with the Holy Spirit. Thank You for saving me from hell and giving me eternal life in heaven, in Jesus' name I pray, Amen."

"I Want to Witness, But What Do I Say at Junior High School?"

Addition – This math problem reminds me of Matthew 6:33: "Seek **first** the kingdom of God...then all these things will be *added* unto you." When I put God <u>first</u> in my life through reading my Bible, worshipping Him and going to church, I can see His hand really moving in my life to provide for my needs and even my wants. He faithfully keeps His promises. I am so glad that He loves me and that I made Him my Lord.   Philippians 4:19

Door – That door reminds me of something Jesus said in John 10: 9. "I Am the door. If anyone enters through Me, he will be saved." So Jesus Christ is the most important door you will ever walk through. In Revelation 3:20 Jesus says, "Behold, I stand at the door (of your heart), and knock"...Have you ever opened the door of your heart and asked Jesus Christ to come in to be your Lord?

Eraser (or Delete Key) – This eraser reminds me of God's mercy. Isaiah 43:25 says: "I am He who blots out your sins, for My own sake and I will not remember them." When a person prays to receive Jesus as their Savior, God will erase (or delete) their sins and give them eternal life in heaven.   Philippians 3:13

Name – My name is _____. What is your name? That is a nice name. Do you know what makes your name even better? It is better if your name is written into the *Lamb's Book of Life* in heaven because then you will have eternal life...I know that my name is there because I prayed to receive Jesus Christ as my Lord and Savior.... So is your name there?   Revelation 21:27

Paper – Did you know paper is made out of wood? They take the wood and grind it to a pulp. Once the wood pulp has been beaten, treated, washed and bleached, it becomes paper. It all reminds me of

Jesus Christ. He was **beaten to a pulp** with a whip 39 times, was **treated** so badly and was **washed in His own blood**. Then He died on a **wooden** cross, but in three days He rose again. Now we have eternal life if we receive Him as our Lord and Savior. His Gospel is now widespread and written on this paper, in which they have so much in common. Have you ever prayed to receive Jesus as your Lord?

Isaiah 53:5

Pencil – The lead in this pencil reminds me of how important it is to be **led by the Spirit of God.** God knows the good plan and the destiny for my life. He knows the answer for this math problem and what I should write for this essay. But you can only be led by the spirit if you have a relationship with God through His Son Jesus... Would you like to pray now?   Romans 8:14; Psalm 32:8

Question – The most important question of all is: How can a person receive eternal life in heaven? It is by believing and then praying to receive Jesus Christ as your Lord and Savior. That is the answer. Does that answer your question?

Subtraction – As I work this math problem and subtract these numbers, it reminds me of a few things that I need to subtract from my life – all my sins. Since I prayed to receive Jesus as my Lord, God will forgive me when I repent of my sins and choose His way...Have you ever prayed to receive Him as Lord? 1 John 1:9

Salvation Prayer: "Heavenly Father, I believe that Your Son Jesus Christ died on the cross for my sins and rose from the dead. I repent of my sins. Jesus, I ask You to forgive me and come into my heart and be my Lord and Savior. Fill me with the Holy Spirit. Thank You for saving me from hell and giving me eternal life in heaven, in Jesus' name I pray, Amen."

"I Want to Witness, But What Do I Say in High School & College?"

Book – a thick book – Our life here on earth is like the first one or two pages on this very thick book. Eternity is like the whole rest of the book. It is a very long time to be spent in the wrong place…Do you know Jesus Christ as your Lord and Savior?

Isaiah 57:15–19

Exam – As I take this exam, I am thankful that I am a Christian because I have the Holy Spirit, Who is my divine helper, on the inside of me and "He brings all things back to my remembrance." Do you need some help on this exam? Would you like to pray to receive Jesus Christ as your Lord? He will help you.   John 14:25–26

Greek Letters – Those Greek letters mean you must be in a sorority (or a fraternity to a guy). It reminds me of the Greek letters – Alpha and Omega. It says in Revelation 1:8 that God is the Alpha and the Omega. He knows the beginning and the end. So we can put our trust in God that His plan is the best plan…Have you ever put your trust in God to receive His Son Jesus as Lord?

Locker Door – I'm glad that I remember the combination to open up this locker because it keeps all my books in it, but the Bible is the most important book of all. The Bible *unlocks* the mysteries to eternal life… Jesus Christ said in John 10: 9: "I Am the door. If anyone enters through Me, he will be saved." So Jesus Christ is the most important door you will ever walk through.

Paper – Did you know that paper is really made out of wood? They take the wood and then grind it to a pulp. Once the wood pulp has been treated, washed, bleached and beaten, it becomes paper. This whole process reminds me of Jesus Christ…He was *treated badly* and then *beaten to a pulp* with a whip 39 times, then died on a *wooden* cross, but now we have eternal life if we believe in Him. And His Gospel is written on this paper – in which they have so much in common.

Pen – You need a pen to write words, so the pen must have been created before the words, right? But in the beginning was the Word and the Word was with God, and the Word was God because Jesus Christ is The Word. All things were created through Him. So the Word created the pens that wrote the words! Have you ever prayed the words to receive Jesus as your Lord and Savior? John 1:1–3

Problem – This math problem reminds me of the worst problem of all. It is that sin problem. Sins like drugs, getting drunk, premarital sex or homosexuality all separate us from God. If we are separated from Him, then we cannot have eternal life and we will all go to hell which is the most problematic fiery place of all! But God sent His Son Jesus Christ as **the Answer** to the sin problem. There is no forgiveness of sins without the shedding of blood. So Jesus shed His holy blood and paid the price on the cross for our sins, so that we could be forgiven and reconciled to God and go to heaven. When anyone admits that they have a sin problem and ask for forgiveness and repents and prays to receive Jesus as Lord, then they will go to heaven. John 3:16, Romans 6:23; Roman 10:9–10; Matthew 6:14

Salvation Prayer: "Heavenly Father, I believe that Your Son Jesus Christ died on the cross for my sins and rose from the dead. I repent of my sins. Jesus, I ask You to forgive me and come into my heart and be my Lord and Savior. Fill me with the Holy Spirit. Thank You for saving me from hell and giving me eternal life in heaven, in Jesus' name I pray, Amen."

†   †   †

"I Want to Witness, But What Do I Say Around Housework?"

Dish Detergent – As I use this detergent to wash these dishes, it reminds me of how thankful I am for the blood of Jesus Christ that washed my sins away, totally forgiven and clean and white as snow inside…Have you ever been washed clean on the inside by Jesus before? It is an everlasting great feeling.

Window Cleaner – As I look through this window while cleaning it, it reminds me of how I cannot hide from God. My heart is like a window and He can see right through it. But I'm not afraid when God points out my sins and my stains because I know that He loves me. So then I just repent and ask Him to change me. Then He makes me clean and clear again.

Mop – As I mop up the mess on this floor, I am so thankful that Jesus took His cross and mopped up the mess in my life. Now my mess has become my message. I am saved by His blood. I am free and healed and complete in Christ…. So have you ever been messed up and just needed a clean up?

Oven Cleaner – It is so amazing how a **white** foam can get all the **black** grease and grime off of my oven to make it clean again. I guess it should not surprise me because Jesus' **red** blood that He shed on the cross got all the **black** sinful stains out of my heart and made it **white** and clean again!

Trash – As I take out the trash, I am so thankful that God took all the trash out of my heart – I mean the trashy bitterness, the rejection, the pride and the trashy lust out of my heart. We all have trash. When I asked God to forgive me for my trash or for my sins, He forgave me and took the trash out, so that I could be in right standing with God and go to heaven… So is *your trash* still inside or has Jesus taken it out?

Vacuum – As I use this vacuum to vacuum up the dust and the dirt, it reminds me of how when I confess my sins, God is faithful to forgive me of my dirty sins just like this vacuum. He just sucks up my sins and He remembers them no more! So are your sins in the vacuum or are they still on the floor?

Shoe Polish – As I shine my shoes, it reminds me of Isaiah 52:7, "Oh how beautiful are the feet of those who bring good news." The Good News is God sent His Son Jesus Christ into the world who willingly went to the cross and shed His holy blood for the sins of the world to reconcile us back to God. Whoever believes and prays to receive Jesus as their Lord will receive eternal life in heaven. That is good news!

Wood Polish – As I spray this to make the wood shine brighter, it reminds me of the wooden cross that Jesus died on. Isaiah 60:1 says "Arise and shine, for your light has come and the glory of the Lord is risen upon you." So are you shining for Jesus?

Dish Rag – This dishrag reminds me of Isaiah 64:6: "my self–righteousness is as filthy rags." My good works will not cause me to be right with God. Only the blood of Jesus will…Are you right with God?

Salvation Prayer: "Heavenly Father, I believe that Your Son Jesus Christ died on the cross for my sins and rose from the dead. I repent of my sins. Jesus, I ask You to forgive me and come into my heart and be my Lord and Savior. Fill me with the Holy Spirit. Thank You for saving me from hell and giving me eternal life in heaven, in Jesus' name I pray, Amen."

CHAPTER SIXTEEN

"I Want to Witness, But What Do I Say When Traveling?"

Airport
Car or Bus
Auto Repair
Gas Station
Train

The hardest part about witnessing is *the transition* from an everyday conversation onto the Gospel track. One way to do it is through relating the Gospel to objects around you like Jesus did many times in Matthew 13. These object evangelism icebreakers will **train** you how to transition conversations onto the Gospel **track.** Jesus is coming soon, so use loving boldness and be compassionate. Then be led by the Spirit using whatever method. You may prophesy or pray for healing or whatever is needed. After the "...", there is an invitation to be saved. Then be bold and encourage them to pray a salvation prayer after you.

"I Want to Witness, But What Do I Say at the Airport?"

Airplane Window – As I look out the window, it reminds me of how God can see everything and He knows everyone. He knows "the haves" and the "have nots." You know, those who *have* prayed to receive Jesus as their Lord and Savior and those who *have not*…so which one are you?

Baggage Claim – I hate it when I lose my luggage. In the same way I know that *God* hates it when one of His children backslides and dies and then He loses them to hell So have you found Jesus yet or are you kind of like lost luggage? Luke 19:10, Matthew 18:11

Passport – This passport reminds me of the fact that I am also a citizen of God's Kingdom in heaven, which is a wonderful beautiful glorious place where God dwells, full of peace, love and joy. I became a citizen of heaven when I prayed to receive Jesus Christ as my Lord and Savior. His name is the passport to heaven…would you like to become a citizen of heaven too?

Pilot – As I see that airplane pilot, it reminds me of Who my pilot is. When I was younger, I tried to "be my own pilot," but it did not work out well. I just crashed and burned. Then I realized that the One that lives above these planes can see everything below and He knows what is best. So I repented and received Jesus Christ as my Lord and Savior. I made God the pilot for my life and let Him take control. I'm glad that my final stop will now be heaven for all eternity...So who is your pilot? Proverbs. 3:5; Psalm 32:8

Security Checkpoint – As I stand here in line, it makes me wonder what it will be like to get into heaven. Those x–ray scanners see thru my carry on to check for weapons or anything illegal in the same way that God sees into my soul to check for sin. But I have peace because I have received Jesus Christ as my Lord and Savior, so I know that when it is my time to die, I will pass the checkpoint at the pearly gates and get into heaven...So will you?

Take Off and/or Landing – I used to get scared at the take off and the landing. But after I received Jesus Christ as my Lord and Savior, the fear of death went away because now I know that if this plane crashes and I die that I will truly land in heaven.... So do you know where you would land?

Visa – Getting my visa approved by the government authority so that I can gain entrance into this country reminds me of how Jesus Christ is the authority that gives entrance into heaven. John 14:6 says that Jesus is the way, the truth, and the life and there is no way to heaven but through Him... Jesus Christ is the most important visa that you can ever get because it is one that lasts for all eternity.

Airline Reservation – Checking on my flight reservation to go to_____(city) reminds me of the reservation that I made to go to heaven someday. When a person receives Jesus Christ as their Lord and Savior, they will be saved from eternal death because their name is written in the *Lamb's Book of Life*, which is the reservation book in heaven... So have you called on God to make your reservation yet in the *Lamb's Book of Life*? Revelation 21:27

Salvation Prayer: "Heavenly Father, I believe that Your Son Jesus Christ died on the cross for my sins and rose from the dead. I repent of my sins. Jesus, I ask You to forgive me and come into my heart and be my Lord and Savior. Fill me with the Holy Spirit. Thank You for saving me from hell and giving me eternal life in heaven, in Jesus' name I pray, Amen."

"I Want to Witness, But What Do I Say Around Auto Repair?"

Dirty Hands – I may have *dirty* hands, but since I received Jesus as my Lord, I know that I have *a clean heart* because I have been cleansed from all unrighteousness and my sins are forgiven...So is your heart clean or dirty?   1 John 1:9

Filthy Rag – This filthy rag reminds me of what the Bible says – that my self– righteousness is as filthy rags (Isaiah 64:6). My good deeds or my good works will not cause me to be right with God and go to heaven. It is only by grace through faith in the Lord Jesus Christ that we are saved from hell. Salvation is really a gift. So have you received this gift?   Ephesians 2:8–9

Jumper Cables – As I watch you connect those jumper cables from your battery to my dead battery, it reminds me of Jesus Christ because He is the bridge between God and man and when I chose to receive Him as my Lord, His resurrection power connected me to God and gave my dead soul resurrection life and eternal life in heaven as well...Do you need a jump to receive eternal life? Let's pray.   2 Corinthians 5:17; 1 John 4:7

Lift /Jack – As I watch you lift up this car, it reminds me the many times I have been **uplifted** in my relationship with God. When I asked Jesus to become my Lord, He became so real to me and now He **lifts** me up and brings me joy even in a bad situation...So has Jesus ever lifted you up?

Wrench – This wrench is the tool that reminds me of how God can turn things around if I just put my trust in Him. The Bible says, "All things work together for good for those who love God and are called according to His purpose."   Romans 8:28

Oil Change – Getting this oil change reminds me of the time that I changed the oil that was in my heart. I was sad and depressed. But when I prayed to receive Jesus Christ as my Lord and Savior, everything changed in my life. Like it says in Isaiah 61:3, God gave me beauty for ashes and *the oil of joy* for mourning and the garment of praise for the spirit of heaviness. It was the best change that I ever made. Now I have God's oil of joy. So do you need an oil change in your heart? I'd be happy to pray with you.

Romans 14: 17

Tools – These tools remind me of the tools of God's Word, the Holy Spirit, His love, joy and peace and good Christian friends to work on repairing and restoring whatever is broken in our lives. Even trials like a broken down car can teach us about God's love and His faithfulness as the car gets repaired and up and running again...Do you know how much God loves you?

Under the Hood – As I look under the hood of this car, it reminds me of how God can look under my outer appearance and looks right into my heart. He wants to repair the brokenness, remove the devil's lies, and get me up and running again.

Tire Change – Changing this tire reminds me of the time when I made the best change of all. I changed and repented for my rebellious attitude and prayed to receive Jesus as my Lord and Savior. Now just like this new tire, I am a new creature in Christ Jesus...Have you ever made that change?   2 Corinthians 5:17

Salvation Prayer: "Heavenly Father, I believe that Your Son Jesus Christ died on the cross for my sins and rose from the dead. I repent of my sins. Jesus, I ask You to forgive me and come into my heart and be my Lord and Savior. Fill me with the Holy Spirit. Thank You for saving me from hell and giving me eternal life in heaven, in Jesus' name I pray, Amen."

"I Want to Witness, But What Do I Say in a Carpool or on a Bus?

Bridge – This bridge reminds me of Jesus' death on the cross for our sins, which created "the bridge" between God and man that reconciled us to God...Those who receive Jesus Christ as their Lord and Savior will have eternal life in heaven?   John 3:16

Car Door – This car door reminds me of what Jesus said: "I Am the door. If anyone enters by Me, he will be saved." Jesus Christ is the most important door you could ever walk through. Have you ever walked thru that door?   John 10:9

Dead End – That sign reminds me of the ultimate dead end – the place filled with torment, pain and suffering and burning flesh for all eternity called hell. Whether you believe it is there or not, there truly is a heaven and a hell. If you receive Jesus Christ as your Lord and Savior, you will be saved from going to hell and go to heaven. C'mon, let's pray.
Romans 10:9–10.

Do Not Enter – Wrong Way – That sign reminds me of: "Do not enter – hell. It is the wrong way." Jesus is the right way – the way, the truth and the life and the only way to heaven.   John 14:6

No U–Turn – That sign reminds me of the fact that after this life on earth is over, there are no U–turns. There is no reincarnation. After you die, you go into eternity to either heaven or hell. There are no U– turns in hell. Let's pray. You never know when your last day on earth will be.   Romans 2:4

One Way – As I see that sign, it reminds me of the fact that there is only **one way** to heaven... Many people think that there are multiple ways, but they are all false. Jesus Christ paid the penalty for our sins on the cross, and so He reconciled us to God, therefore receiving Jesus Christ as your Lord and Savior is the **one way** to heaven. So are you on your way there?   John 14:6

Stop Sign – Stop signs remind me of evangelists who exhort people to stop sinning and live for God. Why? Because they love people and they know that if they do not receive Jesus Christ as their Lord, their final stop for all eternity will sadly be hell. Have you ever **stopped** to ask Jesus Christ to be your Lord?

Traffic Light – This traffic light reminds me of three types of people. The **green** reminds me of the Christians that are **going** to heaven. The **yellow** reminds me of those who are lukewarm. They say are Christians, but they still go to the bars. The **red** reminds me of those people that need to <u>stop</u> their sinning and turn to Jesus Christ or they will go to hell…So which color are you? Do you want to pray to be **green**?

Window – This window reminds me of the windows of heaven. God will pour out His blessings to us through the windows of heaven when we tithe. God expects us to give because He God gave His only begotten Son Jesus, who died shedding His perfect blood, so that we could be reconciled to to God and have eternal life in heaven. …So do you have eternal life in heaven?   John 3:16; Malachi 3:10

Yield – That yield sign reminds me of yielding to the Holy Spirit. That means to obey God instead of selfishly doing what I want to do… Have you ever yielded your heart to Jesus Christ and prayed to receive Him as Lord?   Romans 6:13

Salvation Prayer: "Heavenly Father, I believe that Your Son Jesus Christ died on the cross for my sins and rose from the dead. I repent of my sins. Jesus, I ask You to forgive me and come into my heart and be my Lord and Savior. Fill me with the Holy Spirit. Thank You for saving me from hell and giving me eternal life in heaven, in Jesus' name I pray, Amen."

"I Want to Witness, But What Do I Say at a Gas Station?"

Car Door – As we stand here talking by my car door, I am reminded of what Jesus said in John 10: 9. He said, "I Am the door. By Me if any man enter in, he shall be saved." ... Jesus Christ is the most important door that one could ever walk through. Also our heart is a door that we can open and close allowing what we want to enter in and out of it. In Revelation 3:20 Jesus said, "Behold, I stand at the door (of your heart), and knock; if any man hear My voice, and open the door, I will come in to him, and will sup with him, and He with me." If any man enters in through Jesus Christ, then they shall be spend eternity with Him in heaven.... Have you ever opened the door of your heart to allow Jesus Christ to come in?

Coffee – I drink coffee every day, but the black color sure does remind me of sin. I am so glad it says in Romans 14:17 that the Kingdom of God *is not meat and drink,* but righteousness, peace and joy in the Holy Ghost. So God is not looking at my coffee. He is looking at my heart to see whether I am born again or not. ...Have you ever prayed to receive Jesus Christ as your Lord and Savior?

Gas Pump – As I fill up this gas tank, I was just thinking about how important it is to be filled up with the Spirit of God because this gas will last maybe a week, but getting filled up with the Holy Spirit will last for all eternity. .... Would you like to pray to receive Jesus Christ as your Lord and Savior so that you can be filled with His Spirit?   Acts 19:6

High Gas Prices – This gas is getting so expensive. It is a good thing that you cannot get to heaven through driving your car. I would not have enough money! So I am so thankful that salvation is a free gift by grace through having faith in the Lord Jesus Christ. You just pray "a salvation prayer" and then you will have a free ride to heaven when you die…. So would you like to pray?

Lottery Ticket – I know a sure bet. If you want to go to heaven when you die, a sure bet is receiving Jesus Christ as your Lord and Savior. Then you will definitely go to heaven. So you have nothing to lose …Would you like to pray to receive Jesus Christ as your Savior?   Acts 4:12; John 3:16

Newspaper – The stories in the newspaper are so depressing, but have you heard the Good News of the Gospel of Jesus Christ…His salvation is a free gift. His love endures forever. His mercies are new every morning and great is His faithfulness. Have you ever received Jesus as your Lord and Savior?
                              Ephesians 3:17; Lamentations 3:22

Quik Trip – When Jesus comes again; it will be a quick trip! … Are you ready? *If they don't understand, explain:* I am talking about the rapture, which is when Jesus Christ will come again and take all the Christians with Him up to heaven. It says in 1 Corinthians. 15:52: "It will all happen **in a moment,** in the **twinkling of an eye**, when the last trumpet in the sky is blown…So is Jesus your Lord and Savior?

Salvation Prayer: "Father, I believe that Your Son Jesus Christ died on the cross for my sins and rose from the dead. I repent of my sins. Jesus, I ask You to forgive me and come into my heart and be my Lord and Savior. Fill me with the Holy Spirit. Thank You for saving me from hell and giving me eternal life in heaven, in Jesus' name I pray, Amen."

† † †

"I Want to Witness, But What Do I Say Around a Train?

Railroad Crossing Gate – The red and white striped crossing gate reminds me of the red stripes on Jesus' back. Before Jesus died on the cross, the soldiers whipped Him 39 times leaving red stripes of blood. It was so horrible, but because of His suffering, the Bible promises in 1 Peter 2:24: "By His stripes we were healed." And Psalm 103: 3 says: "Forget not all His benefits, who forgives all my sins and heals all my diseases."...Have you ever been healed by Jesus? Or Have you ever prayed to be saved from hell?

Red Caboose – People are so glad when they finally see the red caboose because they know the train is about finished passing by and then they can cross over and get on their way. It reminds me of Jesus Christ who died for our sins shedding His red blood on the cross saying, "It is finished." The old covenant law is finished and now we have a new covenant based on God's amazing grace. Those who pray to receive Jesus as Lord can cross on over into heaven...so are you ready?

Steam Engine – The steam from that engine reminds me of the power of the Holy Spirit. He came to live on the inside of me when I prayed to receive Jesus as my Lord. He connects me to God causing me to have a relationship with Him…. So have you got that Holy Spirit Steam in you?

Train Headlight – The big head light on the front of the train is so important at night to make sure that the path is clear and that no one is on the tracks. It reminds me of Psalm 119:105 "God's word is a lamp to our feet and a light to our path." Jesus is the Light of the world and He shines bright in my heart because I got born again   So have you ever prayed to receive Jesus as your Lord? Is His Light shining in your heart?   John 8:12

Train Horn – The train whistle that calls people to get on board reminds me of the trumpet call in Revelation 8. The trumpet blows to warn the lost to repent now and pray to receive Jesus Christ as their Lord – to get on that Gospel train now – because He is coming back soon to rapture or "catch away" all the Christians to take them back up to heaven for all eternity…So are you on that Gospel train?

Train of His Robe – When I see a train, many times Isaiah 6:1 goes through my mind: "I see the Lord seated on the throne exalted and the TRAIN of His robe fills the temple with glory" When you pray to receive Jesus as Lord, then you are on the right track with Jesus and **the train** of His robe, or the Holy Spirit, will fill you with His glory.… so are you on the right track with Jesus?

Isaiah 6:1

Train Tracks – As I look at down those train tracks, they remind me of a ladder. If they were vertical, it would be like a ladder that would take you up to heaven. But the truth is, you can't get to heaven on a train. You can only get there on a salvation prayer…So are you on the right track with Jesus?

Waiting – As I wait for this train so I can **cross** the tracks and go on my way, it reminds me of how Jesus died on **the cross** for my sins, so I could be reconciled to God and go on my way to heaven.… So have you ever prayed a salvation prayer so that you will be on your way to heaven? John 14:6

Salvation Prayer: "Heavenly Father, I believe that Your Son Jesus Christ died on the cross for my sins and rose from the dead. I repent of my sins. Jesus, I ask You to forgive me and come into my heart and be my Lord and Savior. Fill me with the Holy Spirit. Thank You for saving me from hell and giving me eternal life in heaven, in Jesus' name I pray, Amen."

Section 3

"After the Icebreaker, Then What Do I Say?"

CHAPTER SEVENTEEN

Truth to Say to
13 False Religions

Astrologists & Horoscope Readers
Atheists & Evolutionists
Buddhists & Hindus
Jehovah Witnesses,
Jewish People
Mormons & Muslims
New Agers &Scientologists
Utilitarian Universalism
Homosexuals & Lesbians

Truth to Say to Astrologists and Horoscope Readers

Deception: Astrology is an ancient practice that assumes that one's life pattern can be "charted" by determining the position of the stars and planets at the time of one's birth. This chart is called your "Horoscope."

Many people in social situations ask: "What's your sign?" in many casual conversations.

Truth to Say: The Bible forbids us from relying on horoscopes, astrologers and astrology:

Deuteronomy 4:19 says: "And beware lest you lift up your eyes to the heavens, and when you see the sun, the moon and the stars, even all the host of the heavens, you be drawn away and worship them and serve them."

Isaiah 47:13–15 In His wrath, God said through Isaiah: "Let your astrologers come forward, those stargazers who make predictions month by month, let them save you from what is coming upon you. Surely they are like stubble; the fire will burn them up. They cannot save themselves from the power of the flame."

Daniel 2:27–28: Daniel answered in the presence of the king, and said, "The secret which the king has demanded, the wise *men,* the astrologers, the magicians, and the soothsayers cannot declare to the king. [28] But there is a God in heaven who reveals secrets, and He has made known to King Nebuchadnezzar what will be in the latter days. Your dreams, and the visions of your head upon your bed, were these:

Deception: Astrology claims to have the solution to:
1. Who am I?

2. What will happen to me in my future?
Astrology offers daily horoscopes to predict a person's future.

Truth to Say: The truth is that men and women were created in the image of God. So we are a three–part being with a body, soul, and a spirit. When a person receives Jesus Christ as Savior, their spirit becomes born–again into the Kingdom of God. Then they are connected to God or "on–line" and thus, they have the ability to be led by the Spirit of God, also called following "your inward witness" or your heart (Romans 8:14). As Christians, we are not to be led by the stars, but we are to be led by the God who created them. God wants us to "walk by faith and not by sight." 2 Corinthians 5:7

Deception: Some Christians flirt with reading their daily horoscope and don't understand the subconscious conflicting danger "or static" this brings to their minds to prevent them from being led by the Spirit of God in their heart.

Truth to Say: Since it is apparent a great deal of astrology has no basis in reality, when you live your life by a horoscope, you run the risk of great financial loss due to what you may spend on astrology and also because of what the astrologers may recommend for you to do as far as: invest now, or buy later, or don't purchase this, etc. Another danger is a person who continually tries to live his life by a horoscope can become very depressed with no hope as he sees life as fatalistic, predetermined from birth, with no way to break free and change.

Deception: If one reads a horoscope, even in a cursory manner, he will be struck with the general and ambiguous nature of the statements, which can be pointed to as fulfilling anything that may happen that day or just about everything. Since there are so many variables and options, the astrologer seems to be "always right." If you break your arm, when your astrologer told you the signs were "good," he can congratulate you on escaping what might have happened had the signs been bad. Conversely, if you go against the signs and nothing happens, the astrologer can insist that you were careful because you were forewarned that the signs were "bad" for that day.

Truth to Say – Astrology must be rejected as both unscientific and unbiblical because:

1. **Conflicting Systems** – There are many systems of astrology, which are diametrically opposed to each other. Astrologers in the West differ from those in the East. Some say there are 8 zodiac signs and others contend that there are 12 or 14 or even 24. So one could go to two different astrologers and receive two totally different courses of behavior for the same day. If you compare horoscopes in daily newspapers you'll often see contradictions.

2. **Missing Planets** – Secondly, in ancient times, *Uranus*, *Neptune* and *Pluto* were unobservable with the naked eye, so most astrological charts are based upon the assumption that there are *seven* planets in our solar system (including the sun and moon).So the astrological theory breaks down, for no accurate horoscope could be charted without considering *all nine* of the planets and influence. In 2006, Pluto was downgraded as not a planet at all.

3. **Twins** are born at exactly the same time and place; they should have the same destiny. Unfortunately, experience shows this is not the case.

4. **No Scientific Verification** – Astrological prediction is criticized because of the fact that its scientific value is nil due to shifting constellations.

5. Astrology is Ineffective - Astrology doesn't work. Only Daniel, a prophet of God, could answer the king's question. The astrologers could not. Daniel 2:10 says, "The Chaldeans answered the king, and said, 'There is not a man on earth who can tell the king's matter; therefore no king, lord, or ruler has *ever* asked such things of any magician, astrologer, or Chaldean."

To Be Set Free from Horoscope Reading, Study These Scriptures:

- **John 14:5 6** - Thomas said to Him, "Lord, we do not know where You are going, and how can we know the way?" Jesus said to him, "I Am the way, the truth, and the life. No one comes to the Father except through Me.

- **Romans 8:14** -   For as many as are led by the Spirit of God, these are sons of God.

- **2 Corinthians 5:7** - For we walk by faith, not by sight.

- **Hebrews** 10:38 - Now the just shall live by faith; But if *anyone* draws back, My soul has no pleasure in him.

- **Jeremiah 29:11** -   For I know the thoughts that I think toward you, says the LORD, thoughts of peace and not of evil, to give you a future and a hope.

- **1 Corinthians 2:9-12** - Eye has not seen, nor ear heard, Nor have entered into the heart of man the things which God has prepared for those who love Him." But God has revealed *them* to us through His Spirit. For the Spirit searches all things, yes, the deep things of God. For what man knows the things of a man except the spirit of the man which is in him? Even so no one knows the things of God except the Spirit of God. Now we have received, not the spirit of the world, but the Spirit who is from God, that we might know the things that have been freely given to us by God.

- **Proverbs 3:5–6**: Trust in the LORD with all your heart, And lean not on your own understanding; In all your ways acknowledge Him, And He shall direct your paths.

- **Psalm 23** - The Lord is my shepherd; I shall not want. He makes me to lie down in green pastures; He leads me beside the still waters. He restores my soul; He leads me in the paths of righteousness For His name's sake. Yea, though I walk through the valley of the shadow of death, I will fear no evil; For You are with me; Your rod and Your staff, they comfort me You prepare a table before me in the presence of my enemies; You anoint my head with oil; My cup runs over. Surely goodness and mercy shall follow me All the days of my life; And I will dwell in the house of the Lord Forever.

Pray this Salvation Prayer: "Father God, I repent for trying to lead and guide my life through a horoscope. Forgive me. I want You to be my Good Shepherd. I trust in You, that if I follow You and Your Word, then I will be following Your good plan for my life. My hope is in You. My trust is in You and not my horoscope. Jesus, I ask you now to come into my heart and be my Lord and Savior. Deliver me from the temptation to be led by my horoscope or by the stars. Teach me how to be led by Your Spirit and by the Word of God. In Jesus name I pray, A–men"

These two books are excellent resources:

"How You Can Be Led By the Spirit of God
by Bro. Kenneth E. Hagin

"Listen to Your Heart" **by Pastor Kenneth Hagin, Jr.**

Truth to Say to Atheists and Those Who Believe in Evolution

Deception: God does not exist.

Truth to Say: How do you know? Do you know everything? Do know all the information that there is to know? No, you have limited knowledge. But did you know that there are *doorways* to more knowledge? For e.g., in order to clearly see the stars in the sky, you use *the door* of a telescope; in order to know more about your brain, you use *the door* of an X–ray in order know more about the cells in your body, you use *the door* of a microscope. Isn't that right? In John 10:9 Jesus Christ said that *He was the door* to Father God. So in order to know more about God, you have to go through the door of Jesus Christ. When you receive Jesus Christ as your Savior, your spirit will be born into the spirit realm of the Kingdom of Heaven, which opens the door to God. Then you will know that He exists. He knew you in your mother's womb and He loved you even before you ever loved Him.

Deception: There are so many terrible things that have happened to me. There is so much suffering in the world. God is not just. So I don't believe in God.

Truth to Say: The truth is that God gave human beings a free will – to either do good or bad, to worship God or to not worship God because love is not truly love unless it is *freely* given. God did not want to make us worship Him like robots. Many times parents make bad choices and their children suffer horribly. This is not God's will and yet it happens. Many children get angry and rebel because they know that the way they have been treated was not fair. But it is not God's fault. God loves you. The Bible says that God heals the broken hearted (Psalm 147:3) and when you receive Jesus Christ as your Savior and forgive those that have hurt you, God will turn things around for you. You must be patient, wait for His timing, and trust in Him. This God–given free will is a Law that He cannot break, but God is just. He could have sent us all imperfect humans to hell, but He intervened through sending His only begotten Son Jesus Christ to this earth to die on the cross to pay the price for our sins. So that those that believe in Jesus would be reconciled to God and go to heaven. That is how much God loves us.   Read Romans 12:19.

Deception: I don't believe the Bible is true nor the Word of God.

Truth to Say: *Prophecies fulfilled* is one of the methods the Bible uses to authenticate itself as the Word of God and that is something that is lacking in all the other religious writings. For example, the writings of Buddha don't have any predictive prophecy about the things of the future. In the Koran, we find only one prophecy: that Mohammed would return to Mecca. But he himself fulfilled that while still on earth. In the Old Testament there are at least 333 prophecies about Jesus Christ. Hundreds of years later in the New Testament all 333 prophecies were fulfilled through Jesus, proving that the Bible is true.

Deception: I do not believe that God created Adam and Eve. I believe in Evolution.

Truth to Say: Evolution was a theory, but advanced technology has disproved it. Darwin said: *"If it could be demonstrated that any complex organ existed which could not possibly have been formed by numerous, successive, slight modifications, my theory would absolutely break down."* Researcher Michael Behe found through electron microscopes several examples such as: the cell, cilia, the blood clotting system, the bacterial flagellum and the vision in the eye, which cannot be formed by numerous, successive, modifications because the removal or the reducing of one part would cause the whole complex system to not function. They are irreducibly complex. They defy evolutionary origin. This proves that humans were formed by Intelligent Design and I believe that the Intelligent Designer is the Creator, who is God Almighty.

Truth to Say to Witness to Buddhists

Deception: Siddhartha Gautama, the founder of Buddhism, was born about 560 BC during the time of Ezekiel in the Bible. He called himself "Buddha" meaning, "the enlightened one." Buddhism came out of Hinduism. It did away with the caste system.

Truth to Say: Buddha was right that existence brings suffering. Many times suffering comes because of sinful choices that are made. Some Christians have suffered a lot emotionally and physically, but they have found that their loving relationship with God through His Son Jesus Christ and the healing power of the Holy Spirit has brought great comfort to their suffering. In John 15:15 Jesus said to His disciples before He ascended to heaven that God will give you all another Comforter, (Who is the Holy Spirit), "that He may abide with you forever." The Holy Spirit abides within Christians and brings healing comfort to them all.

Deception: Buddha discovered **Four Noble Truths**. The first two noble truths are:
1. Existence Brings Suffering
2. The cause of suffering is the craving desire for pleasure (happiness and prosperity).

Truth to Say: Yes, existence brings suffering, but it also brings joy in many ways. In Ezekiel 36:26 says, "I will give you a new heart and I will give you new and right desires." Psalm 37:4: "Delight yourself in the Lord and He will give you the desires of your heart." Prosperity helps spread the Gospel.

Deception: The 3rd Noble Truth: The way to escape from suffering is to get rid of the desire for pleasure.

Truth to Say: Jesus Christ rid us from eternal suffering. God sent His Son Jesus Christ, who paid the price for our sins, satisfying the wrath of God through shedding His perfect holy blood and dying on the cross. You escape suffering in hell through praying to receive Jesus as your Lord and Savior. Here on earth, God wants us to be joyful in Christ. Happiness often depends on outward circumstances, but when a person is in Christ, one can always be joyful because that joy comes from within your born again spirit. God desires for us to be joyful. Psalm 16:11 says: "In God's Presence is fullness of joy." Proverbs 17:22 says: "A merry heart does good like a medicine." Nehemiah 8:10 says: "The joy of the Lord is our strength."

Deception: The 4th Noble Truth: The way to be rid of desire is to discipline one's mind and to live correctly, following the Eightfold path for your life.

Truth to Say: God want us to have godly desires. Christians discipline their minds through *actively* memorizing scriptures and then applying them to their lives to live for Christ. Buddhists *passively* blank out their minds through yoga, which causes demons to enter in. You do not want demons to control you. Then your life will not go God's way. You want the Holy Spirit to control you and be the Lord of your life, right? Then you must get delivered from yoga and be set free.

Deception: Buddhists believe to receive "salvation", you must go through a series of reincarnations, a chain of rebirths, in which each soul, through mastering the Eight–fold Path, can rise to a higher state. The deny the authority of the Vedas (that the Hindus believe in)

Truth to Say: We are human, so we all sin. Our sin separates us from God. Hebrews 9:22 says without the shedding of blood, there is no forgiveness of sins. Jesus Christ paid the price for our sins through shedding His holy blood on the cross for all mankind, so that we could be forgiven and reconciled again to God. Salvation from hell or eternal life in heaven is a free gift. You just believe and pray to receive Jesus Christ as your Lord and Savior. After you are saved, then God does want you to do good works to help your fellow man (like the Eight fold path), but it is not how you receive salvation.

Truth to Say to Witness to Mormons

Deception: Mormonism is just another Christian denomination.

Truth to Say: No, it is not. There are vast differences, which is why Mormonism is often called "a cult"

Deception: In 1820 at age 15, Joseph Smith was told by a "spirit" to not join any of the churches around him because their creeds were all wrong and an abomination in God's sight. "If it had not been for Joseph Smith and the restoration, there would be no salvation. There is no salvation outside the church of Jesus Christ of Latter–day Saints" (from Mormon Doctrine, p. 670).

Truth to Say: No, I do not believe that all the churches from the death of Christ until 1820 were all wrong and only what Joseph Smith says is right. Churches may be wrong in envying one another or arguing over minor issues, but I know that Jesus Christ's shed blood on the cross paid for my sins & reconciled me to God. I have a personal relationship with God through the power of the Holy Spirit. That creed has never been wrong.

Deception: A "person glorious beyond description" led Joseph Smith to a book written on gold plates containing "the fullness of the Gospel" as delivered by the Savior. Two stones called "Urim & Thummin" were given to translate *Doctrines and Covenants* (which is false doctrine). Regarding the Book of Mormon, they believe: "The book of Mormon is more correct than the Bible," (History of the Church, vol. 4, p. 461.)

Truth to Say: 2 Corinthians 11:14 says "And no marvel; for Satan himself is transformed into an angel of light." A spirit of divination is a method that familiar spirits use to pervert the Gospel. Revelation 22:18 says: "For I testify…if any man shall **add** unto these things, God shall add unto him *the plagues* that are written in this book." So since *The Book of Mormon* & *The Pearl of Great Price* were added, then I know they are false. The Bible is the inerrant Word of God.

Deception: Regarding **Jesus Christ** they believe: "The birth of the Savior was as natural as are the births of our children; it was the result of natural action." (Journal of Discourses, vol. 8, p. 115).

Truth to Say: No, that is false. The Holy Spirit overshadowed the Virgin Mary and it was an immaculate conception. This is a vital truth to any Christian denomination and cannot be disputed. The conception of Jesus Christ was a miracle. Mary was a virgin.

> Regarding **God,** they believe that God used to be a man on another planet near the star Kolob

Deception: Regarding **God,** they believe that God used to be a man on another planet near the star Kolob (Mormon Doctrine, p. 321; Joseph Smith, Times and Seasons, vol. 5, p. 613–614; Orson Pratt, Journal of Discourses, vol. 2, p. 345; Brigham Young, Journal of Discourses, vol. 7, p. 333)

Truth to Say: The Bible says in Matthew 6:9 "Our Father, which art **in heaven,** hallowed be thy Name." God lives in heaven because He created the heavens and the earth. The Mormon so called "prophets" have been greatly deceived.

Deception: Mormons believe that if they are obedient to the laws and ordinances of their "gospel" that they will become gods with a planet of their own. They believe **"As man is, God once was, and as God is, man may become."** ("Articles of Faith" by James believe: After you become a good Mormon, you have the potential of becoming a god (Teachings of the Prophet Joseph Smith, p. 345–347, 354).

Truth to Say: We do not become gods. That is such false doctrine! God is omnipotent (all powerful) and He is omniscient (all knowing). He knows everything and we will never know everything like God does. The truth is God wants us to grow in our relationship with Him through reading the Bible and have godly character. He has called us to walk by faith and not by sight. He wants us to be loving and kind and forgiving. He wants us to walk in the fruits of the spirit and be obedient to Him. That is what God wants.

Deception: Regarding the **Holy Ghost,** they believe: The Holy Ghost is a male personage (A Marvelous Work and a Wonder, Le Grand Richards, Salt Lake City, 1956, p. 118; Journal of Discourses, vol. 5, p. 179).

Truth to Say: No, the Holy Ghost is a Spirit. The Bible says that God is a Spirit in John 4:24. The truth is we can know God personally through praying to receive Jesus Chris as our Lord and Savior. Then we will be united to Him, through spirit– to Spirit. It is called becoming born again, which is when our spirit becomes born into the Kingdom of God when we pray to receive

Deception: Regarding a mother goddess, they believe there is a mother god (Articles of Faith, James Talmage, p. 443).

Truth to Say: There is not a mother goddess in the Bible. That is not Christianity.

Deception: They believe that there are many gods (Mormon Doctrine, p. 163).

Truth to Say: That is false doctrine. The truth is there is one God. He is manifested in three forms that we call the Trinity: Father, Son and Holy Ghost.

Deception: They teach that Jesus Christ had a church organization, but it sinned and fell from grace and thus, went "into apostasy" and was "taken from the earth." So their focus is on "the restoration of the organized Temple with registered membership" on earth once again in Salt Lake City.

Truth to Say: When you become a Christian, Jesus comes into your heart to be your Lord. 1 Corinthians 6:19 says your body is the temple of the Holy Ghost. A Christian is already a true member of the Church and their name is written in the Lamb's Book of Life (Revelation 21:27). There is no way the church could be "taken from the earth." Jesus says in Matthew 16:18: "Upon this rock I will build my Church and the gates of hell shall not prevail against it." No sin is too great for the blood of Jesus to forgive and save.

Deception: Joseph Smith claimed to receive the Melchisadek and Aaronic priesthoods. He professed to restore these back to the body of Christ. The Lord gave him ordination instructions and then a "holy angel" came to confirm his priesthood.

Truth to Say: I do not believe that the "holy angel" was from God. Satan came come as an "angel of light" to deceive like it says in 2 Corinthians 11:14. Jesus Christ did away with the Melchisadek and Aaronic priesthoods in the Old Testament Law because they are no longer needed. Jesus Christ made atonement for mankind's sins through shedding His blood on the cross. He fulfilled the Law. So the priesthoods do not need to be restored.

Deception: Joseph Smith decided that "God gave him a revelation" and used the Bible out of context convincing many people (the Hendrikites) that Jesus would return to Independence, Missouri. (From book: *Delivered from Mormonism*, by Bill Ketchum, p 4)

Truth to Say: The Bible says in Zechariah 14:4 says that Jesus will return and set His feet on the Mt of Olives. Also, when the Mormons started constructing the temple there in Independence, MO, the leader went home and died that very night! Then later another man led the building of the temple and he went home and died as well. After these men died, the people gave up building the temple. These tragic deaths reveal the truths of Revelation 22:18 that if any man adds to the Bible, God will judge him and add to him the plagues in the Bible. It is true.

The following truth below was extracted from a Chick Tract called "The Visitors" (1984) published from www.chick.com.

Deception: Mormons teach that God was once a man. Brigham Young said, "If our Father and God should be disposed to walk through these aisles, we should not know Him from of the congregation. You would see a man and that is all you would know about Him" (from Journal of Discourses, Vol. II, pg 40.)

Truth to Say: The Bible says that God is a Spirit in John 4:24 and the truth is we can know God personally through receiving Jesus Christ as our Lord and Savior. Then we will be united to Him, through spirit to Spirit. It is called becoming born again, which is when our spirit becomes born into the Kingdom of God when we pray to receive Jesus Christ as our Lord and Savior. We can also know God better through reading our Holy Bible. The Bible says in 1 Kings 8:10–11 when the priests came out of the holy place of the Temple, the Presence of the Lord filled the Temple "so the priests could not continue ministering because of the cloud; for the glory of the Lord filled the house of the Lord."

Deception: They do not teach polygamy anymore, but they do believe that God the Father has many wives (from "The Seer" by Orson Pratt, pg 172)

Truth to Say: The truth is that God has never had a wife! The Virgin Mary was not even God's wife. She was the chosen vessel to bear the Son of God, Jesus Christ. And even in that Immaculate Conception, the Holy Spirit hovered over her and miraculously caused her to become pregnant with God's seed. God and Mary were never married.

Deception: They believe that God the Father is now on a planet near the star Kolob, with His wives having spiritual children. (Pearl of Great Price, Abraham 3:9, 16), They believe this because it was revealed though a prophet of theirs.

Truth to Say: Their so–called "prophets" have been greatly deceived. Matthew 6:9 declares: "Our Father who art **in heaven,** hallowed be thy Name." It is true God created the planets, but He lives in heaven.

Deception: The Mormons also teach that Satan and Jesus are brothers. This was taught by Prophet President Kimball. (Ensign magazine, December 1980, p 5)   They really believe that Jesus and Satan are spirit brothers and we were all born as siblings in heaven to them both, (Mormon Doctrine, p. 163.)

Truth to Say: The Bible says in Colossians 1:16–18 that Jesus is God, the Creator of everything in heaven and earth (including Lucifer). There is none beside Him.

Deception: The Mormons also teach about how there was a war in heaven, which was when Jesus and Lucifer approached God with their plans of Salvation.   They believed that there were many gods present.   Joseph Smith called it a "Council of Gods." Lucifer's plan was to **make** the people worship God. But Jesus' plan was to **show** the people how to worship God. Lucifer's plan was rejected and Jesus' plan was accepted. (Pearl of Great Price, book of Moses, 4:1–3"

Truth to Say: This is a conjured up story by the Mormons. The Bible says in Isaiah 45:5: "I Am the Lord, and there is none else, there is no God beside Me." There was no council of gods and Jesus Christ is not the Savior simply because "His plan was accepted." The Bible says in John 1:10 that "He (Jesus) was in the world, and the world was made by Him and the world knew Him not." Jesus created the universe. He created the world. That is the truth.

Deception: The Mormons believe that Lucifer became Satan when he rebelled and was thrown out of heaven with a third of the spirits. Then they were sent to this planet near the star Kolob. This is where the demons came from.

Truth to Say: Yes, Lucifer rebelled, but not from a planet in the sky. Lucifer was thrown out of heaven with one third of the angels, which then became demons because they rebelled and disobeyed God. Then God created hell for the devil and his demons to dwell in, so hell is where demons come from.

Deception: They believe that of the remaining two–thirds of the spirits, one third was faithful and stayed with Jesus in the battle. The other third didn't fight as valiantly. They believe that all of these spirits are really spirit children that came from God and all of His wives.

Truth to Say: All of this is a conjured up story and is not in the Bible. God does not have many wives!

Deception: The Mormons believe that the spirit children who were faithful to Jesus in the battle up in heaven are born as babies with white skin ("Doctrines of Salvation", Vol. 1, J.F. Smith, p 61). They believe that the spirit children who did not fight valiantly during the battle in heaven are babies born with black skin. ("Mormon Doctrine" by Bruce R. McConkie, pp 526–527, 1966 edition)

Truth to Say: This is a terrible thing to say. First of all, there was no battle in heaven. Isaiah 14:12–15 reveals that God simply cast the devil out of heaven and he fell to the lowest depth of the pit. The Bible says in 1 Samuel 16:7 "But the LORD said to Samuel, "Do not look at his appearance or at his physical stature, because I have refused him. For the LORD does not see as man sees; for man looks at the outward appearance, but the LORD looks at the heart." Their so–called "prophets" have been greatly deceived. Babies with black skin and babies with white skin are equally valuable and precious to the Lord.

Deception: When Mormons marry they want to have large families because they believe that there are many spirits waiting for human tabernacles, and each child will become a home for one of those spirits. (Mormon Doctrine, by B.R. McConckie, pg 698 and Pearl of Great Price, Abraham, 3:22–28.

Truth to Say: God wants us to have children that we desire to have and that we can afford to take care of. Any accidental pregnancies I believe are God's divine hand as well, but not so that all of these "spirits" can have a human temple to dwell in. That thinking is skewed.

Deception: They believe that Jesus Christ had many wives…the two sisters of Lazarus and Mary Magdalene. (Journal of Discourses, Vol. 1, pp 345 and Vol. II, pg 210)
Truth to Say: That is not true and it is not in the Bible.

Deception: They Jesus had many wives because they believe that Jesus could not become a god unless He was married. (Mormon Doctrine, by Bruce R. McConkie, pp 117–118)
Truth to Say: This is so crazy it makes me laugh. In the Bible, in John 1:1–3 and Revelation 1:8 show that Jesus Christ has always been God and He always will be God. It says in Hebrews 13:8 that "Jesus Christ is the same yesterday, and today, and forever." When Jesus Christ comes again, He will take up or capture and carry away (also called the Rapture) all the Christians that are born again on up to heaven. In Ephesians 5:27 Paul refers to the Church at *the Lord's Bride* that shall be without spot or wrinkle, holy and without blemish. After the Rapture, we will all attend, up in heaven, the Marriage Supper of the Lamb. Jesus will allegorically marry the Church someday.

Deception: Joseph Smith's revelations were from God.
Truth to Say: Truthfully, Joseph Smith's family was deeply involved in the occult. He was arrested in 1826 for the occult practice called "Glass Looking". When Joseph Smith was killed, he was carrying an occult talisman of Jupiter in his pocket. (Early Mormonism and the Magic World View" by Quinn, pp 66–73.) The Bible says in Deuteronomy 7:25–26, Deuteronomy 18:10–12, Leviticus 19:31 and Isaiah 47:10–14 that any involvement with the occult is an abomination. The One who created the world – He is Almighty God.

Deception: Joseph and his brother Hyram were Masons. Joseph Smith jumped from a 1st degree to a sublime degree in only one day. This is why Masonic symbols are on the walls of the Mormon temples. (History of the Church" by Joseph Smith Vol. 4, pp 551–552. and "White Sepulchers" by Schnoebelen & Spencer)

Truth to Say: Masons are of the occult. Mormonism is really nothing but a modern day version of Baal worship. It is a mixture of Babylonian and Jewish religions, Masonry and Catholic tradition. They claim Apostolic Authority, like the Vatican. They even have 12 apostles living in Salt Lake City, Utah.

Deception: Masonic symbols are also on the undergarments worn by Mormons who have gone through the temple, where they learn their secret handshakes, their blood oaths, their secret names which they need to get to heaven.

Truth to Say: The Word says in Ephesians 5:11–12, "Have no fellowship with the unfruitful works of darkness, but rather reprove them for it is a shame even to speak of those things which are done of them in secret." See also: Deuteronomy 13:1–10.

Truth to Say to Witness to Muslims

It is difficult to win a Muslim to Christ because if they convert to Christianity, then their whole family will disown them and consider them "dead." They could even be killed for their faith in Christ. They have to surrender ALL and make the decision to fear God more than their family. If you do win a Muslim to Christ, make sure that you and other Christians become his/her "new family." (Matthew 12:50). They need to be properly discipled and have a network of friends and spiritual family support.

Before you try to witness to a Muslim, pray and bind the spirit of Islam, the antichrist spirit, the lies of the enemy and the "god of this world that is blinding their eyes to salvation." And pray for the eyes of their heart to be enlightened. Loose the love, the truth and the power of God upon their hearts in Jesus' name. Only God can change someone's heart. Pray for the Holy Spirit to touch their heart as only He can do. Many Muslims are supernaturally getting saved through Jesus appearing to them in their dreams or an angel appearing to them in their dreams. Pray for that to continue!

Telling them your testimony of how you came to know Jesus as your Savior can be effective.

My friend Bill Shepherd tells me that this technique is very effective. He says: **"You believe that Jesus Christ was a prophet?** (wait for them to agree.) Prophets tell the truth. Right? (and waits for them to agree...)** *Well, in John 14:6 Jesus Christ said that He was "the way, the truth and the life and there is no way to the Father, but through Him." So what do you think of that?*

One of the most effective ways for a Muslim to be saved is if they supernaturally experience a miracle healing or hear a word of knowledge through a prophetic word that causes their heart to receive Jesus as Lord. One of the most helpful things to know is how to answer the three questions that Muslims often ask:

Three Questions Muslims Ask:

1. Has the Bible Been Changed?

No, the Bible has not been changed. The reason why Muslims believe that the Bible was changed by Christians and Jews is because the Koran does not say what the Bible says and so one of them has to be wrong. Allah claims to have written both the Bible and the Koran and says, "He is the guardian of His own word including the Torah and the Gospel." Allah and his Koran are not very good guardians if the Bible has been changed.

Answer: The Koran was supposed to be a confirmation of the Bible. So, how can the Koran confirm a book that has been changed? The Koran says in Sura 6:115: "Perfected are the Words of your Lord in truth and justice and none can change his Words." The Koran states that the Bible is God's Word. The Torah, the Gospels, the Psalms and the writings of the Prophets are recognized as Scripture. Sura 2:91 says: "It (the Koran) is the truth corroborating their (the Christians and Jews) own Scripture." Sura 3:2–3 says: "He has revealed to you the Book (Koran) with the truth confirming the Scriptures that have come before it, for He (Allah) has already revealed the Torah and the Gospel for the guidance of men and the distinction between right and wrong." Sura 21:105 says, "We wrote in the Psalms after the Torah was revealed."

I want you to notice this! This is the one of the greatest benefits when witnessing to Muslims, if not the greatest witnessing tool! The Koran commands Muslims, Christians and Jews to read and obey the Bible!! The quote is here, so remember Sura 5:58

Sura 5:58 "People of the Book, you will attain nothing until you observe the Torah and the Gospel and that which is revealed to you by your Lord." This verse is a great way to witness to get them to read the Bible

2. Why Does the Bible Say that Jesus Christ Was Crucified?

The Koran denies that He was crucified. Sura 4:157 "The Jews have said, "verily we have slain Christ Jesus, the son of Mary, the Apostle of Allah; yet they slew him not, neither did they crucify him, but he was represented by one in his likeness…They did not really kill him; but Allah took him up to himself."

Answer: First of all, no one took the life of Jesus. **He gave His life willingly to save man** from sin. John 10:18 says, "No one takes it (my life) from Me, but I lay it down on my own accord. I have authority to lay it down and authority to take it up again." So the crucifixion did not just happen. It was prophesied for thousands of years. For e.g.: Isaiah 53: 3–7 prophesied it would happen and 1 Peter 1:10–11 says: "Concerning this salvation, the prophets…predicted the sufferings of Christ and the glories that would follow." **So Jesus knew that He would die for the sins of the world**. Matthew 16:21 says: "Jesus began to explain to His disciples that He must go to Jerusalem and suffer many things at the hands of the elders, chief priests and teachers of the Law and that He must be killed and on the third day be raised to life." **The sacrifice of blood is God's way of paying for sin.** Hebrews 9:22 "In fact, the law requires that nearly everything be cleansed with blood and without the shedding of blood there is no forgiveness." **God is the only one "good" enough to pay for men's sins**.

Matthew 1:22–23 says, "All this took place to fulfill what the Lord had said through the prophet: "The virgin will be with child and will give birth to a son, and they will call him Emmanuel, which means, "God with us." No good works will bring you into a right relationship with God. Only through praying to receive Jesus Christ as your Lord and Savior will you be saved from eternal damnation in hell. Jesus said in John 14:6 , "I Am the way, the truth and the life and there is no way to heaven, but through Me."

3.   Why Does the Bible Say Jesus is the Son of God?

Answer: First of all, God has no son in the sense of God having sex with Mary. It's not what you think in that way. Why? Because God is a Spirit. Matt 1:18 says that Mary was found to be pregnant through the power of the Holy Spirit. She was overshadowed by the Holy Spirit. When Jesus left heaven and humbled Himself to come to earth to be born and live as a human, He came to show us the Father and to shed His perfect sinless blood and die on the cross for our sins so that we could be reconciled to God. On earth, Jesus was submitted to His Father, so in this sense, it was a special relationship, similar to a "Father– Son" relationship. But Jesus is God just like God is God and the Holy Spirit is God.

The Almighty God is one God in three different personalities. For e.g.: ice, water and steam. God is three in One. When He was on earth, Jesus was fully God and fully man. The Bible Says that there is only ONE God:

In 1 Corinthians 8:5– 6 it says: "There is no God, but one. For even if there are so–called gods, whether in heaven or on earth, **yet for us there is but one God**, the Father, from whom all things came." The Bible says that Jesus is the Son of God because God <u>said</u> Jesus is His Son in Matthew 3:17: "And suddenly a voice came from heaven saying, "This is My beloved Son, in whom I Am well pleased." God is one God in three different manifestations or personalities. Acts 10:38 demonstrates this trinity when it says: "How *God* anointed *Jesus of Nazareth* with the *Holy Ghost* and with power who went about doing good and healing all that were oppressed of the devil."

In Matthew 28:19 Jesus Christ affirmed the trinity: "Make disciples baptizing them in the name of the *Father* and of the *Son* and of the *Holy Spirit.*" Paul also emphasized the trinity in 2 Corinthians 13:14:- "The grace of the Lord Jesus Christ, and the love of God, and the communion of the Holy Ghost, be with you all."

Muslims See Allah as Judge, Not as a Loving Father

There are 99 names for Allah. Not one of them is "Father." Not one of them is "Love." Muslims see Allah as a distant, capricious judge, not a loving Father who takes delight in His children. Allah of the Qur'an offers a master–slave relationship, while God of the Bible offers adoption into a Father–child relationship.

Truth to Say: When I became a Christian, God adopted me into His family, into the Kingdom of Light and so He is now my Heavenly Father. I call him Father. It says in Romans 8:15 (NIV) *"The Spirit you received does not make you slaves, so that you live in fear again; rather, the Spirit you received brought about your adoption to sonship. And by him we cry, "Abba, Father." "*

Six Differences between Jesus Christ and Muhammad that Can Help in Witnessing:

1. Jesus Christ forgave sins. Muhammad did not forgive any sins.

2. Jesus Christ is omniscient. He knows everything. Compared to that, Muhammad knows little.

3. Jesus Christ did miracles and healed many people. Muhammad did not do any miracles nor did he heal anyone.

4. Jesus Christ has all authority. Muhammad has temporal authority.

5. Jesus rose from the dead. Muhammad just died.

6. Jesus Christ claimed He was God. Muhammad claimed he was a prophet, a messenger of God.

Another Effective Way to Witness to Muslims Is to Cast Doubt on Their Own Beliefs

One of the best ways to do this is to ask questions about their faith in a gracious respectful manner. Do not ridicule or tear down their Koran, Muhammad or their customs or beliefs because you will only drive a wedge between you and them and then they will not listen. In other words, do not tell a Muslim something and make them mad. Ask them a question and make them think. The following are some questions to make them think:

1.   If the God of the Bible is the same as the god of the Koran, then how can my sins be forgiven so I can be reconciled to God? You know, ,there is no forgiveness of sins without the shedding of blood.
2.   If I were a Muslim, how could I know *for sure* that I will end up in paradise or heaven? Is the only way to really know for sure is if I actually kill someone for Allah?
3.   If the God of the Bible is the same god of the Koran (Sura 29:46), why is the symbol for Islam a crescent moon and the symbol for Christianity is a cross? Did Muhammad die on the moon?
4.   Did Muhammad ever heal anyone or perform any miracles? Did he forgive anyone of his or her sins? Jesus did.
5.   What if I miss praying five times a day? Would I have to pray 10 times a day the next day?
6.   Many say that Muhammad was a prophet. Prophets in the Bible were holy. Many, like Jesus Christ, were not even married. Why did Muhammad have so many wives? (He had eleven).
7.   In the Exordium, it says, "Guide us in the straight path..." That reminds me of Isaiah 40:3: "Prepare the way of the Lord; make His beaten paths straight." Do you think he was searching for Jesus Christ?
8.   Why does the Koran depict heaven as a place where sexual desires are fulfilled? Sura 55:54 says "therein are bashful virgins

whom neither man nor Jinnee will have touched before." But the Bible says in Revelation 4:8 that the angels in heaven surround the throne of God saying, "Holy, holy, holy!"

9.   Someone read in this book by Salman Rushdie that once there were actually some "satanic verses" in the Koran saying that his family could worship the three goddesses, the daughters of Allah, but these verses were taken out. Did you ever hear about that? Has the Koran been changed?

Five Pillars of Islam

1ˢᵗ Pillar Deception: The "Shahada" or profession of faith to which every Muslim must witness: "There is no God but Allah, and Mohammed is the messenger of God."

Truth to Say: The Bible says in Acts 1:8 – "But you shall receive power when the Holy Spirit has come upon you; and you shall be my witnesses" (which are like messengers). Acts 4:33 says, "with great power the apostles gave witness to the resurrection of the Lord Jesus."

2ⁿᵈ Pillar Deception: The "Salah"– daily ritual prayer. Dedicated Muslims stop 5 times every day and repeat a total of 17 prayer rounds.

Truth to Say: In the Bible in Matthew 6:7 says: "and when you pray, do not use vain repetitions as the heathen do, for they think that they will be heard for their many words. You only pray five times a day, but in the Bible, it says in 1 Thessalonians 5:17 says to: "Pray without ceasing." We Christians stay connected to God spirit to Spirit, *through abiding in the Lord*, fellowshipping with His Spirit who is within us, like the Bible says in John 15:5: "I Am the Vine and you are the branches."

3ʳᵈ Pillar Deception: The Payment of Zakat   A tax for the poor which is 2.5% of their income plus fasting one meal at Festival of Eid.

Many Muslims seek to avoid this task.

Truth to Say: Christians tithe, which means they give 10% of their income to God. Malachi 3:10: says, "Bring all the tithes into the store house" (God's church). Christians who tithe give 10% of their income to God, which is so much more than the 2 ½ percent that Muslims give to Allah or their god.

4ᵗʰ Pillar Deception: The "Sawn" of fasting in the month of Ramadan. There is no eating, smoking, or sex during daylight unless you are ill, traveling, nursing or pregnant. The purpose of the fast is to contribute to a mastery or world concerns and fosters compassion for the poor.

Truth to Say: Isaiah 58:6 says: "Is this not the fast that I have chosen: To loose the bonds of wickedness, to undo the heavy burdens, to let the oppressed go free and that you break every yoke?" Matt. 6: 16– 18 "moreover, when you fast, do not be like the hypocrites, with a sad countenance. Assuredly, I say to you, they have their reward. But you, when you fast, anoint your head and wash your face, so that you do not appear to be fasting, but pray to your Father who is in the secret place; and your Father who sees in secret will reward you openly."

5ᵗʰ Pillar Deception: The "Haij" or pilgrimage. Once a year many Muslims travel to Mecca in remembrance of Abraham's sacrifice of Ishmael (not Isaac). The journey is to be made by every Muslim at least once in his/her lifetime if he can afford it.

Truth to Say: Genesis 22:7–14 s a y s that Abraham obeyed God and prepared to sacrifice his son Isaac, not Ishmael, before an Angel of the Lord stopped him. In Genesis 22: 9–14, Ishmael and Hagar were sent away. Muslims are making this pilgrimage or journey to remember something that is not even true. Sigh. At communion, when we partake of the bread and the wine, (symbolizing the body and blood of Jesus), we remember Him. Since the Lord dwells in our hearts, there is no better place to travel than to our local churches to worship Him.

Truth to Say to Witness to New Agers

Deception: New Age represents the self–conscious spiritualization of the human potential movement. Their main concern is to be whoever they believe they are authentically are.

Truth to Say: "Spiritual experiences" from God or the Holy Spirit only come if you know Jesus as your Lord. Any other spiritual experience is not from God, but from demons. Would you like to pray and receive Jesus as your Lord and Savior?

Deception: New Agers abide by secular humanism which says: Man is the standard by which all life is judged. Thus values, law, justice, good, beauty, and right and wrong all are to be judged by man– made rules with no credence to God or the Bible.

Truth to Say: Since man's wisdom is limited, there is no way we can solve all of our own problems. Since God created the world and all of us, He has all the wisdom, all the power and all the knowledge. So we must humbly seek and honor God and abide by His moral standards and rules in the Bible. God is the Judge.

Deception: There is no absolute truth. Everything is relative. It may be true for you, but it is not true for me.

Truth to Say: Individual circumstances are important, but everything is neither relative nor absolute. You cannot say, "God exists for me, but does not exist for you." We don't create our own reality. Absolute truth does exist. The Bible says in John 14:6 that Jesus Christ is the only **true** way to heaven.

Deception: Spiritual truth comes from within. It is something to be discovered within the sanctity of the self rather than in an external aid or tool.

Truth to Say: Jeremiah 17:9 says: "The heart is deceitful above all things, and desperately wicked: who can know it?" Proverbs

28:26 says, "He that trusts in his own heart is a fool, but whoso walks wisely shall be delivered." Truth comes from the Bible. Truth is Jesus Christ.

Deception: We are in charge of our lives.

Truth to Say: Christians gladly submit their lives to God, also known as, their Heavenly Father because they know He loves them and He knows what is best for them.

Deception: We can communicate with the dead for guidance, knowledge and confirmation.

Truth to Say: We can receive guidance and some knowledge of the future from the Holy Spirit (1 Corinthians 2:10). God forbids communicating with the dead or familiar spirits, who are from the devil. It is an abomination to the Lord. Deuteronomy 19:10–13

Deception: New Age affirms its faith in both spiritual seeking and in validating private experiences and offers a new form of mysticism of becoming a god.

Truth to Say: I agree we should be godly, but it is not godly to want to be a god. There is no other God besides God. He is all– powerful and all knowing and He is perfect. God wants us to walk in godly character.

Deception: We have a right to make decisions that reflect personal inner needs and desires. We are no longer expected to automatically follow the dictates of authority.

Truth to Say: Psalm 37:4 says, "Delight yourself *in the Lord* and He will give you the desires of your heart. Commit your way to the Lord, trust also in Him and He shall bring it to pass." Your needs will be met when you follow God, Who loves you.

Truth to Say to Witness to Scientologists

Deception: Ron Hubbard is the founder of Scientology and he was in several films himself over his lifetime. *"Scientology"* was conceived by Hubbard. It means in Latin: *scio* – the study of knowledge. Ron Hubbard quotes: "what is true for you is what you have observed yourself. And when you lose that, you have lost everything."

Truth to Say: The Bible says in Rom 12:1–2 to: "Renew your mind with the Word of God so that you may *know*, the good, the acceptable and the perfect will of God." The truth is – when you observe the Bible and apply it to your life, then you will gain everything.

Deception: Dianetics was introduced into the much broader field of Scientology to provide some kind of "therapy" around 1950. The goal of Scientology is true spiritual enlightenment and freedom through their "counseling" which has different terminology than what in normally used.

Truth to Say: To come into "true spiritual enlightenment" one must become born–again through believing and praying to receive Jesus Christ as their Lord and Savior. Then one needs to study the Word of God to understand who they are in Christ because true freedom comes through Him alone.

Deception: In Scientology, the **auditor** is "the counselor." A **preclear** is a person undergoing counseling for whatever reason. They put new names to common day terms.

Truth to Say: This sounds like what a pastor is called to do for members of his congregation if he does any counseling. Also the Holy Spirit can lead us and guide us to the truth that will destroy the lies from our past or from the demonic spirits that were meant to entangle us. The truth will set use free. Psalm 119:105 says, "The Word is a lamp to my feet and a light to my path." There are many pastors and life coaches that are out there today helping Christians become all that God has called them to be. We become strengthened by standing on the promises of God and God's power and His grace working through us, not trusting in ourselves and in our own strength.

Deception: The Auditor uses an **E–meter** – a device that measures the spiritual state or change of state of a person that helps locate the areas of spiritual distress needed to be handled when asked a whole series of questions about their past relationships and past experiences. The auditor never tells the preclear what he should think about himself, nor offers his opinion because of the goal of not evaluating their behavior nor being "judgmental."

Truth to Say: The Bible says that the way that we delete and defeat these bad memories is in found in 2 Corinthians 10:4–5: "Casting down imaginations and everything high thing that exalts itself against the knowledge of God and bringing every thought captive to the obedience of Christ." The auditors do not evaluate nor judge their preclear, so they do not give them any Biblical guidance. But it says in 2 Timothy 3:16– 17 that "all scripture is God–breathed and is useful for teaching, rebuking, correcting and training in righteousness." Also it says in Romans 12:1–2 we are to "renew our minds with the Word of God." I can see why Holly wood stars are so attracted to scientology because a lot of them do live sinful lives and in scientology, no guidance from the Bible is given to help them understand God's mercy and also His divine judgment for the sinful things they continually do.

Truth to Say to Witness to Unitarians & Universalists

Deception: In 1961 the Unitarians and Universalists merged to become one Association. The UU do not have a creed, but they have statements of purpose, one which includes a covenant to promote: "a free search for truth and meaning." So in UU there is a religious pluralism. They promote being accepting and tolerant of each other's beliefs. Anything goes.

Truth to Say: I understand your search for truth. I've been there and I found that Jesus is the Truth. And He was Jewish too and yet, He was tolerant of different cultures and **customs** that were not Jewish and often talked to non–Jews, like the *Samaritan woman* at the well (John 4:5–30). Jesus was so tolerant that the Pharisees complained, calling Him "a glutton, a winebibber, a friend of tax collectors and sinners." (Matthew 11:19; Luke 15:2). The truth is Jesus was tolerant in talking to outcasts because He loved them and wanted them all to know the truth and have eternal life in heaven. But Jesus was intolerant of false doctrine because He knew that it would send people to hell. Now the devil and his followers are tolerant of all kinds of false doctrine. I believe the Bible doctrine that says: "Jesus Christ is the Son of God and He is the way, the truth and the life and there is no way to the Father, but through Him (John 14:6)." The devil hates God's creation, so he wants all people to go to hell.

Deception: They allow every person to believe or do whatever is right in their own eyes as long as he/she is sincere about it.

Truth to Say: The Bible says in Jeremiah 17:9, "The heart is deceitful above all things, and desperately wicked: who can know it? (Romans 1:21). You can be sincerely wrong. So I believe that false doctrine comes from men's hearts. You cannot find the truth in your heart or even your own personal experience. Truth comes from God's Word because God is the Creator and we are His creation. God is the Potter and we are the clay. (Isaiah 45:9–13). He is the Father and we are His children. Therefore, we must put our trust in the Bible and refrain from trusting our own hearts to find the truth. You can be sincerely wrong.

Deception: A UU survey was done that shows the stats of their theological perspectives:

Humanist   46.%

Nature/Earth 19%

Theist   13%

Christian   9.5%

Mystic   6.2%

Buddhist   3.6%

Jewish   1.3%

Hindu   0.4%

Muslim   0.1%

Other*   13.3%

*atheist, agnostic

Truth to Say: Proverbs 28:26 says, "He who trusts in his own heart is a fool, but whoever walks wisely shall be delivered."

Proverbs 3:7 says, "Do not be wise in your own eyes; fear the Lord and depart from evil."

Proverbs. 21:2 says, "Every way of a man is right in his own eyes, but the Lord weighs the hearts." Yes, God will judge our hearts. One way to know how He will judge us on an issue is to know what the Bible says about that topic. Proverbs 12:15 says, "The way of a fool is right in his own eyes, but he who heeds counsel is wise."

Deception: The Unitarian Universalists largely believe: *"if it feels good, then do it."* They throw caution to the wind. They do not think about the long–range destruction that will happen from their emotional "feel good" selfish choices that they make in the present moment.

Truth to Say: Just because I think or feel something doesn't mean it is true or right. Many kids do not feel like going to school every day, but they go. After years of being married, many married people do not feel the same way they did about each other on their passionate honeymoon, but love is not a feeling. Marriage is an unselfish choice to stay committed to each other, forsaking all others, for better or for worse, for richer or poorer, in sickness and in health until death do you part. If you choose to love your spouse, you won't physically nor verbally abuse them nor commit adultery. You will keep your vows in the fear of God.

Deception: The Unitarians believe in the oneness of God or the unity of God. They do not believe in the Trinity: Father, Son and Holy Ghost.

Truth to Say: I believe in one God and that there are three manifestations of His Presence. It is like: water, ice and steam. See: Matthew 28:19 and 2 Corinthians. 13:14. You see, God is like the *ice.* He is our Rock and He is up in heaven, so we cannot see Him. **Jesus Christ** came to earth and said, "He who has seen Me has seen the Father." Jesus is like the *water* (John 7:37). When a person asks Jesus to come into their heart to be their Lord and Savior, what happens is the **Holy Spirit** comes into their heart (John 14:15–17). That is how God can truthfully say in Hebrews 13:5: "I will never leave you nor forsake you." because the Holy Spirit is God. The Holy Spirit is like the *steam.*

Deception: The Unitarians reject the divinity of Jesus, but do recognize him as a great moral teacher, like Moses or Buddha. They also deny the miraculous elements in Scripture.

Truth to Say: Jesus Christ is divine because He was born of the Virgin Mary. He was fully God and fully man. He committed no sin, thus, He was the perfect sacrifice for our sins, shedding His holy blood and dying on the cross (so that our sins could be forgiven and we could be reconciled to God) and God raised Him from the dead, which makes Him deity.

Deception: The Universalists believe that God would not deem any human being unworthy of divine love, and that salvation was for all. They believe in universal salvation: that *all* will go to heaven. It is also called: "the doctrine of Inclusion."

Truth to Say: The question is not whether God loves us or not. The question is: *Do we choose to love Him?* God gave us the choice when He gave us our own free will. Like I said earlier, love is a choice. Jesus said in John 14:23 says: "If anyone loves Me, he will keep My Word; and my Father will love him, and We will come to him and make Our home with him..." God is loving, but do not ignore He is also our Judge. God loves everyone, but everyone does not choose to love God. So they choose the devil's side and therefore will go to hell

Deception: Universalists believe that there are no torments of hell.

Truth to Say: Hell is where the devil lives – a real place full of pain and suffering, torments, fire and brimstone. You may not believe hell exists, but that doesn't mean that you will not go there. The choice is *your* choice, not God's choice, to make. I urge you to receive Jesus as your Savior and go to heaven. Eternity is a long time to be spent in the wrong place.

Deception: They do not believe the Bible is the exclusive source of truth, but see it as mythical or legendary. They respect the sacred literature of other religions, science, art and social commentary.

Truth to Say: Prophecies fulfilled is one of the methods the Bible uses to authenticate itself as the Word of God. In the Old Testament there are at least 333 prophecies about Jesus Christ. Hundreds of years later in the New Testament all 333 prophecies were fulfilled through Jesus, thus proving that the Bible is true.

Deception: Whatever their theology, UU agree that being active leaders in the struggle for racial equality, civil liberty, international peace and equal rights for all people matter more than true beliefs about God.

Truth to Say: God believes in equal rights for all people. That is why salvation is not through good works because people do not have equal abilities to do good works. People have different talents and gifts; and different levels of income, intelligence, athletic ability and social status. But no matter what, God knows that everyone has an equal right to believe whatever he/she chooses. The truth is our sin separates us from God. Hebrews 9:22 says, "Without the shedding of blood, there is no forgiveness of sins." So God sent His Son Jesus Christ, Who shed his holy blood on the cross, paying the price for our sins. Whoever chooses to love God through believing and receiving Jesus Christ as their Lord and Savior will be reconciled to God and have eternal life. The choice is yours.

Truth to Say to
Witness to Homosexuals

Fifteen years ago a prominent pastor/evangelist from Orange County, CA was caught in a homosexual act. When the article came out about him admitting this moral failure in *Charisma* magazine, I was shocked because I had read several of his books that are in all major Christian bookstores and they were edifying, encouraging and totally in line with the Word of God! I could not understand why and how someone like him could fall into that? To his credit, this pastor went though counseling for a couple years and he has recovered. Although he lost his thriving church, he has been restored back into his traveling teaching ministry and is doing well.

After that incident, I read several books and articles on the topic to try and understand the root causes of homosexuality and I also read many encouraging testimonies of men that "came out straight."

Jesus ministered to the "lost of the lost." To the unclean leper He said, "I am willing. Be clean!" Jesus also ministered to the Samaritan woman at the well who shamefully had five husbands. Jesus ministered to the outcasts of society.

When I read the truth about the root cause(s) of these men having same sex attractions (SSA), I became less judgmental. When I read over and over that they did not choose these same sex attractions and did not want these same sex attractions and feel ashamed, humiliated and embarrassed and loathed themselves for having them, I became sympathetic. When I read that they did not know how to get rid of the same sex attractions and many were suicidal over it, a divine compassion rose up in me. Mercy triumphs over judgment.

If those struggling with SSA are raised in a Christian home, they often do not want to tell anyone that they have SSA for fear of being judged, ridiculed and ostracized. They need help, but are afraid to ask for help. They have tried to change, but they do not know how to change and so many struggle with a victim mentality.

I realized that be many pastors and Christians have little idea how to minister to or counsel them to help them understand how to make their same sex attractions go away. Therefore, the church in general has not provided a safe environment for healing and wholeness to take place and this grieves my heart. Most struggling homosexuals and lesbians are angry because they have only encountered judgmentalism, rejection, ridicule and name calling in the church. Many Christians have verbally abused them calling them: "faggot, queer, sissy, dyke, and pervert." This has added insult to the already profound brokenness inside them. The church has driven many away out of fear and ignorance. Realizing this, the Lord put it on my heart to write this chapter. I also wrote this chapter for those who are struggling with same sex attractions to give them **hope** that their same sex attractions (or SSA) can greatly diminish or go away altogether. I did not have enough room in this book to include all of the wonderful information that I gathered, so I put it on my website: www.iwanttowitness.com under Contacts – to Homosexuals – and I encourage you to read it.

We have done right in telling homosexuals and lesbians that their gay behavior is scripturally wrong. We cannot be tolerant and allow them to believe that it is OK to continue to live the gay lifestyle and think nothing of it and also be a Christian. That is hypocritical.

At the same time, to tell them they are wrong to have these same sex attractions without helping them or counseling them to understand the solution to make them go away is quite confusing, frustrating and even infuriating to them.

The gay church denomination is in grave error. They have totally misread the Bible out of context and twisted the scriptures so that their interpretation is what they want it to say: that they can be born again and at the same time maintain homosexual and lesbian sexual relation-ships and live the gay lifestyle. Several churches and. institutions have been deceived into believing that these men and women with same sex attractions are born gay and so they are now reaching out to accept both the homosexual person *and* their homosexual behavior. These churches are: the United Church of Christ, the Episcopal Church, Lutheran Church, Presbyterian Church USA, Unitarian Universalism, Metropolitan Community Churches and reform Quaker or society of friends. They have backslid and gone by the wayside. The motivation is sincere. However, by accepting their homosexual behavior, these churches are in actuality condemning these men, women, and children to a life of suffering, pain and perhaps even hell.

I encourage you to not be like them and have courage to stick to the scriptures and stand for the truth. Do not allow your church to backslide into their waywardness like these other churches have done. Do not allow "being nice" or political correctness to take precedence over truth. I encourage you to remain steadfast standing on the truth from the inerrant unchangeable incorruptible Word of God.

Men with SSA Come From All Walks of Life

Through all the research I have done, I have come to understand that guys who have same sex attractions (SSA) are all different. They come from all walks of life and work in all kinds of occupations and nationalities. You really cannot stereotype them. Some are tall and muscular, and others are short and skinny. Most men who struggle with SSA are hurt, broken, and ashamed and some are fearful of men. Others wear masks and seem happy, but they are really hurting on the inside. Some have suicidal thoughts. If you have suicidal thoughts at times, please read pages 88-89 "Truth to Say to Suicidal People" because God loves you and He wants you to live!

Far less are the ones that are hard core and angry and aggressively want their "rights" to marry another homosexual man. Now that it is legal to be married, perhaps they are less angry. Most erroneously believe that they were born gay. Some erroneously believe that they can be born again and at the same time maintain homosexual and lesbian sexual relation-ships and live the gay lifestyle. Some are introverted and others are extroverted and yet they are all tangled up on the inside. They are different because there are a dozen different reasons as to why they have same sex attractions. Many were sexually abused. A study by Sheir and Johnson (*Sexual Victimization of Boys, 1988*) reported that 58 percent of male adolescents who later became same sex attracted suffered sexual abuse as children, while 90 percent who did not suffer sexual abuse did not become same sex attracted.

One guy I talked to hates his same sex attractions and loathes himself so much that he tried to commit suicide three times. The reason for his SSA stems from the fact that his father died when he was three years old. And yet he is a Christian who sincerely loves God.

So I want to encourage you to not judge them as all the same. I want to encourage you to be discerning and gently talk with each one and find out where they are at. For a clue, you could ask them about how their relationship was with their father.

When you find a guy (or a girl) that hates having same sex attractions and sincerely wants to change, then help them understand that you are on their side and are willing to walk the road with them towards their inner healing from same sex attractions. It is a process.

I have heard pastors say to men struggling with SSA to find a pretty girl and just get married. The advice sounds good, but that does not really stop the SSA. If the root cause of the SSA are not uprooted and if they do not bond in a godly healthy way with the same sex, then they will still have SSA even when they are married to a beautiful woman.

In Richard Cohen's book, **Coming Out Straight,** (p 68) he says, "Those who want to come out of homosexuality will not accomplish this without the help of others. True and lasting healing will take place when God's love is manifested in experience through people."

What the Bible Says About Homosexuality:

- **Genesis 19:5-7** and they called to Lot and said to him, "Where are the men who came to you tonight? Bring them out to us that we may know them carnally." So Lot went out to them through the doorway, shut the door behind him, and said, "Please, my brethren, do not do so wickedly!"

- **Leviticus 18:22**: You shall not lie with a male as with a woman. It *is* an abomination

- **Leviticus 20:13 (NIV)** If a man has sexual relations with a man as one does with a woman, both of them have done what is detestable.

- **Romans 1:21, 26-27**: Although they knew God, they did not glorify *Him* as God, nor were thankful, but became futile in their thoughts, and their foolish hearts were darkened. For this reason God gave them up to vile passions. For even their women exchanged the natural use for what is against nature. Likewise also the men, **leaving the natural use of the woman, burned in their lust for one another,** men **with men committing what is shameful**, (emphasis added) and receiving in themselves the penalty of their error which was due

- **1 Corinthians 6:9–10:** Do you not know that the unrighteous will not inherit the kingdom of God? Do not be deceived. Neither fornicators, nor idolaters, nor adulterers, **nor homosexuals, nor sodomites**, nor thieves, nor covetous, nor drunkards, nor revilers, nor extortioners will inherit the kingdom of God

- **Timothy 1:10–11** (NLT) for the sexually immoral**, for those practicing homosexuality,** (emphasis added) for slave traders and liars and perjurers—and for whatever else is contrary to the sound doctrine that conforms to the gospel concerning the glory of the blessed God, which he entrusted to me

It is Not a Civil Rights Issue

Being a homosexual or lesbian or transgender is not a civil rights issue. This erroneous thinking has gained even more credence in their eyes because the liberal Supreme Court justices legalized gay and lesbian marriage on June 26, 2015 by a vote of 5-4, but it will never be legal or right in the eyes of God because the Word of God does not change. You cannot change the color of your skin or the nation you were born in, but you can change your sexual orientation. The truth is there are many testimonies of men and women have overcome SSA!

The Truth is – No One Is Born Gay

Many homosexuals believe they were born "gay." This belief often supplies them with comfort, relieving them of any responsibility to change. However, there is no solid scientific evidence that people are born homosexual. The overwhelming majority of gay people are completely normal genetically. They are fully male or fully female.

The first lie that must be cast down is that no one is born gay. You must understand that you were not born gay if you want to be free.

Homosexual behavior comes from real human needs going unmet. In short, the need to bond with their father to establish his sexual identity did not happen. Homosexual behavior takes hold when those needs get met in ways other than the Lord intended. It is the same thing as people turning to alcohol or drugs to find comfort when they are broken and their emotional needs are not met.

In Richard Cohen's book, *Coming Out Straight*, on pages 18-24, he looked at three homosexual studies and reveals that the studies that have been done to find a gay gene or gay-part of the brain have been proven faulty, inaccurate, not conclusive and even biased because they were done by researchers who were self-proclaimed homosexuals. The ones that seemed to find something have not been replicated. Trust me in this. No one is born gay.

Simon LeVay's study, *"A Difference in Hypothalamus Structure Between Heterosexual and Homosexual Men"* was published in Science magazine in August 1991. Simon LeVay, who is himself a homosexual, professed to have found a group of neurons in the hypothalamus that appeared to be twice as big in heterosexual men than in homosexual men. He studied cadavers and theorized that this part of the hypothalamus has something to do with sexual behavior, therefore he concluded, sexual orientation is somehow biologically determined.

This study had several critiques. First of all, he did not verify the sexual orientation of his control group, which is poor science. All 19 homosexual subjects died of AIDS, and we know that the HIV/AIDS virus may affect the brain, causing chemical changes therefore, rather than looking at the cause of homosexuality, we may be observing the effects of HIV or AIDS. Of his own study Levay himself said.

"It is important to stress what I did not find. I did not prove that homosexuality is genetic or find a genetic cause for being gay. I did not show that homosexuals are born that way, which is the myth and the mistake that people make in interpreting my work nor did I locate a gay center in the brain" (Cohen, 19).

The Bailey-Pillard study: *A Genetic Study of Male Sexual Orientation* was reported in the General Archives of General Psychiatry in December 1991. They studied the prevalence of homosexuality among twins and adopted brothers where at least one brother was homosexual. They found that 52% (29 pairs out of the 56) of the identical twins were both homosexual, 22% (12 out of 54) of the fraternal twins were both homosexual and 11% (6 of 57) of the adopted brothers were both homosexual. They also found 9% of the non-twin biological siblings were both homosexual. The authors therefore concluded that there is a genetic cause to homosexuality.

The biggest flaw of the Bailey-Pillard Study is the interpretation of the researchers. Since about 50% of the identical twins were not homosexual, we can easily conclude that genetics does **not** play a major part in their sexual orientation. If it had, then 100% of the twins should be homosexual since identical twins have the same genetic makeup. We might just as easily interpret the findings to mean that environmental influences caused their homosexuality. Biologist Anne Fausto-Stirling of Brown University stated: "In order for such a study to be at all meaningful, you would have to look at twins raised apart. It is such badly interpreted genetics."

Another critique by Dr. Simon LeVay stated "In fact, the twin studies… suggest that it is not totally inborn (homosexuality) because even identical twins are not always of the same sexual orientation."

Dr. Bailey himself stated, "There must be something in the environment to yield the discordant twins." Another critique is the research is failed to investigate the roles that incest or sexual abuse and other environmental factors play in determining same-sex attractions. If they had found that incest was more common among identical twins than fraternal twins or non twin blood brothers, this could have helped explain the varying rates of homosexuality.

Dean Hamer et al, of the National Cancer Institute, published his study, *A Linkage Between DNA Markers on the X Chromosome and Male Sexual Orientation* in Science Magazine, July 1993. The media reported that the gay gene was discovered as a result of the study. The researchers studied 40 pairs of homosexual brothers and suggested that some cases of homosexuality are linked to a specific region on the X chromosome (Xq28) inherited from the mother by her homosexual son. Thirty three pairs of brothers shared the same pattern variation in the tip of one arm of the chromosome. Hamer estimated that the sequence of the given genetic markers on Xq28 is linked to homosexuality in 64% of the brothers.

There are several critiques of this study - Dr. Kenneth Klivington, assistant to the President of the Salk Institute in San Diego states: "There is a body of evidence that shows the brains neural networks reconfigure themselves in response to certain experience. Therefore, the difference in homosexual brain structure may be a result of behavior and environmental conditions.

Secondly, there was no control group. This is poor scientific methodology. Hamer failed to test the heterosexual brothers. What if the heterosexual brothers had the same genetic markers?

Thirdly, it has not been proven that the identified section of the chromosomes has a direct bearing on sexuality or sexual orientation.

Fourthly, one of Hamer's fellow research assistants brought him up on charges, saying that he withheld some of the findings that invalidated his study. The National Cancer Institute is investigating

Also a Canadian research team using a similar experimental design was unable to duplicate the findings of his study. Hamer himself emphasizes: "These genes to not cause people to become homosexuals. The biology of personality is much more complicated than that."

Finally, Dean Hamer, et al is all self-proclaimed homosexual men. Therefore Richard Cohen suggests that behind their work is a strong motivation to justify their same-sex attractions. There are other studies that have been done by homosexual researchers (which is a bias in itself) and the same findings have never been replicated.

If homosexuality is a normal sexual orientation, then why is only 1 to 3% of the population homosexual and not 50%? Why are there more homosexual males than females?

Therefore theory that there is a genetic cause for homosexuality has been generally discarded today. No serious scientist suggests that a simple cause-and-effect relationship applies. There is a preponderance of scientific evidence conducted over the past eight years that shows that homosexual it is an acquired condition.

The best evidence to disprove the theory is experience. Thousands of men and women throughout the world have changed from homosexual to heterosexual orientation. The National Assoc for Research and Therapy of Homosexuality conducted a survey of 860 respondents and found that those who want to change their sexual orientation may succeed.

The LGBT (Lesbian, Gay, Bi-Sexual, Transgender) community loves to push this false idea that there is a biological cause for their same sex attractions, so they can blame God, (instead of themselves or the devil for it) and continue on in their sinful alternative lifestyle (Cohen, 19-24).

God's Original Design

In this "broken home/single mom" society, many boys grow up without a father-figure in the home, which is not God's original design. A father-son bond is needed in early childhood in order for a boy's true sexuality to develop. Early childhood is the stage when a boy bonds with his father. It is at this age, the boy comes to realize or identify that that he is a boy and so he wants to be like his father. It is then that he develops a bond with his father and he wants to play with the boys and hang out with the boys who are like him! He looks up to his Dad to become a man right along with his Dad! In this early stage when a boy is establishing his identity as a boy, they think: "I am a boy and the girls are not like me. They are *girls*. They are different. They usually don't want to play with what I want to play with and they are just so irritating! They talk too much too! They are like the enemy! Ugh! *Girls*!" It is totally normal for young boys to feel that way. When a young boy sees a man and woman kissing and he rolls his eyes and says: "Eeww! Girls are gross!" then you can be thankful because you know he is developing a healthy gender identity that he is a boy. All young boys need that same sex attachment or bonding with their father or a male role model to help them understand their sexual orientation.

Then when he becomes a teenager and his hormones kick in, he will feel a switch on the inside and start having feelings for girls or be attracted to girls. Opposites attract. This may be puzzling at first. "Oh! I was wrong! Girls are mysterious and they are sexy! They are beautiful and oh, so fine! Now I understand why Mom and Dad kiss!"

For those who suffer with SSA, when their hormones kicked in, they never felt that switch. When they find out they are different, it is the most dreadful feeling because no one wants same sex attractions.

How Do Same Sex Attractions Develop?

Michael Saia's book, **Counseling the Homosexual,** describes a **5 phase model** that leads to the development of same-sex attachment disorder:

Phase 1: The child feels, perceives or receives rejection from the same-sex parent. They feel his disappointment, his disapproval and his distance. In short, his heart gets wounded or broken at a very early age, many times before he can remember. He withdraws from the relationship because he feels hurt or rejected. Your brain does not fully develop to store memories until ages four to six, therefore, experiences of detachment, which occurred in the first years of life, are lodged deep in the unconscious mind. That is why many homosexual individuals say: "for as long as I can remember, I felt different" and believe they were born gay. The emotional wounding could be:

- **Emotionally Absent Father** - Your father was there, but your father didn't spend time with you or seem to care about you because he was working a lot. Children spell love - TIME
- **Divorce** – You had to live with your mother & you really missed seeing your Dad every day. **Many Broken Promises** – Your father said he was coming to see you, but he didn't show up. This happened again and again and again.
- **Physical Abuse** by your father - of your mother and maybe you and your siblings caused the rift/wall between you and your father.
- **Sexual abuse** or molestation by a family member or friend created learned and reinforced behavior which also offered "a substitute for love" that they did not receive from their father. Sad statistics: 70% to 80% of homosexuals experienced sexual abuse.
- **Mother Wound** – When there is a divorce, the mother is often left emotionally bankrupt and she seeks to meet her emotional needs from her son.
- **Name Calling by Peers** - They believed the name calling by peers – fag, queer, sissy, homo, dyke
- **Media Wounds** – Perhaps the worst part about SSA is not the disorder itself but the ignorance surrounding it. Many people with SSA are fooled into thinking that they were born gay, and they often blame their unhappiness on the lack of acceptance society has of gays. In reality their suffering is more from deep emotional scars and unmet emotional needs than from any prejudice around homosexuality. Healing and wholeness cannot be reached without education, support and work. Many individuals suffering SSA disorder or Same Sex Attraction Disorder (SSAD) are completely unaware of its complicated origin and even worse of the fact that even embedded learned responses of SSA can be changed. Many individuals are drowning in the deluge of propaganda, half truths and lies of gay activists

- **Temperament** – Highly sensitive, artistic, gender non-conforming behavior, so they played with girls instead of boys as a child
- **Hetero-emotional Wounds** – Mother says: I wish you were a girl
- **Sibling Wounds** – Your brothers and sisters calling you names, putting you down, abusing you.
- **Body Image Wounds** – late bloomer, shorter, skinnier, larger or physical disabilities. The truth is masculinity comes in all shapes, sizes, levels of athletic ability, and interests.
- **Adoption** – feeling unloved or rejected by your birth mother
- **Intrauterine Experiences** – Your mother attempted to abort you and thus the baby felt unloved and unwanted in mother's wound perhaps because the father was having an affair. (Info from Richard Cohen's book – *Coming Out Straight,* pgs 29, 50-52)

Phase 2: The child takes revenge (instead of forgiving) and rejects the same sex parent back by putting a shield or a wall around his heart to protect or defend himself from any more emotional pain or wounding. The child does not realize that putting up a wall does a lot more harm than good. With the wall there, there can be no bonding between them and their father which begins the same sex attachment disorder – or SSAD.

Phase 3: Then the child rejects his gender identity, thinking unconsciously:*"If men are that way, then I do not want to be like them!"* And gets angry and then vengefully rejects his gender identity. "The detachment prevents him for internalizing his own sense of gender identity. He has cut off psychologically and emotionally from his father, his role model of masculinity (Cohen, pg 37)

Phase 4: The child rejects himself because he is the same gender of the parent he just rejected. Again, he unconsciously says, *"If daddy is not good, and he is a man, then I am not good, because I am a boy."* So they do not want to attach to or connect to who they really are. This makes him feel different.

Phase 5: The child then rejects others of the same gender as a defensive reaction of self protection against further wounding. So because of the wound, he prefers to play with the girls who are safe instead of the boys, which forms the same sex attachment disorder.

After this 5 stage process, they feel separated for parents, separated from self, separated from their body and others thinking: *"I don't fit in. I do not belong. I'm different from the rest. I am neither a boy nor a girl."*

If you have SSA and nothing in the Phase 1 list relates to you, then you need to understand the truth that you were not born with same sex attractions. You were born holy and pure because your spirit came straight from heaven. The truth is there is a wound in your psyche or soul down deep somewhere that was made when you were a toddler before you can remember, perhaps before age four. You must repent for your wrong fearful, angry, vengeful reactions as a toddler or small child. You must repent for unconsciously putting up a wall around your heart to "protect yourself" from further wounding because this wall prevented you from bonding with your father and with the same sex.

Jeremiah 30:7 says, "I will restore health to you and heal you of your wounds," says the Lord, "because they called you an outcast"

When young boys do not bond with their father and have that void in their soul, when they reach adolescence, they still want to attach with or bond with the same sex and yet, the early boyhood stage when boys bond with their father and understand and receive their sexual identity has already past. They are now in their teens and their hormones have kicked in and they now find that they are not attracted to girls. The switch did not flip for them. They have homosexual feelings.

Then they may spend a lifetime trying to fill those unmet needs for attachment through same sex sexual relationships. It is proven that sex never heals or fulfills the deeper love need simply because they are the unmet needs of a child. If you question him, the active homosexual would not say he is looking for his father's love in the arms of another man. This is often a hidden, unconscious drive very deep in their soul.

Many turn to gangs because their dad was not there for them and they get in a lot of trouble, but many join gangs for the same sex bonding that they never received as a young child.

The truth is - only through an intimate relationship with Jesus Christ, learning to allow God to hold you, to love you, to care for you, affirm you AND healthy healing through non-sexual same sex bonding is how true and lasting change will occur. Same sex attractions can all boil down to your response to the wounding. There are a dozen ways a young child's heart could be wounded. The wound or the void that develops in your inner soul can only be healed through forgiveness.

Different Methods of Healing Homosexuality

Sue Bohlin is a Bible teacher who is on the Board of **Living Hope** ministries and is a writer and speaker for Probe ministries. In her article, *Can Homosexuals Change? - A Christian Perspective*, Bohlin writes: "Many people who tried to change their homosexuality could win contests for praying and reading their Bibles. They really did try very very hard. But the prayers are often misdirected: "God, change me. Take away my desires. Let me start liking people of the opposite sex." Unfortunately, as well-intentioned as this prayer is, it's a lot like trying to get rid of dandelions in your back yard by mowing them. They keep coming back because you're not dealing with their **roots**. The basic cause of a homosexual orientation isn't genetics or choice; it's a wrong response to being hurt. It's about protecting oneself and trying to get legitimate needs met in ways God never intended. True change can only happen with the hard work of submitting to God, allowing Him to expose the deep hurts and needs of one's heart, which means facing horrible pain, and inviting Him to bring healing to those wounded places. **That's why intimacy with Christ is the answer**. Helping someone get set free from same sex attractions is not a simple matter and it would be disrespectful to imply that there is an easy solution to the complex issue of homosexuality. Among those who claim that change is possible, there are three main schools of thought on how to get there.

The first is the deliverance ministries. They say that homosexuality is caused by a demon, and if we can just cast out the demon, the problem is gone. Sounds like an easy fix, but it ends up causing even more problems because homosexuality isn't caused by a demon. The person who was "delivered" may experience a temporary emotional high, but the same temptations and thought patterns that plagued him before are going to return because the root issue wasn't dealt with. Only now, he's burdened by the false guilt of thinking he did something wrong or that he's not good enough for God to "fix" him.

A second and more effective treatment for homosexuality **is reparative therapy.** There is a lot of wisdom to be found here because many therapists believe that homosexuality has its roots in hurtful relationship patterns, especially with family members, and many homosexual men and women report exactly that. But reparative therapy is often just behavior modification, and it deals only with the flesh, that part of us independent of God. Reparative therapy can make people feel better, but it can't bring true inner healing.

The third and I believe best way to bring about real and lasting change is **a redemptive approach.** Ministries who disciple men and women into an intimate relationship with Jesus are able to lead them into inner healing because *God* transforms His people." - Sue Bolin.

I agree with Sue Bolin and am taking the redemptive approach to write this next section on Healing Homosexuality.

Steps to Healing Homosexuality

Healing from same sex attractions is a process and it is similar to peeling an onion one layer at a time.

Layer 1 - You Must Repent and Become Born Again

First of all, if you want to start the journey toward freedom from same sex attractions, then you will need to repent for your sins and then pray and receive Jesus as your Lord and Savior. When Jesus started His ministry He said, "Repent, for the kingdom of heaven is at hand"(Matt 4:17). Repentance means to intentionally change one's mind or one's will to turn away from sin and turn to God and obey Him.. This is the most amazing promise: 1 John 1:9, "If we confess our sins, he is faithful and just to forgive us our sins, and to cleanse us from ALL unrighteousness." There is no sin too great for God to forgive Proverbs 28:13, "He that covers his sins shall not prosper: but whosoever confesses and forsakes them shall have mercy."

Becoming born again means a total change of heart where you are sorry for your sins and so you repent of them and then you become a new person through in Jesus Christ. 2 Corinthians 5:7 says, "Therefore, if anyone is in Christ, he is a new creation; old things have passed away; behold, all things have become new."

Now you can stop calling yourself a "homosexual" or "gay" because you are a new creation. Romans 4:17 says "God, who gives life to the dead and calls those things which do not exist as though they did." Remember that God created the world with His WORDS, "Let there be light" and there was light! We are created in His image and have that same power to create with our words. So instead you can truthfully say: *"I am a beloved son of God and sometimes I struggle with SSA, but I am more than a conqueror through Christ who loves me" (Roman 8:37)*

When you become born again, then the Holy Spirit comes to dwell in your heart, which is God's power that enables you to live a life that conforms to the Word of God and enables you to fulfill God's will for your life. When you become born again, God wants you to do what Luke 3:8-9 says: "Bear fruits in keeping with repentance." Now that your past failures have been forgiven, you need to leave them there, forget our pasts and press forward towards the things God has for you.

Philippines 3:13, says, "...this one thing I do, forgetting those things which are behind, and reaching forth unto those things which are before."

Layer 2 - Stop the Homosexual Behavior

Now that you are born again, the Holy Spirit that is now on the inside of you will help you and empower you to stop the homosexual behavior and overcome temptation. He will convict you to do the obvious - avoid gay bars and gay bathrooms to avoid temptation. Secondly, avoid and cut off the sexual relationship with your current gay lover. You can still be non-sexual friends, but stop the gay sex. Of course, stop any other affairs or one night stands too. Thirdly, get rid of gay porn and avoid stores that sell it and get some kind of internet program that filters out unwanted website or ads from popping up -

Layer 3 - Develop a Support Network

Making a decision to leave the gay lifestyle is not easy and so developing a support network is vital. The support network can be made up of parents, brothers, sisters, relatives, spouse, and close friends, your pastors and church members that will help in the process of change where you can share about your situation and needs. You may need to move out and find a new place to live. As you go through the process of healing, there may be ups and downs. Therefore you need email addresses and phone numbers in your smart of people you can reach out to when you are feeling weak or tempted. There are four types of friendships that will help in the process of healing:

1. heterosexual friends that know about the struggle and are supportive
2. hetero sexual friends that do NOT know about the struggle and are good friends
3. Mentors who assist in the process of re-parenting the individual
4. Fellow strugglers who are coming out of homosexuality

An attraction to a heterosexual friend is a perfect opportunity for healing and growth. Heterosexual, sexually attractive male friendships with men for whom you feel an erotic attraction offer of the greatest opportunity for healing. Only through such associations can there be a transformation from erotic attractions to true friendship. It is the demystifying of the distant male that leads to healing.

This transformational shift from (from eros to philia) from sexual to fraternal (from eros to philia) is THE essential healing experience of male homosexuality.

A support group would be very helpful if not vital in the healing process. You can look for a support group in your area and there also is a list at the end of this chapter of different ministries that have support groups such as Homosexuals Anonymous. If there is not a support group geared towards "homosexual healing" from that list in your area, then I highly suggest finding a **Celebrate Recovery** group, which is similar to Alcoholics Anonymous, but it is all Christ-centered on the Bible. Those who go have found hope and help in the power of Jesus Christ to overcome our issues of anger, grief, alcoholism, guilt and shame, financial loss, divorce, dysfunction families, sexual abuse, drug abuse, eating disorders and many more. Go to **www.celebraterecovery.org** and find the CR locator. Type in your zip code and you will find one in your area.

At www.livehope.org there are support groups online.

If you go to a 12 step group and have to identify yourself, you can just say: "Hello my name is _____ and I am a son of God" because, like I said earlier, it is important to say who you are in Christ.

You need to understand that the prevailing attitude of the secular mental health profession is very liberal in support of being homosexual. Unrepentant homosexuals use the American Psychiatric Assoc. to tout that they are "normal" and so homosexuality should be embraced as "an alternative lifestyle."

The truth is in Joe Dallas' book, *A Strong Delusion – Confronting the "Gay Christian Movement* (pp123-124) he writes: "The APA did not state that homosexuality is normal. The resolution that the APA Board of Trustees voted on in 1973 agreed that only clearly defined mental disorders should be included in the DSM and that if homosexuals felt no "subjective distress" about their sexuality and experienced no "impairment in social effectiveness or functioning" then their orientation should not be labeled a disorder. The psychiatrist who authored the resolution flatly denied that the APA was thereby saying that homosexuality was normal."

In other words, do not go to a liberal mental health support group like that. It would all be counterproductive, helping you slide back into believing the lies of the enemy and back into homosexual sin.

How the Church Can Help in the Support Network

Churches must involve itself in the healing process of these brave men, women and adolescents who want to change. Those who want to come out of homosexuality will not accomplish this without the help of others.   Parents are the first representatives of God for their children. They are the invisible manifestation of an invisible God.   They symbolize our role model for masculinity (Mr. God) and our role model for femininity (Mrs. God). God represents an extension of the father-figure. If a child rejects his parents, it follows that they may easily reject their parent's religious beliefs. This distances them from God, from parents, authority figures, and a sense of belonging to the world.   Therefore a defensive detachment from father or mother may lead to a defensive of detachment towards God. (Cohen, *Coming Out Straight*, pg 52).

Therefore they need to be taught know the truth about God's true character and how that differs from the character of the sin-based nature of their parents and study God's true nature and how He feels about them and how much He loves them.

If you read the previous sections, now you know the causes of same sex attractions. Usually the problem was developed through same sex parent's rejection, a wounded heart (or sexual abuse) and then a defensive wall built around their heart when they were a young child, which prevented them from bonding with their father and prevented them from developing their true gender identity. It is not anything a guy can "catch like a cold" by being close to one. It is not contagious. As the pastor, I encourage you to teach your church members how to treat people who they suspect are struggling with SSA:

1. Teach the youth and men that the root cause of those struggling with same sex attractions (SSA) started because they felt wounded or rejected by their same-sex parent in their early childhood or they were abused. Since SSA started with a root of rejection, it needs to be healed

with the love of God and kindness and acceptance by godly healthy same sex friends that treat them like one of the guys. They need to feel like they belong and do guy stuff with godly friends.

2. Teaching the youth and the men in your church (or women) to not be afraid of a feminine guy or a woman whom you suspect may have SSA. Homosexuality and lesbianism is not contagious. It may seem like SSA can rub off, but actually it is simply two guys with that same void or wound in their heart "being attracted" to one another.

2. Teach them to NOT call him/her any homosexual terms or names nor gossip about them, but to do the opposite and encourage them through compliments and encouragement such as: "You're the man!" and "high five" them and "call things that be not as though they were."

3. Teach your youth to be a friend or a big brother and the men in your church to be a father figure to those you suspect may have SSA. They need a godly healthy role model, because they did not have that when they were a child, in order to increase their heterosexual feelings and feel secure in their masculinity. Now that they are older, they need to play "catch-up" in the development of their gender identity.

4. Teach those struggling with SSA the truth about their Heavenly Father's character and how He differs from the sin-based character or nature of their parents. Teach them the true nature of the Holy Spirit as well and how He feels about them and how much He loves them.

For those seeking healing of same sex attractions, you really need to find a Bible believing church that believes that homosexuality is Biblically wrong and that change is possible through the Word of God and the power of Jesus Christ and healthy godly same sex relationships. When you go to church or anywhere, I encourage you to:

- Talk like heterosexual guys talk. Watch a few Army movies and find your deeper original voice that God gave you and talk like that.
- Sit like a guy sits, with your left ankle on your right knee. Do not cross your legs like women do.
- Do your best to fit in and model the guy's behavior.

- Remember you are at church to renew your mind with the Word of God and to make healthy same sex friends, so do not make a pass at a guy you may be attracted to at church. You will only offend them and lose your potential friend who will think you are weird because of your behavior.

Physical Exercise or Playing Sports is important for individuals coming out of homosexuality. It is an opportunity to hang out with heterosexual males and that increases your feeling of masculinity as you participate in a sport, even if it is weight lifting at the gym. A workout partner could be a part of your support network.

Read Books - I encourage you to read books on the causes and treatment of homosexuality. There is a list at the end of this chapter.

Read Testimonies - I have also included many Testimonies of men who have been set free from homosexuality. I encourage you to look them up online and read them. They will give you great hope!

Counseling is important as well. The best therapist is preferably a Christian who has been delivered from homosexuality. Look at the ministries listed in Resources at the end of this chapter

Layer 4 – Develop An Intimate Relationship with Christ

Developing an intimacy with Jesus Christ is a total surrender of all your carnal desires to Him and asking God for His desires and His will in your life, which includes your sexual orientation. You accept that God made you a man and you embrace your manhood. You surrender your whole will to Him like Jesus did in the garden of Gethsemane: **"Not My will but Yours be done."** (Luke 22:42)

In developing an intimate relationship with the Lord Jesus, you submit to Him and let Him be in control and take the driver's seat of your life. It means renewing your mind with the Word of God through reading it every day. You must realize that God is your Heavenly Father and you are a son of God.

It means having a hunger for the Word where you want to listen to Christian TV and podcasts and Christian music to build up your spirit. It means casting down the lies of the enemy and replacing them with God's truth from the Word. It means walking in holiness. When you are tempted, you run to God or call or text other Christians to help you. If means you welcome correction, even though it hurts, because you want to be right with God. It means being obedient.

It means being seated with Christ in heavenly places. Therefore, we rule and reign with Christ. Jesus has given us the keys to heaven and so we can take authority over the devil's lies and his spirits of perversion Matthew 18:18 says, "whatever you bind (lock up) on earth is bound in heaven, and whatever you loose (unlock) on earth is loosed in heaven." So you can pray and take authority over your same-sex attractions like a military sergeant or an angry coach and command:

"I bind these same sex attractions and the evil spirits of perversion and sin and I command all these unclean spirits to go back to hell in the name of Jesus Christ. And I loose upon myself - holiness and purity and right feelings that line up with the Word of God. I'm normal, straight and healed in Jesus' name."

Having an intimate relationship with Christ means singing and worshipping God from your heart. Then power of the Holy Spirit and His manifest presence will touch you with His love as you spend time worshipping Him. He becomes your best friend and you find comfort through the presence of the Holy Spirit and you will learn how to be led by His Spirit. Dennis Jernigan overcame homosexuality through praise and worship and has written many anointed songs. I also like *"Mended"* by Matthew West and *"Never Too Far Gone"* by Jordan Feliz. There are so many wonderful praise and worship songs and Soaking songs out there that you can find in Christian music stores or iTunes.

There is so much power in speaking the Word of God. It is the sword of the spirit. Proverbs 23:7 says "As a man thinks in his heart, so is he." **The battle is in the mind**. Since you are now born again, it is so important to receive God as your Heavenly Father and catch a revelation of the fact that you are His son. I exhort you to speak these confessions of "who you are now in Christ" also read "A to Z Affirmations from Your Heavenly Father." It will build you up.

Confess Who You Are in Christ. You Are a Son

- I am a new creature in Christ (2 Corinthians 5:17).
- I am a son of God through my faith in Christ Jesus (Galatians 3:26)
- Since I am born again, I am no longer a slave to fear, but I am a adopted as a child of God and because I am a son, God has sent forth the Spirit of His Son into my heart which cries out "Abba! Father!" (Romans 8:15)
- I am not a stranger anymore, but I am a fellow citizen with the saints and a member of God's household (Ephesians 2:19)
- God loves me and so He disciplines me. He scourges every son whom He receives. God deals with me as a son. I know that every father disciplines his son. Therefore I shall respect God and honor Him and live a godly life for His glory. (Hebrews 12:6-7, 9)
- I have received Jesus as my Lord and Savior, therefore God gave me the right to become a child of God (John 1:12-13)
- I am forgiven of all my sins and washed in the Blood (Eph. 1:7).
- I am the temple of the Holy Spirit; I am not my own (1 Cor. 6:19).
- I have put off the old man and have put on the new man, which is renewed in the knowledge after the image of Him Who created me (Colossians 3:9-10).
- I am greatly loved by God (Romans 1:7; Ephesians 2:4; Colossians 3:12; 1 Thessalonians 1:4).
- I am holy and without blame before Him in love (Ephesians 1:4; 1 Peter 1:16).
- I have the mind of Christ (1 Corinthians 2:16; Philippians 2:5).
- For God has not given us a spirit of fear; but of power, love, and a sound mind (2 Timothy 1:7).
- It is not I who live, but Christ lives in me (Galatians 2:20

- I have received the spirit of wisdom and revelation in the knowledge of Jesus, the eyes of my understanding being enlightened.

Layer 5 - Find the Root Lie that Created the Wound and the Wall around Your Heart

This is the hardest part of the healing. You need to go back as far as you can remember and locate the bad memory that created the wound at the root of the problem and the lie that the wound created. You may have to ask your mother what happened when you were little because **your brain does not develop enough to store memories until you are 4 or 5 years old.** This is why homosexuals think they were born gay because "as far as they can remember" they have had these homosexual feelings. **But a lot can happen before you are 4 years old that you just do not remember.** It would be most helpful to talk to your father personally, if at all possible, to get his side of the story. There are always two sides to every story. You may want to ask him: Why did you leave us? or why were you not there for me? When you hear what he has to say, you must forgive him. Even if you do not have the opportunity talk to him, you must forgive him anyway even if you never hear an apology from him. Only forgiving him will set you free. Unforgiveness will keep you bound.

If she does not know, then your intimate personal relationship with God through the power of the Holy Spirit can reveal to you the painful memory in His timing. The true source or the root of your emotional pain must be found. Then you must face it. You cannot heal it if you cannot feel it. Once you remember the painful memory, what was your reaction to it? What did you believe about it?

Most of the time, there are lies embedded somewhere in the memory when a person is wounded. As long as the lie remains buried in the memory, the lie will cause pain every time they are triggered by a similar life situation. If we believe a lie to be true, then it will play itself out as though it were true.

Proverbs 23:7 says, "As a man thinks in his heart, so is he." When one does not truthfully understand WHY that wound came to be there or truthfully why the terrible experience happened to them, then through a bitter root judgment the devil will attach his lies to the wound instead to "help them understand," but it is a false understanding based on his lies. The devil and his demons then spins a web of lies around about that wound building lie upon lie upon lie. This may take years to develop. Then when that person reaches puberty, the devil and his demons attach *feelings* to the lies to perpetuate the lies so that they seem true until there is a web of lies in your mind that makes you believe that you are a homosexual. When a person understands the lie(s) at the root of the same sex attraction, and the bitter root judgment is removed with mercy and forgiveness, then change is possible! The web of lies can then be dismantled and the truth from God's Word will greatly diminish the same sex attractions. Then you will find release from the pain and can receive God's peace.

Examples of Lies that Attach to the Wound

The following are some examples of lies the devil may have told you as a child to help trigger your memory and the truth is in italics.

- My father does not love me or accept me. *Truthfully every father loves his son. He may be just irresponsible or busy working or angry at your Mom*
- If my father loved me, he would be here for me. They would not have gotten divorced. *Truthfully they did not divorce because your father does not love you. You do not know the whole story. The divorce was not your fault. He did not love his wife right or maybe she did not love him. Perhaps he was abusive towards her or maybe there was an affair, but truthfully, every man loves his son and you can believe that your father indeed loves you.*
- My father would have gotten custody of me if he really loved me. *.The Judge is the one who decided who got custody. You do not know how hard your father fought to get custody of you or to get visitation rights to see you.*
- If my father really loved me, he would spend more time with me, etc. (children spell love with TIME). *Truthfully, many fathers are*

hurting on the inside. It is hard to be there for others when you yourself are hurting. Many fathers have to work long hours to pay the bills, to pay for your child support. Many fathers live far away from their children, in another state. Some fathers are in prison, but your mother does not want you to know that. Some fathers are hurt, ashamed and disappointed with their lives and instead of forgiving and praying and turning that emotional pain over to God, they turn to drugs and alcohol instead. You need to pray for your father to be born again and set free from all sin and to trust in the Lord for strength, peace and joy.

- If my father really loved me, he would not have forgotten my birthday. And this is his week for visitation to come pick me up and see me. He says he's coming to see me and then he breaks his promises over and over again! *When a man is not born again, he thinks about himself before he thinks about others. Forgive him for forgetting your birthday. Maybe something came up at work. Maybe his finances are so low that he does not have the money to come see you. When a man is hurting on the inside, it is hard for him to reach out. When he does not have God's love on the inside of him, it is hard for him to love others. Perhaps his father was not a good father to him, so he did not know how to be a good father to you. Pray for this generational curse to be broken.*

- That guy came on to you because you're gay. *The truth is that guy "came on to you" because HE is gay. Not you! Do not be confused.*

- You cannot fight well because you're gay. *Do not be confused. Do not be insecure. Truthfully, guys that have had practice and training to fight are ones that fight well. You can watch You Tubes and learn how to fight better. But seriously, if you learn how to fight and use those skills on some punk kid at school, you can be expelled and get behind.. If you drop out of high school, you will not get a good job. If you do not get a good job, you will be miserable doing something you do not like that pays very little. Stay in school and get a college degree, then going to work will be a joy and you will enjoy your life*

- You cannot play ball well because you're gay. *Do not be confused. Do not be insecure. Truthfully guys that play ball well have practiced a lot. All you need to do is practice and stand on Philippians 4:13. After practice, then practice more at home if you want, but playing sports is supposed to be fun. Truthfully, some guys are not good at sports because God has gifted them in other areas, but that does not mean you're gay. Very few guys make it to the pros anyway, so it is a waste of time. Just focus on what you are good at.*

- Those kids are right. You are gay. You are a fag. You are a wimp. *Truthfully, that is a wrong opinion, based on a lie, which is not reality. For e.g., let's say the bully said you were wearing a **red** shirt, but in reality, you are wearing a **blue** shirt. You KNOW your shirt is blue. In the same way you KNOW you are normal and straight. So do not let their wrong opinion become your opinion of yourself because they are lies. Your shirt is blue. You are normal and straight. You see, many kids are insecure and so they cut down other kids to make themselves feel taller or better. Just ignore them and forgive them and embrace the truth – You are straight and they are insecure. They need to get born again, go to church and learn to respect others and be kind.*

- I feel abandoned, unwanted, unloved, unsafe and insecure. *God will never leave you nor forsake you. Ephesians 1:6 says, "You are accepted in the Beloved." Your Heavenly Father loves you. Pray Psalms 91 and God's angels will protect you. You will be secure when you know who you are in Christ.*

- This homosexual sex is what love is really all about. It is the love that I did not receive from my father – *The truth is men who have a wound from not receiving their father's love are very susceptible to sexual abuse because it becomes a substitute for their father's love. The truth is God wants you to bond with godly men in a healthy way and receive your Heavenly Father's love through His manifest Presence when you sing and worship Him.*

- You enjoyed that forced sexual abuse because you really are gay. *Truthfully when anyone is touched in the "pleasure center" of their private parts they will be aroused That is normal So do not associate your sexual orientation with a man who "aroused you" while he was sexually abusing you. You are not gay. Do not be confused. It is terribly wrong the way it happened. It was not your fault. God designed for a man and a woman to wait until they are married to experience the sexual pleasure of making love. The sexual organs fit together perfectly as God designed sexual intercourse to happen.*

- I was born this way. I might as well embrace it and be proud of it – *God did not give you these same sex attractions. Truthfully no one is born gay. Why would God create something that He calls an abomination?*

- Being gay is the "in" thing. I can be accepted. *Truthfully, God loves you, yes, but if you want to go to heaven, you will repent and pray for God to help you change to be who He created you to be and do His plan for your life.*

- A lot of people are like me at the gay bars, a whole gay community! *Truthfully, only 2% of men self-identify themselves as gay.*

- I can make myself happy by being my genuine self. *Truthfully, you were created in God's image and being gay is the devil's image of you.*

The above "lies and the truth" are common examples. Perhaps the lie at the root of your pain I did not touch on. Well then I encourage you to pray and ask God to help you remember the root cause of your pain. What is the painful memory? And what lie or lies were attached to the memory? Then ask God to uncover and reveal the truth to you.

Forgive Whoever Was There in the Bad Memory

After you remember the painful memory, the right response is: to forgive your father for not being there for you or forgive the one(s) who abused you or forgive whatever the painful memory was for you. Unforgiveness is an open door to the enemy. When you forgive, God will close the open door to the devil and God will move on your behalf. When you forgive, the defensive wall around your heart will come down. God will heal and restore your heart. God will heal the memory. If you are having trouble forgiving, a few of my favorite books are:

- *Do Yourself a Favor and Forgive* by Joyce Meyer.
- *Total Forgiveness* by RT Kendall
- *The Bait of Satan* by John Bevere.

Forgiveness is first of all an act of the will. It is not hypocrisy to will to forgive when the emotions are screaming for vengeance. Be obedient to the Lord regardless of how you feel. If you refuse to harbor spite or dwell on the offense, evil emotions will be starved. Moreover, the Lord Himself will set your heart right. Right emotions will eventually come if you surrender to the Lord. A conscious, deliberate, willful choice to forgive is the *only* thing that can free a heart from the bondage of bitterness.

Undoubtedly, there are Christians who have called you terrible names in childhood and adulthood who you really need to forgive. Perhaps you **were** having same sex attractions, but that gives them no right to call you: fag, queer, homo, dyke, etc. That is just totally wrong and not what a Christian is supposed to do.

On behalf of all of them, I am so sorry and I want to apologize to you for their name calling. Many Christians are like in kindergarten when it comes to renewing their mind with the Word of God and so they are still carnal and insensitive. Anytime they call you a bad name, do not dwell on it, but forgive them and then, do what it says in 2 Corinthians 10:4-5, cast down the bad name/label and replace those lies with the truth by confessing "who you are in Christ" on page 251.

I applaud you that despite their carnal judgmental behavior, that you courageously decided to not let them become a stumbling block, but still decided to become a Christian.

What people do not understand remains a mystery to them and mystery brings fear. People many times people fear what they do not understand. When there is something that they are not familiar with, they assume the worst about it. They are subconsciously afraid that they may "get it." And they are appalled at the unnatural behavior of homosexuality as well. They are judgmental and ignorant because they have never walked in your shoes. They think that you want the SSA and are just rebellious towards God, therefore out of righteous indignation; they want to hold signs at gay parades. They think that you are crazy and rebellious for thinking that God made you gay or you were born gay. What they do not understand is your reality: that you have most likely had SSA since before you can remember, so it seems to you that you born with SSA – even though it is not true. They fear that because of your sin that God will judge and destroy our nation like Sodom and Gomorrah. But I think that God wants pastors and

Christians to understand, be sympathetic and do what they can to help people with SSA. I know it may be really hard, but the Jesus says to "forgive them, for they know not what they do."

Learn to Forgive Others Because:

1. **Jesus tells us to forgive.** It is always best to obey the Word of God because Jesus suffered, died and was resurrected so that we could receive the forgiveness of our own sins. Mark 11:25 says, "And when you stand praying, if you hold anything against anyone, forgive them, so that your Father in heaven may forgive you your sins." It is so smart to forgive, because when we forgive those who have wronged us, our prayers will be answered. The wound or the void that develops in your inner soul can only be healed through forgiveness.

2. **Unforgiveness is like a wedge or a dividing wall between you and God.** You do not want anything to stand in the way of your relationship with God because you need Him to live victoriously to overcome SSA and also to have eternal life. If God can forgive us all the awful things we've done, we can forgive others for the things they have done. Matthew 6:14-15 says, "For if you forgive other people when they sin against you, your heavenly Father will also forgive you. But if you do not forgive others their sins, your Father will not forgive your sins." It is a serious thing to not have your sins forgiven, so you should always forgive those who sin against you. Do not repay anyone with evil, but overcome evil with good.

3. **Forgiveness leads to your emotional healing from SSA.** Holding onto resentment and not forgiving your father or those who abused you is sinful and stands in the way of your emotional and even physical wellness. They say that bitterness is the root cause of cancer

4. **Forgiving Empowers God Take Vengeance for You** Forgiving releases the shackles of sin and opens the door for the Lord to intervene in your situation. It releases God's hands and His angels to go to war on your behalf to repay with vengeance those who hurt you.

2 Thessalonians 1:6 says, "it is a righteous thing with God to repay with tribulation those who trouble you." When you forgive, you open the channel of God's love to operate through other godly men who can bless you as well with that love and time and attention that you long for that your father did not give you. They can fill that void in your heart that your real father left there. God will make it up to you.

5. **Forgiveness closes the door to the enemy and all tormenting spirits**. If you harbor unforgiveness you will be holding onto bitterness and judging others and sinning opening a door to the enemy to get into your life and cause havoc. Proverbs 24:29 says, "Do not say, 'I'll do to them as they have done to me; I'll pay them back for what they did.' Also Romans 12:19 says: "Vengeance is the Lord's and He will repay."

6. **Forgiveness is for your benefit,** not for the benefit of the person you are forgiving. Do yourself a favor and forgive. Unforgiveness is like drinking poison yourself and yet expecting the other person to die.

7. **Choosing not to forgive keeps you stuck in your past**, preventing you from moving forward. Without forgiveness you are constantly stuck in your past. You can move forward if you pull up the **bitter root judgments** - Hebrews 12:15 (NAS) "See to it that no one comes short of the grace of God; and that no root of bitterness springing up causes trouble, and by it many be defiled." If you do not forgive and you do not stop judging those who wronged you, then you will do the same thing later on because the bitter roots (aka generational curses) were never forgiven of and pulled up. You must extend grace, mercy and understanding to your wrongdoer or you will waste years of your life in bitterness when you could have lived your life in peace and joy.

8. **Forgiving helps you stay productive and fruitful.** Once you have forgiven those who wronged you, then suddenly you will find you have more time for thinking useful productive and happy thoughts instead of useless negative and self-centered complaining.

9. **Forgiveness is a free gift** that costs you nothing to give and receive! In Matthew 18:21-22, Peter came to Jesus and asked, "Lord, how many times shall I forgive my brother or sister who sins against

me? Up to seven times?" Jesus answered, "I tell you, not seven times, but seventy-seven times" Paul says in Colossians 3:13, "Bear with each other and forgive whatever grievances you may have against one another. Forgive as the Lord forgave you."

10. **Forgiveness leads to purification of the spirit.** 1 John 1:9 says, "If we confess our sins, He is faithful and just and will forgive us our sins and purify us (or cleanse us) from all unrighteousness."

Forgiving God

When we talk about forgiving God, we're not talking about standing in judgment of God and accusing Him of wrongdoing or accusing Him of sinning against us. We are talking about forgiving Him because this helps us deal with our own anger, resentment, and bitterness that we experience when we get hurt; when things didn't go our way; when we prayed for the same sex attractions to go away and they did not; when our loved one did not get healed, but died; when our spouse left us when we prayed and prayed for the marriage to work out.

We know that God isn't in the wrong. Perhaps the same sex attractions did not go away because the root of the sin was not dealt with and forgiven and repented of.

Even when we're angry at Him, He still loves us and yearns for us to turn to Him for the comfort and encouragement we need. Forgiving God is not the same as forgiving other people, for one main reason: While other people may hurt us because of sin or bad motives, God is always good. He always does what is just and right with a pure motive – which is to draw us closer to Him. James 4:8 says, "Draw near to God and He will draw near to you."

We must remember that God has given everyone a free will because He did not want robots to worship Him, but true worshipers. We know that love is not truly love unless it is freely given. So God gave everyone a free will to make that decision to choose to whether to believe in God and worship and serve Him or to obey the devil and do the sinful destructive things that he wants people to do. Many times people use their free will and sin against God and others by their sinful wrong actions and decisions. We cannot control what people do. We can only control how we respond and the Word of God commands us to forgive. The devil plots his evil by tempting people to do sinful terrible things that in turn deeply hurt their loved ones. The devil does this in vengeance to get back at God and hurt Him by hurting the people He created to make them mad and bitter at God so they will turn away from Him and backslide or miss going to heaven. Sadly many times the devil is successful and many people have turned away from God, even those who were raised in church. This grieves God's heart big time. Many people love God for what He does for them instead of for who He is. Through His shed blood on the cross and His resurrection, Jesus Christ is our Lord and Savior. This is why Job is such an outstanding man of God. God allowed the devil to take almost everything away from Job, except his life, and Job still worshipped God. He did not understand why all the tragedy happened, but he still made the right decision refused to curse God to praise God and put his trust in Him.

Truthfully, God can only control someone who chooses to listen to the Holy Spirit (or his/her conscience) and then obeys God doing what God tells them to do. In short, God controls those who are led by His Spirit who indwells the born again believer. Romans 8:14 says, "For as many as are led by the Spirit of God, these are sons of God." As far a divine protection goes, there are many testimonies of people who escaped the Twin Towers disaster in Sept 11, 2001 because they were led by the Spirit. One born again believer lady I talked to testified that she felt led by the Spirit to go buy a bagel up the street for breakfast instead of eating inside the Twin Towers building that day. Her close relationship with God led her away from the disaster and saved her life. This is what Psalm 91:1 – "He who dwells in the secret place of the Most High shall abide under the shadow of His wings." The secret place is basically having an intimate relationship with God where you pray to God and also listen what the Holy Spirit is saying back to you and then obey Him. God was able to control her because she listened and obeyed the Holy Spirit's promptings, but He could not control the terrorists who flew their planes into the building because they were listening to and obeying the devil's evil plots and plans.

You Must Forgive Yourself

When the bad memories from childhood come back to you, then you must forgive your father and you also must forgive yourself for your wrong reaction that was probably subconscious at that time that build a wall around your heart when you were a toddler or a very young boy that prevented you from bonding with your father. Forgive yourself for judging him as a child without knowing all the facts. Perhaps the facts were that the reason why he was not around was not because he did not love you nor care about you, but because he was a traveling salesman. We must remember that our memories are highly fallible and plastic. And yet, we tend to subconsciously favor them over objective facts. Forgive yourself for not believing the facts.

Forgive yourself for engaging in homosexual acts because you were deceived into thinking that it was the way to receive your father's love that you did not receive when you were a boy.

If you are unforgiving towards yourself, then you open that door for tormenting spirits to come against you because you are not really accepting the work that Christ did for you on the cross. Matthew 18:23-35 tells us how the unforgiving person is turned over into the hands of tormenters (or tormenting spirits).

Failing to forgive yourself will put blinders on your spiritual eyes. It will cause you to see things through the eyes of guilt, shame and condemnation. It will ruin your faith. Romans 8:1 says, "There is therefore now no condemnation to them which are in Christ Jesus..."

The key to forgiving yourself is to believe that you have been forgiven and do not forget it.

Jesus Took Your Shame on the Cross

Many men feel a lot of shame for having unwanted same sex attractions. That shame separates and prevents intimacy with God. To overcome, you need to stop thinking about your past homosexual thoughts and sinful acts of the past. When you ask God to forgive you, then you are forgiven and the sin has been dealt with and washed away. Therefore, if you think about it anymore, then you are meditating on something that no longer exists! Isaiah 1:18, "Come now, and let us reason together, says the LORD: though your sins be as scarlet, they shall be as white as snow; though they be red like crimson, they shall be as wool." Instead of feeling shameful, begin to praise God for the solution to the problem, and think about how you have been washed clean from those failures! Instead of meditating on a lie, begin to meditate on the truth in God's Word concerning your past. Shame is one of those things that the Bible speaks of as an imagination or lie that must be cast down (2 Corinthians 10:5) and replaced with the truth.

Single Moms – Find a Godly Role Model for Your Son

Your son needs a godly male role model in his life. You have to make the effort to bring a godly role model into his life. He cannot do it alone. If the father of your son or your husband is not around, or if you are divorced, do not despair. Pray and ask God for a godly role model for your son. I encourage you to find a godly man, an uncle, your boyfriend, you neighbor's dad, youth group leader or scout leader or a coach. Make him get involved with sports, cub scouts, children's church or youth group at church. You may re-marry and his step-father can be a good godly role model for him as well. You can greatly help your son when he is a child by not allowing him to play with girls. Make him play with boys, even if he does not want to. If the boys pick on him, help him with "who I am in Christ" confessions on page 252 and Affirmations from A to Z on page 291. Explain to him that insecure boys pick on other kids to make them feel better about themselves and it is wrong and they need to be saved. Pray with your son to pray for his enemies or any bullies. Encourage your son that he can be "a light" for Jesus. Teach your son to forgive his father for not being there for him. Lead him in a sinner's prayer to receive Jesus as His Lord and Savior and God as His Heavenly Father. When he forgives his father, then God will make it up to him. Teach your son to pray, sing and worship God, read the Word and trust in God.

Books to Help You Witness to Them

The Gay Gospel? How Pro-Gay Advocates Misread the Bible by Joe Dallas
The Game Plan, The Men's 30-Day Strategy for Attaining Sexual Integrity by Joe Dallas
Messy Grace by Caleb Katenbach
When Homosexuality Hits Home by Joe Dallas
Coming Out of Homosexuality by Bob Davies
Leaving Homosexuality – by Alan Chambers

You cannot deny or argue with someone else's testimony because it is their personal experience. Many homosexuals make fun of or deny these people have been delivered and set free from homosexuality. I think that is because it easier to embrace the lies (that it is not sin and I was born this way) and yield to the world's acceptance of the sinful "alternative lifestyle" rather than repent, surrender your life to Christ, and walk in the truth from the Word of God. Reading these encouraging testimonies will give you great hope that change is possible and you too can change or your SSA can greatly decrease you and you can come out straight.

Testimonies of Homosexuals Healed through Christ

- Testimony of Dennis Jernigan in his book called: *Giant Killers* – " http://www.dennisjernigan.com/djtestimony

- Testimonies from People Can Change www.peoplecanchange.com

- Testimony of Donnie McClurkin – http://ex–gaytruth.com/ encyclopedia/donnie–mcclurkin/

- Testimony of Richard Cohen www.comingoutloved.com

- Testimony of Stephen Bennett www.sbministries.org

- Testimony of Kegan Wesley – www.keganwesley.com

- Testimony of Lee Preston http://www.m2m4purity.com /index.php/about/

- Testimony of DL Foster is in his book: *Touching a Dead Man* www.witnesstotheworld.org

- www.focusonthefamily.com/lifechallenges/understanding– homosexuality/stories–of–hope–and–change/redeeming–love

- Testimony of Dean Bailey – www.beyondtheshadesofgray.org

- Testimony of Stephen Black http://www.stephenblack.org /2015/02/27/stephen–blacks–testimony–2013–from–homo sexuality–to–holiness/

- Testimony of Eric Garner – www.ericgarnersetfree.com

- Testimony of Nathanael Flock - www.cbn.com/700club/ features/amazing/nathanael_flock061209.aspx

- Testimony of Victor J Adamson – www.victorjadamson.com

- www.facebook.com/pages/Ex–Homosexual–Through–Jesus– Christ/227709067265250

- http://ex–gaytruth.com/ex–gaytestimonies/

Book–Length Testimonials

- *Coming Out Loved* by Dr Richard Cohen
- *Beyond Gay*, by David Morrison
- *Born That Way?* By Erin Eldridge
- *Closing the Closet: Testimonies of Deliverance from Homosexuality* by Talbert Swan
- *Free Indeed* by Barbara Swallow
- *Healing Homosexuality: Case Studies of Reparative Therapy*, by Joseph Nicolosi
- *Out of Egypt: Leaving Lesbianism Behind*, by Jeanette Howard
- *A Place in the Kingdom*, by Garrick and Ginger Hyde
- *Portraits of Freedom: 14 People Who Came Out of Homosexuality*, by Bob Davies
- *You Don't Have to be Gay*, by Jeff Konrad
- *A Strong Delusion: Confronting the "Gay Christian" Movement*
- *The Poetic Testimony of an Ex-Homosexual* by Dominique Evans

Helpful Ministries for Those Struggling with Same–Sex Attractions

- Focus on the Family - Resources Concerning Homosexuality
  http://media.focusonthefamily.com/topicinfo/homosexuality_resources.pdf
- Focus on the Family -Understanding Homosexuality
  http://www.focusonthefamily.com/lifechallenges/understanding-homosexuality/leaving-homosexuality/resources-groups-and-support-for-men-and-women-with-same-sex-attractions

- -Focus on the Family - Leaving Homosexuality - http://www.focusonthefamily.com/socialissues/sexuality/leaving-homosexuality/leaving-homosexuality
- Focus on the Family - Understanding Same-Sex Attractions http://www.focusonthefamily.com/socialissues/sexuality/understanding-same-sex-attractions/understand-same-sex-attractions
- Focus on the Family - Homosexuality, Theology, Church http://www.focusonthefamily.com/socialissues/sexuality/homosexuality-theology-and-the-church/homosexuality-theology-and-the-church
- How to Talk With Your Children About Homosexuality http://www.focusonthefamily.com/socialissues/sexuality/how-to-talk-to-your-children-about-homosexuality/how-to-talk-to-your-children-about-homosexuality
- www.dennisjernigan.com/needhelp
- www.hopeforwholeness.org/
- http://www.restoredhopenetwork.com/
- Living Hope Ministries – www.livehope.org/
- Genesis Counseling www.joedallas.com
- Homosexuals Anonymous – http://www.ha–fs.org/
- Jayne Bowman – www.real–soulutions.com
- Richard Cohen, M.A. – www.gaytostraight.org
- SBM Worldwide – www.sbministries.org/
- First Stone Min. – Stephen Black – www.firststone.org
- www.wifeboat.com - help for wives of men who struggle
- Pastor DL Foster — www.witnessfortheworld.org/
- Hope for Homosexuals.com – familypolicy.net
- www.desertstream.org founded by Andrew Comiskey
- For Catholics – http://couragerc.org/courage/
- Assisting Families & the Church www.harvestusa.org
- JONAH International – www.jonahweb.org/

- PATH: Positive Alternatives www.pathinfo.org/□
- People Can Change – www.peoplecanchange.com/
- P–FOX – Parents & Friends of Ex–Gays – www. pfox.org/

More Resources: Informational Articles about the Risky Homosexual Lifestyle

- Matt Barber: The "Gay" Death style –pearceyreport.com/ corporateresourcecouncil.org/
- Expert Research Finds Homosexuality More Dangerous Than Smoking – lifesitenews.com/
- Study: Homosexual Lifestyle Strongly Linked to Depression, Suicide – lifesitenews.com/
- The Negative Health Effects of Homosexuality by Timothy J. Dailey, Ph. D. – orthodoxytoday.org/
- Sex Diseases in Many Gay Men Go Unfound, Experts Say – by Lawrence K. Altman – nytimes.com/
- Superbug Linked To Homosexual Behavior' – Society hasn't learned from the AIDS pandemic' – wnd.com/
- "Drug–resistant staph found to be passed in gay sex" Superbug can cause life–threatening disfiguring infections." www. reuters.com/
- Gay Bowel Syndrome – conservapedia.com/

Truth to Say to Witness to Lesbians

Deception: Many lesbians think: "I was told that I was born this way or God made me this way."

Truth to Say: Lesbianism is a counterfeit coping mechanism – a false way to love and nurture oneself. Despite the media's spin, scientifically there is no evidence for a gay gene. Actually, psychologists say that your sexual identity is *socially developed.* Why would God create something that He calls an abomination? (Genesis 19:1–11)

Deception: Some lesbians think: "I think my mom and dad wanted a boy, so I did my best to fulfill that role and became a tomboy...I wanted to be loved and accepted." Or: "My mother did not meet my emotional needs." Or: "I was sexually abused."

Truth to Say: Psalm 139:13 says: "For You (God) formed my inward parts; ...I will praise you, for I am fearfully and wonderfully made; Marvelous are Your works..." Rejecting your sexual identity is rejecting whom God made you to be. Change begins with receiving Jesus Christ as your Lord and becoming rooted and grounded in God's love (Eph. 3:17–18). God wants to uproot the lies that were planted in your heart when you were abused. He is so glad you are a girl and He loves you.

Deception: Some think: "I did not like my mother. My dad abused her and I did not want to be like her. I see women as weak and vulnerable. Acting like a man makes me feel more protected and strong and confident

Truth to Say: Acting like a man will not make you any stronger or protect you more. Men and women both need divine protection. Meditate on Psalm 91. The Bible says to men and women: "I can do all things through Christ Who strengthens me." Receiving comfort and strength from God is what will make you strong, courageous and confident. Isaiah 40:31 says: "Those that wait upon the Lord will renew their strength..." Psalm 18:2 says "the Lord is My Rock."

Ways to Overcome Lesbianism and Be Set Free:

1. Forgive your parents who you perceived rejected you for not being a boy and/or forgive those who abused you. Receive the love and acceptance of God through anointed praise and worship.

2. Do not share your attraction with the woman to whom you are attracted.   .Romans 13:14 says to "make no provision for the flesh." If you tell her, you are forging the possibility of a sexual relationship with her and you do not want that. Attractions come and go. Feelings die down as you truly get to know a person. If you tell the "object of your affection" how you really feel, she may treat you differently or distance herself or cut you off completely

3. Avoid places that can lead directly into sin: lesbian or gay bars or bookstores, parties, and other such places.

4. Renew your mind with the Word of God.

2 Corinthians 10:5 says you must "take captive every thought," every imagination and fantasy and make it obedient to Christ. Cast down the lie and replace it with truth using a Bible scripture Memorize God's word and say it out loud. Think on Philippians 4:6–8 and think on things that are true, honest and just, things that are pure lovely and holy and of a good report.

5. Learn to abide in the Vine. Read John 15 Learn to bond with and depend on the Lord. Sing praise and worship songs to Him and learn to receive His love through His manifest presence. When you think about how much you love God, often His Presence will come and He will comfort you and fill you with His love. God's love will heal your soul

6. Have Healthy Female Friendships. At first, avoid having a "best friend." Straight women often admire and complement other straight women freely and it is not a sexual attracttion. Wearing makeup and feminine looking clothes will help you feel feminine to embrace your womanhood identity. Then slowly "the right feelings" will follow.

Say out loud these scriptural confessions that are on page 252 in the previous chapter until you receive revelation that you are a woman of God and He has a plan and a purpose for your life. Christians, as you read these testimonies below, you will learn how to effectively minister to lesbians. Also see "Helpful Ministry Links" on pages 267-268.

Testimonies of Lesbians Whom Christ Set Free

- Testimony of Jeanette Howard – in her book: *Out of Egypt: Leaving Lesbianism Behind*
- **Testimony of Charlene Cothran – Ex–Gay Activist** http://blog.godreports.com/2014/12/lesbian–publisher–gay–activist–found–deliverance–in–christ/
- **Testimony of Melissa Fryrear** – http://www.cbn.com/ 700club /features/amazing/melissa_fryrear072309.aspx
- **Testimony of Rosaria Champagne Butterfield** is in her book: *The Secret Thoughts of an Unlikely Convert*
- **Testimony of Janet Boynes** is in her book: *Called Out*
- **Testimony of Anne Paulk** who overcame, got married & had 3 sons is in her book: *Restoring Sexual Identity*
- **Testimony of Karen Abbott** – www.settingcaptivesfree.com/ courses/door–of hope/testimonials/234/
- **Testimony of Erica Pike** http://www.endtime.com/ end time– magazine articles/miraculous–deliverance–homosexuality/
- **Testimony of Wendy** – www.charismanews.com/opinion /%20clarion–call/46013–a–former–lesbian–s–moving– testimony–of–breaking–free–from–homosexuality
- **Testimony of Debora Barr** – http://americansfortruth.com
- /2012/11/29/the–ex–lesbian–testimony–of–debora–barr/
- **Testimony of Jackie Hill** "My Life as a Stud – Former Lesbian, Now Christian" on You Tube: https://www.youtube.com/watch?v=ERmsmv5gdrU
- **Testimony of Erin Eldridge** in her book: *Born That Way?*

References for Truth to Say
to 13 False Religions

A Ready Defense by Josh McDowell (Here's Life Publishers, 1990)

Where Was God When Pagan Religions Began? by Lester Sumrall (LeSEA Publishing, 1980)

A Missionary that did not want to be named (for his protection) gave a seminar in November 2001 on "Witnessing to a Muslims"

The official Scientology Website

Homosexual and Lesbian sections were written with the help of LPC Jayne Bowman. **www.real–soulutions.org**

Other References have been noted.

CHAPTER EIGHTEEN

Witnessing Using Prophetic Evangelism

Prophetic Evangelism, I believe, is one of the most powerful ways to win someone to the Lord. After you have transitioned the conversation into the Gospel using an object evangelism icebreaker, you can listen for God to give you a prophetic word. But before you can really prophesy, you first need to know how to be led by the Spirit of God in your own life. Rom.ans 8:14 says that "as many who are led by the spirit of God, they are the sons of God." Therefore if you are born again, then you are in the Kingdom of God and you are connected to God by His spirit and so you can hear from Him. He will lead you and guide you when you listen with your spirit.

In 1959 the Lord Jesus Christ appeared to Bro. Kenneth Hagin, Sr. the founder of RHEMA Bible Training College, and He offered some insight Romans 8:14. The Lord told him: *"The number one way that I lead all of my children is by the inward witness."*

The inward witness of the spirit to **GO** ahead and do something feels like a velvety–like feeling in your spirit. It is a comfortable good feeling, like a "green light" or the go–ahead signal in that direction.

The inward witness to **STOP** will feel like a scratchy feeling or you will have a check in your spirit, which is like an uncomfortable feeling that something is not right, like taking a bath with your socks on! That is the red light or a stop signal to <u>not</u> go in the direction you are thinking about. (*How You Can Be Led By The Spirit of God*, Hagin, 29)

Following the inward witness is not like following your head or what you see, hear or feel in the natural. In fact, the out ward circumstances may seem fine to go on ahead, but sometimes the Lord will direct you to <u>not</u> go somewhere because He knows everything and He sees the roadblocks or the obstacles ahead. So it is better to be led *by your spirit*. Believers should be led by the inward witness every day.

The second way the spirit guides us is through the inward voice, also called the still small voice. Your spirit has a voice and it will speak to you. Just like your physical body has a voice. We call this voice of the inward man, "your conscience" as well. (Hagin, 43)

The third way God leads us is by the Spirit of God speaking to us. This voice is more authoritative. Sometimes it is so real it almost seems like it is *an audible voice.* You may look around to see who said it. (Hagin, 82)

I have only experienced this audible voice once in my whole life. I had met a RHEMA graduate who told me all about RHEMA Bible Training College in Tulsa, OK. I was interested in going, but my Mom at age 50 was bedridden with bone cancer in Charlotte, NC, (my hometown) and Tulsa, OK was an 18–hour drive away! I had been accepted to Duke Divinity School, but the money just wasn't there for me to go and yet Duke was only 3 ½ hours away. I loved my Mom so much. I did not know what to do. Then one day in June 1993, while driving with my Dad in his car, the Lord spoke to me in an audible voice: *"Just go to RHEMA."*

It was so loud that I asked my Dad, "Did you hear that?"

He replied, "Hear what?" I couldn't believe that he did not hear it!

When it comes to witnessing, after you experience and know how to be led by the spirit of God for your own life, it will be easier to be able to hear from God when He talks to you about other people whom He wants you to witness to.

Jesus Used Prophetic Evangelism

Some people may not have even heard of prophetic evangelism before, but Jesus used it in the Bible. John 4 17-18 God gave Jesus a word of knowledge and He prophesied, "You have well said, 'I have no husband.' For you have had five husbands, and the one whom you now have is not your husband; in that you have spoke truly."

In short, she was amazed and she got saved and became a great evangelist saying, "Come see a man who told me all things that I ever did. Could this be the Christ?"

Jesus stayed there two days and many Samaritans in her village came out to see Him and they also believed in Jesus telling the woman, "Now we believe, not because of what you said, for we ourselves have heard Him and we know that this is indeed the Christ, the Savior of the world."

In John 1:47 Jesus saw Nathanael coming toward Him, and said of him, "Behold an Israelite indeed, in whom is no deceit!" Nathanael said to Him, "How do You know me?" Jesus answered and said to him, "Before Philip called you, when you were under the fig tree, I saw you." Nathanael answered and said to him, "Rabbi, You are the Son of God! You are the King of Israel!" God had given Jesus a word of knowledge concerning Nathanael and it caused him to follow Jesus. We are called to do the works of Jesus. 1 Cor. 14:31 says: "You may all prophesy." So today we can prophesy too.

Witnessing with a Word of Knowledge

A word of knowledge is supernatural revelation by the Spirit of God of facts in the mind of God concerning people, places or things. It is always present of past tense. (The Ministry Gifts, by Kenneth E. Hagin) Be mindful that a word of knowledge is given only *as God wills*. He decides when He wants to manifest the gifts through us. Since God knows that witnessing using a word of knowledge is one of the most powerful ways to witness, so He often does give words of knowledge if we will just tune our spiritual ears to listen to Him. Those that have a prophetic gift or anointing are more likely to be used in this way, but God can use anyone. Do not underestimate yourself.

One time I was in the elevator with another prayer partner and I felt a pain in my knee for no reason at all. I did not fall or stumble. So I asked him if he had pain in his knee. He said he did. And so I asked him if I could pray for his knee and he said, "Sure, go right ahead!" So I prayed a fiery prayer as I laid hands on his knee and after praying, he told me that the pain in his knee went away! And so did mine! That was a word of knowledge for healing that God has given me for this co-worker and he was so thankful. I was glad there was nothing truly wrong with my knee! God can use you too just like He used me.

Three Ways to Receive a Word of Knowledge

The way to receive a word of knowledge is to listen to God. Be quiet and be still. Cut out the "inner noise" which are worries and cares from your daily life and cast them upon the Lord. Pray in tongues under your breath and tune into the Lord. I guess you could say, "put your spiritual ears on" and focus on the Lord. Imagine yourself sitting on His lap and Him giving you His perspective insight. There are three main ways that God can deliver the word of knowledge to you: Hearing, Seeing and Sensing.

I.   HEARING – The first way that God can deliver a word of knowledge to you is through hearing His voice, the still small voice, or the inward witness. Once in a great while, it may be the audible voice of God. *For example:* One time I was at the altar silently praying for the woman in front of me to the woman in a gentle loving tone of voice: "I believe God is telling me to tell you that He will help you do it again." Then I asked her, "Does that mean anything to you?" She started crying and said, "I'm down here because I did quit drinking once, but I started drinking again." So then we both rejoiced realizing that God was saying He wasn't condemning her and her chances were not up, but He was going to help her quit drinking again

II. SEEING – The second way that God can deliver a word of knowledge to you is through seeing a spiritual vision or a flash of a mini–vision picture. If you are on the streets the Lord could bring a person into your pathway from a dream you had the night before. I have never experienced the two other types of visions which are: trances and open visions, probably because they are too deep of a manifestation and there are distractions out on the street where many times you have to keep walking. For example, one time, when I was about to pray for a woman at the altar at church, the Lord showed me a vision of a broken table leg from a kitchen table. When God shows you something, you need to be sure to ask Him: "What are you showing me? What does this mean?" The Lord was showing me that this lady's heart was broken. That was the word of knowledge. Now when ministering out on the streets, it would be encouraging to lovingly say something like: "God is showing me that you have a broken heart and He wants to comfort you and pour out His love upon you." That would a great way to start witnessing to a young lady and bring her to a saving knowledge of Jesus Christ. But in this instance, I knew that telling the lady that the Lord revealed to me that she had a broken heart would not really help nor encourage her because she already knew that her heart was broken.

So I asked the Lord for **the thought behind** the word of knowledge: "Lord, **why** is her heart broken?" Then I thought about how the table leg looked like one from the kitchen table, so I knew the brokenness had something to do with her family, like a wayward son or daughter. So knowing this I asked the Lord: "OK. Now I know why her heart is broken. What do you want me to say now? The Lord told me to tell her: **"The Lord wants you to trust Him."** So I told her: "The Lord wants you to trust Him," then the Lord continued on with the vision.

I saw Him take the broken table leg and He replaced it with a new one. This new table leg was translucent and sparkling and glorious–looking. It symbolized the Lord giving her strength and grace for the situation that He was going to "hold her up" as she put her trust in Him to bring her children back to the Lord. Then I told her about the vision I had and the new glorious table leg that God was giving her. Then she started crying as she then told me about all the problems she was having in her family with her teenage children that were raised in church and knew God, but they were rebelling and straying away from Him and it was breaking her heart.

She told me: "That prophetic word really ministered to me and encouraged me because I really did felt like I was collapsing under the strain of all of my worries, but now I know it is all going to be OK. God is in control and I can lean on Him and trust in Him to take care of my kids." Then she gave me a big hug.

II. SENSING – The third way that God can deliver a word of knowledge to you is through sensing something. You may have sudden inspiration from God where you just know that you know in your spirit. This can come through a spontaneous thought floating through your mind at the spur of the moment or you may have **an** *impression* in your emotions, your mind or spirit that you perceive. Don't be disturbed by this description. Although our feelings are often inaccurate indicators of reality, God created our emotions *and will sometimes speak to us through them for others.* We might feel a grief or a sorrow as we pray for someone in a meeting or for a waitress at a restaurant. God is allowing us to feel what they are feeling so that we can minister to them. As we recognize and identify these prophetic feelings, we can see people saved, healed and delivered. At other times we will feel what the Lord feels for someone to whom we are ministering. We may experience profound joy or a sense of divine protection over them. We can prophesy to them that God rejoices over them with singing (Zephaniah 3:17) or that the Lord is protecting them (Psalm 91).

When you are receiving revelation from God, be patient and listen to God until He is finished speaking or revealing the whole revelation to you. Then ask the Lord: **Is this for me to share or is it a secret that You just want me to pray about?** If God wants you to share it, then ask God for wisdom on how to deliver it in *a loving way* to whomever you are witnessing to.

So when you are witnessing, you can ask the Lord to give you a word of knowledge for the person that you are witnessing to: "Lord, what does this person that You want me to witness to need prayer for? In what area of their life do they really need You? Is it a financial breakthrough or a healing or prayer for a family member or healing of a broken heart?" Then be courageous and ask God for wisdom to know how to deliver the word of knowledge.

Allow God to use you. Remember to prophesy in a respectful and sensitive loving manner. We do not have a videotape to really see and hear what tone of voice Jesus used in John 4:17-18 when He prophesied to the woman at the well. But you can tell from the woman's reaction that He was not angry, judgmental nor condemning in His tone of voice. If He was, when He prophesied these words: "You have well said, 'I have no husband.' For you have had five husbands, and the one whom you now have is not your husband; in that you have spoken truly" she would have run away in fear and shame carrying much condemnation. So we know that Jesus was kind and loving and respectful because even when He revealed her sinful past, she stuck around and was drawn to Him.

1 John 4:8 says that "God is love". and 1 John 4:18 says "perfect love casts out fear."

If you receive a word of knowledge, I exhort you to deliver it with a loving, caring respectful attitude like Jesus did and then you will get similar results like Jesus did.

Love Is the Way to Prophesy

When you read 1 Corinthians 12, you will see that Paul is describing the Gifts of the Holy Spirit. In 1 Corinthians 14, he describes how to prophesy in a group with others taking turns. So if we read it in context, 1 Corinthians 13 is really describing how to prophesy with the love of God. Paul wrote it to teach the church how to interact with one another when using the gifts of the Spirit in a loving way. Most examples of how to prophesy were in the Old Testament consisting of harsh prophets who thundered God's judgments in a spirit of anger. Since we are on the New Testament side of the cross now, prophetic people are now called to prophesy (which is to encourage, edify and comfort) with a spirit of love and mercy and grace. Prophesying without the love of God is misrepresenting God because, like I said earlier, 1 John 4:8 says that God is love. In the New Testament, the love of God is the true prophetic motivation. Perhaps the Corinthians were prophesying in angry harsh tones like the Old Testament prophets did. Maybe this is why Paul wrote the famous love chapter. Knowing this, Paul wrote 1 Corinthians 13 which says (NIV): "If I speak in the tongues of men and of angels, but have not love, I have become a resounding gong or a clanging cymbal. If I have the gift of prophecy and can fathom all mysteries and all knowledge, and if I have a faith that I could move mountains, but have not love, I am nothing."

This is my commentary of what I believe Paul was thinking when he wrote the following verses in 1 Corinthians 13:4-8:

Love is patient. This means that love is long suffering as well. If there are several prophetic people present, then you must be patient to "wait your turn" to prophesy. As you read 2 Corinthians 11:24–27, you will see how much Paul suffered for the Gospel, but God's love suffers long. Jesus said in Matthew 5:44 "to love your enemies, bless those that curse you, do good to those who hate you and to pray for those who persecute you" and that takes patience.

Love is kind. To be kind means to be: sympathetic, forbearing, of a pleasant nature, benign and gracious to others. Prophetic people need to phrase their prophetic words **in a kind tone of voice** because prophesying is encouraging, edifying and comforting.

Love does not envy. Love does not envy the evangelist who does mighty healing miracles. Love does not envy another's prophetic gift or anointing. In 1 Corinthians 12:11 the Lord gives the different gifts of the spirit to each one, just as He determines. It is His decision and His will. The Lord showed me that when you envy another's gift, you are questioning God or striving with Him. Isaiah 45:9 says, "Woe to the man who strives with His maker." Instead of complaining and envying in your heart, you need to repent and be thankful and content with what you do have and concentrate on developing that. When you are faithful in the anointing that you do have, God will give you more. Love does not compare itself to others in a competitive way. He who compares himself with others is not wise (2 Corinthians 10:12). Many people do not understand the trials, the attacks, and the persecution that prophetic people go through because of the anointing they carry that the enemy so hates. God requires them to make much higher sacrifices as well. So be happy being whom God made you. Paul said in Philippians 4:11: "I have learned to be content whatever the circumstances."

Love does not boast. Do not boast in having a prophetic gift. You must remember that when you have any spiritual gift, that it was given to you by His grace. You did not work to get it. You did not earn it as a prize, therefore there is nothing to boast about. Do not boast of how much you gave in the offering either. Love testifies and boasts of what God has done. When you lay hands on the sick and they are healed, God gets the glory.

Love is not proud. I imagine Paul might have been thinking of the prideful pastor saying to a prophetic minister in 1 Corinthians 12: 20–21: "I have no need of you." Truthfully we need every part of the five–fold ministry working together in order for the church to operate at its maximum potential. Do not be prideful that you have a prophetic gift or anointing or even that you are a pastor, evangelist or teacher either. Remember Psalm 75:6–7 and 1 Peter 5:6 – **"God resists the proud, but gives grace to the humble. Humble yourselves therefore under that mighty hand of God, that He may exalt you in due time."**

The more grace you receive, the more anointing you will receive to minister on His behalf. If you are prideful, you will pollute your prophetic gift. Pride is what caused Satan to fall. When I prophesy, many times I am in as much awe as the person receiving the prophetic word because in all humility we both *know* that the prophetic word did not come from me, but from God and so we give Him all the glory.

Love is not rude. To be rude means to be impolite or discourteous. It says in 1 Corinthians 14:32, "for you can all prophesy in turn." So be mindful of others and be courteous so that everyone can contribute what God puts on their heart. If you are upset with someone, forgive him or her before prophesying over them, lest the prophetic word comes out in a rude manner.

Love is not self–seeking. Love is giving and self–sacrificing. Your motive for prophesying should be to serve others, to edify, encourage or comfort others seeking nothing for yourself in return. A few prophetic ministers that I have watched seem to prophesy with the intent to seek money in return. Only the Lord knows their hearts and so I do not judge them. When ministering, check your heart, knowing that God knows exactly why you are doing what you are doing. Walk in the fear of the Lord. God will supply your financial needs by His spirit <u>not</u> through prophetic control or manipulation.

Love is not easily angered. If you are a Pastor and receive a flaky, strange, false or judgmental prophetic word, remember that love is not easily angered. It would be best if you would gently say: *"I appreciate you trying your wings and stepping out in faith. That did not make sense to me, but I will put it on a shelf and it may make sense to me later.*

I encourage you to continue seeking God and use your gifts for His glory."
Also you cannot prophesy in love if you are angry at someone or
bitter about something. You must repent of any bitterness if you
want your prophetic words to be untainted and pure as gold.

Love keeps no record of wrongs. You must forgive
everyone for everything if you want to prophesy with purity and
with accuracy. When you think about all the terrible things that Paul
went through in 2 Corinthians 11:24–29, it is amazing that he wrote
this love chapter at all. If you are having difficulty forgiving, ask God
for grace through showing you something about that person or
something about their past that will help you understand them
more. Paul understood his persecutors, because **before** he was
radically saved on the Road to Damascus in Acts 9:3, he was the same
way! Imagine what it would be like to walk in their shoes. I believe
that the more you understand someone, the easier it is to forgive him
or her. Remember that hurt people hurt people.

Love does not delight in evil, but rejoices with the truth. I
have found that many people who "delight in evil" enjoy judging
someone who falls into sin, especially if it is a pastor, and then
capitalizing upon it. Pastors are notorious for cutting down other
pastors in their city to build up their own church, especially if they
committed some kind of moral failure or sin. We need unity. The
army of God is the only army that shoots down and tries to kill their
own wounded soldiers. How? They kill with their reckless words
that pierce like a sword (Proverb 12:18). Judgmental insecure
weak pastors seem to forget that we are not fighting each other,
but we are fighting the devil in our collective battle to win the world
to Jesus Christ.

It says in Galatians 6:1, "Brethren, if a man is overtaken in any
trespass, you who are spiritual, restore such a one in a spirit of
gentleness, considering yourself lest you also be tempted. Bear
one another's burdens, and so fulfill the law of Christ."

The problem is many Christians and even pastors are not truly
spiritual, but are still walking in the flesh. Let's do what the Bible
says and walk in love.

Love always protects.   In 2 Corinthians 11:33 the Christians protected Paul and let him down in a basket through a window so that he could escape his persecutors. Now aren't you glad that they protected Paul? If they had not protected him, we may not have much of the New Testament that we have today! If you have a prophetic anointing, God may reveal to you the sin of a pastor or church leader, but remember that love protects. The purpose of God revealing it to you is for you to pray or intercede that they will get right with God. It is not so that you can spread gossip. I would not even tell another intercessor. If God wanted them to pray, then He would tell them too. I believe that telling others about some sin that God has shown you in a church leader's life borders on "touching God's anointed." So just pray for the Pastor or church leader in question. If they hurt you in any way, forgive them and trust in God to bring about restoration or vengeance for you.

If you have a correcting word for the pastor, so not tell him in front of his congregation. It does not matter if it is a moral failure, financial misappropriations, teaching heresy or error or uncontrolled anger, etc, you still do not tell him in front of his congregation nor spread any gossip or rumors, for that could bring him public shame and could scatter the flock.

Remember that love protects. Pray and pray and intercede first and if God tells you to, then obey God and set up an appointment and tell him in his office with an elder there. To tell you the truth, normally pastors and ministers will not receive a corrective prophetic word from someone unless they are on their same level in ministry, so use wisdom..

If when you are ministering at a service and God shows you a sin in another church member's life, turn the microphone off and then quietly address the issue and minister the prophetic word or vision so that no one can hear. After you quietly deliver it, be sure to ask, "Does this make sense to you?" Do not assume that you know what the vision means. Some prophetic people get visions, but they get the wrong interpretation of what that vision really means. For e.g., if you see a vision of a stethoscope, you may assume he is a doctor, but it could also mean that he sells medical equipment.

Love always trusts. Trust is relying on God and putting your faith in Him. You have to trust the Lord in prophesying. It is a walk of faith. You not only have to trust Him to give you the prophetic word, you also have to trust Him in *how* you will you be able to deliver it. The winter of 1998 the Lord prompted me to go to a Rick Renner meeting and prophesy over him and his wife Denise. The only problem was it was very icy and I hate driving on ice. I prayed Psalm 91 and drove only 15 – 20 mph, but I finally got there. Because of that treacherous drive, I was determined to obey God and prophesy over them and not wimp out. I told an usher that I had a prophetic word for them and so he closed a couple of French doors to get me alone with them and away from the crowd. I got my little tape recorder out and started prophesying in song. They were so receptive and so encouraged by the prophetic word, which was all about remaining in the peace of God in the midst of the storm. Then *they encouraged me* that I had a precious gift and to keep prophesying.

Trust in God's favor for you to prophesy to another minister. For example, my friendship with Rev. Curry Blake and his wife, Dawn Blake, (who is the overseer of John G. Lake Ministries) gave me favor to prophesy over his friend evangelist David Hogan. He is a missionary to Mexico and has raised over 25 people from the dead. That intimidated me, but I bound up the spirit of the fear of man and loose peace upon myself in Jesus' name and then prophesied over him in song. He was so touched and encouraged by the word that he had tears in his eyes. I am so glad I obeyed God. If you trust God, He will make a way and He will make room for your gift to prophesy.

Love always hopes. A prophecy should always give hope. Hope is so underestimated. It is the anchor of the soul. You have to have *hope* to even be able to stir up your faith. Hope is where it all begins. When all else fails, when you have hope, you will make it.

Love always perseveres. In the face of persecution, love perseveres. In the face of horrific persecution, Paul said that the love of Christ compels him (2 Corinthians 5:14). When you are walking in the prophetic anointing, you need to persist in spite of difficulties. Because of bad past experiences, many pastors have a rift with prophetic people. The healing of this rift or wound between pastors and prophets takes perseverance. I thank God for those who champion the cause of restoring the desire and the operations of the prophetic ministry back to Jesus' Bride.

Love Never Fails. If you say a prophetic word with the love of God, it will not fail to strengthen, encourage and edify the person receiving it, even if it is a little off. Remember to speak words laced with God's Love.

Remember that in 1 Corinthians 14:1 and in vs.3 it says: "Pursue love, and *desire spiritual gifts, especially that you may prophesy*...He who prophesies speaks edification, and exhortation and comfort to men."

> **One prophetic word can change your life – for the better!**

How Do I Know If I Am On Target?

Many prophetic people that minister wonder, how do I know if I am on target with the word I think I have for this person?

You just ask! For example, if you think you have a prophetic word about a person's son you might ask, "Do you have a son?"

If the answer is "yes" and what you think you've heard from the Lord is that their son is sick, you could proceed with: "Does he have any physical problems?" Then if they say "yes," then you can say: *"The reason why I am asking these questions is just to make sure that I am truly hearing from God. Now I know that I am. Let's pray for him to be healed because I <u>know</u> that God wants to heal* *him. But before we pray, is Jesus your Lord and Savior?"*

Praying with a person about a word of knowledge can be so powerful and effective in winning the lost.

One prophetic word can change a person's life, so be bold and prophesy or share the word of knowledge that you hear or see or sense from the Lord. You can say something like: "I see ___ or I hear___ or I sense ____ that the Lord is saying...."

Then be sure to ask: *"Does this make sense to you? Does this mean anything to you?"* Ask for feedback.

As you are learning, I would not try to interpret what you see in a vision or mental picture right away. Don't assume that you know what the interpretation of the vision or mental picture means. Ask them questions instead. Then you will know whether you were on target or not and can be encouraged or learn from your mistakes. Be wise as a serpent and harmless as a dove and completely humble in your approach. As you practice, you will understand more and more. Remember it says in 1 Corinthians 14: 3 that prophesying is to comfort, encourage, edify and exhort. So be kind and loving in your tone of voice. Judging and criticizing unbelievers will push them away. They usually already know that they are in sin. You usually do not need to tell them that they are in sin. They need to hear about how they can be delivered and set free. They need to hear about the awesome love and power of God that will heal them from their addictions, their emotional pain and rejection.

The Prophetic Word Must Be Redemptive

Many times, God will show you the problem – like they are on drugs or they are a homosexual or that they never had a father, etc. You do **not** prophesy the problem that you see, **you prophesy the solution.** They need to hear the edifying, encouraging, comforting word that is redemptive or the words that are the solution They need to hear about the awesome love and power of God and that being set free begins with praying to receive Jesus Christ as their Lord and Savior.

For example, if you see that they are sad, then prophesy the redemption: *"God wants to give you joy, set you free, and turn your mourning into dancing."*

If you hear they are fatherless, then prophesy: *"God wants to be your Heavenly Father, to love you and take care of you."*

If you see that they are lonely, then prophesy: *"God will never leave you nor forsake you. You are not alone."*

If you sense they are broken hearted, then prophesy: *"God loves you and wants to fill you with the height, the depth & the width of the love that He had for you. He is the true lover of your soul."*

I hate to say anything restricting because I just want the Holy Spirit to just have His way, so this is just my opinion, but I would refrain from prophesying anything about wedding bells or prophesying about *who* someone is going to marry. This I what Kenneth E. Hagin, Sr. says on this issue:

"Through the years, I've seen so–called prophets tell people whom to marry and not to marry. I never saw one case work out right. And, oh, the tragedy I've seen in this area." (*The Ministry Gifts*, p 33)

Memorize Scriptures by Topic to Prophesy

It is so important to memorize scriptures by topic so that you can prophesy a redemptive, encouraging, edifying, and comforting word using scriptures in the area where they are struggling, for example:

Anger - Ephesians 4:26-7 Be angry and sin not. Do not let the sun go down on your anger. Neither give place to the devil. James 1:19 Let every man be quick to listen, slow to speak and slow to be angry.

Anxiety - 1 Peter 5:7 Cast all your cares upon Him, for He cares for you. Philippians 4:6 - Do no be anxious about anything.

Finances - Isaiah 48:17 I Am your Redeemer, the Holy One of Israel, who teaches you to profit, who leads you by the way you should go.

Philippians 4:19 My God shall supply all your needs according to His riches in glory through Christ Jesus

Loneliness - Hebrew 13:5 - I will never leave you nor forsake you

Depression - Psalms 37:3-4 Trust in the LORD, and do good; dwell in the land and feed on His faithfulness. Delight yourself in the Lord and He will give you the desires of your heart. Jeremiah 29:11 For I know the plans I have for you, declares the LORD, plans for your welfare and not for evil, to give you a future and a hope.

Many children have grown up without a father figure in their home. They never received the "Words of Affirmation" that they needed to gain the confidence to do what they are called to do and fulfill their God–given destiny. So the following pages contain "Words of Affirmation from A to Z from the Father's Heart" that will help you when you are prophesying. Memorize this list of photo copy it and take it with you. You have my permission. It is very helpful.

A to Z Affirmation From the Father's Heart

A   I have **A**dopted you and I love you unconditionally. You are my child and I **A**ccept you. Romans 8:15. Ephesians 1:6

B   You are my **B**eloved. I will **B**less you. You are **B**eautiful to Me and you are wonderfully made. Psalm 139.

C   I have **C**hosen you to be here for such a time as this. Be **C**ontent with My timing. Do not **C**ompromise to keep your friends happy. Do My will and make Me happy that you are out of trouble and walking in My will and in My freedom.

D   You have a **D**estiny. You can **D**o all things through Me who strengthens you. Do not be afraid or dismayed. Philippians 4:13

E   I Am able to do **E**xceedingly abundantly above what you ask or think. I will give you favor. Trust in Me. Ephesians 3:20

F   Forgive those who have hurt you. Put them in My hands and I will fight for you and turn things around. You are in My Family now. I Am your Faithful Heavenly Father who will never leave you nor forsake you. Matthew 6:14, Psalm 27:10

G   From My viewpoint, your Grade is either "pass or fail" and you passed because you received Jesus as your Lord, so you will pass on into heaven someday. I have given you My Gift to the world, Jesus Christ, and other Gifts and talents as well, so use them for my Glory. I encourage you also to be a Giver. John 3:16

H   I Am the Lord your Healer (Exodus 15:26) and I Am Holy, so you be holy as I Am holy, so do not engage in sexual relations with anyone until you are married and homosexuality is terrible sin.

I   Nothing is Impossible with Me. Your Inheritance is in heaven, so do not fight over earthly inheritances and keep the peace. I shall provide for you. I will be faithful to you.

J   You are a Joint–heir with Me, with Christ. So, receive My Joy and rule and reign for Me. Forgive and I will bring Justice to you.

K   Do not fear. Listen to Me and I will Keep you safe under the shadow of My wings of divine protection. Psalm 91

L   I want you to understand how much I Love you – the height, depth, width and the length of My Love for you. Ephesians 3:17

M   Just believe in Me and Miracles will happen.

N   You are Never Alone. My Presence shall go with You and give You rest. I may convict you of sin, but there is No condemnation in Christ Jesus, so receive my Love – Romans 8:1

O   Always listen to Me in your heart and Obey Me. That shows me that you love Me when you obey Me. John 14:26

P   I have a Plan and a Purpose for Your life. You're a Piece of the jigsaw Puzzle of life. You are Precious and significant. Others around you need what you have. Jeremiah 29:11

Q Never **Q**uit. I will help you. C'mon, let's try again. Be **Q**uiet and you will hear My still small voice comforting you.

R Be sure to **R**enew your mind through reading the Word of God every day. Then **R**eapply what you **R**ead to your life. It will make you like Me and you'll be **R**adically blessed.

S **S**ing and Worship Me in **S**ong. Wait to have **S**ex until you are married. Fornication is sin. If you are married, do not commit adultery or I will judge you. 1 Corinthians 7:2

T Be **T**hankful for all that you have. Do not fear, but **T**rust in Me with all of your heart, even when you do not understand what is going on. Proverbs 3:5–6

U You are **U**nique. You are not weird, but valuable. It pleased Me to make you one of a kind. Do not be influenced by peer pressure. So do not compare yourself to anyone else. Galatians 6:4

V You are **V**aluable to Me. The price I paid for you was the blood of Jesus Christ. It is more precious than all the gold. Remember to forgive those who hurt you. **V**engeance is Mine and I will repay you and make it up to you. Romans 12:19

W You are **W**orthy to be saved and I Am **W**orthy to be served Because I created the world and I created you. Sing and **W**orship Me. Since you are in Christ, you are always a **W**inner in My eyes. Two thumbs up!

X **Expect Me** to move in your life. Be filled with faith and hope, not doubt and unbelief. Expect good things to come your way. I Am able to give you favor by my grace. Psalms 5:12

Y **Y**ield to My Spirit. Do not **Y**ield to the lust of the flesh, the lust of the eyes nor the pride of life. My **Y**oke is easy and My burden is light. Matthew 11: 28–30.

Z Be **Z**ealous to do good works and witness to the lost.

We All Make Mistakes

When you begin to operate in the gift of prophecy, you can all expect to make some errors and blunders or mistakes, especially when you are in learning situations. Accepting your mistakes will free you to keep growing and become an effective believer who can bless others through prophesying. Jesus was the only perfect spokesman for God ever use in an earthly ministry.

One of the greatest temptations we can experience when we begin to prophesy it to quit. Many churches have. Don't condemn yourself if you are not as polished or as anointed as another. Don't compare yourself to another. It takes time to learn about prophesying, how to deliver your prophetic word, and to mature in the gift of prophecy. If you quit, you will just be hurting yourself and others down the road who could have greatly benefited from a prophetic word from you. However, if you decide to continue to prophesy, as you grow, you will be able to bless many others in powerful ways.

1 Peter 4:11 says: "If anyone speaks, let him speak as the oracles of God. If anyone ministers, let him do it as with the ability which God supplies, that in all things God may be glorified through Jesus Christ."

Have confidence in God and believe that He can use you. God wants you to speak His words.

CHAPTER NINETEEN

Plans of Salvation Using

Coffee
Grades
Individual Medley

The following are three fun creative ways to share the Gospel all the way through, from beginning to end, using:

1. the making of coffee with a coffee maker

2. the making of good grades or bad grades

3. swimming the event called the Individual Medley, which is butterfly, backstroke, breaststroke and freestyle.

From the time I was seven until I was seventeen, I swam year round a on swim team in Charlotte, NC, called the Mecklenburg Aquatic Club, so I was not surprised when the Lord gave me these creative ideas so that even *swimmers* can witness to the lost at swim meets, where there is a lot of down time.

Plan of Salvation – Coffee

As I drink my coffee, I was just thinking about how the coffee grinds remind me of Genesis 2:7 which says that "the Lord God formed man from **the dust of the ground**, which is a lot like **coffee grinds**. In the same way that no one wants to eat coffee grinds all by themselves, (yuck!), God sees our sins as "yuck!" and so our sins separate us from God. This grieves God because He loves us because He created us to fellowship with Him.

God is like the Coffee Maker. God knew that someone would have to pay the price for our sins, so that we could be forgiven and reconciled to God, but there is no forgiveness of sins without the shedding of blood. God knew a sacrifice needed to be made. So in God's timing, God sent His Son Jesus Christ who did many healing miracles and He also turned the water into wine.

In John 7:38 and in John 4:10 He told the woman at the well that He was the Living Water, so **Jesus, this Living Water**, shed His blood and died on the cross paying the penalty for our sins. He is the hero that saved us all from going to hell and He saved us from just eating coffee grinds! When someone asks Jesus Christ to come into their heart to be their Lord and Savior, their sins are forgiven; they are reconciled to God and will spend eternity in heaven, not hell.

Receiving Jesus as Lord is allegorically like when the Coffee Maker switch is turned over to "ON" to make it start, the unbeliever prays a salvation prayer and turns their life **over** to Jesus Christ to make a brand new start.

Then the Living Water flows through the dusty coffee grinds, and out comes **a new creature in Christ Jesus or fresh brewed coffee!** This coffee is made even better with cream and sugar. Psalm 34:8 says, "Oh taste and see that the Lord is good!" So that is how coffee is created which is so similar to how a new creature in Christ Jesus is created as well.... So have you ever turned that Coffee Maker switch to ON to allow the Living Water to flow through you?

Plan for Salvation – Grades

Most of the time, if a person studies hard, then they will make an "A." But if a person makes an "F," it is like a huge deadly sin and makes our parents mad too. In the same way, our sins, or our "F's," separate us from God. (Romans 6:23).

According to the world's standards, I thought that to be right with God or to achieve salvation, a person would have to be perfect and make straight A's. Then I was so glad to find that *God does not think like the world does!* (Romans 2:4) God knows that salvation "by works" or making straight A's is *not fair* because no one is perfect. God knows that people have different abilities to study and have different IQ levels. Some cannot write well, but are good at math. Some are not good at math, but can write well. Others may have ADD and some are handicapped. (Romans 3:23)

But God loves us so much that He set the standard for entering the Kingdom of God on a "Pass or Fail" system! There was a high price that God paid to give us this grace (Ephesians 2:8–9). He sent His Son Jesus Christ, who died on the cross and shed His blood for our sins. That means the B's, the C's, the D's, & the F's and any other sins we have done. Jesus took those sins on the cross for us, so that we would be saved from "works" or the whole letter grade system. Then He rose from the dead and put the pass/fail system into place!

Now those that receive Jesus Christ as their Lord and Savior, will be reconciled to God and will *PASS* receiving eternal life in heaven. Those that choose *not* to receive Jesus as their Lord will *FAIL* and go to hell. Under God' system, those that make straight A's and choose *not* to pray to receive Jesus Christ as their Lord, *will still fail* and go to hell. So choose Jesus Christ & pray to receive Him as Lord today!

Note: *Making good grades will help you get into a good college so you can major in and advance in a career where you feel called by God. So please study and do the best that you can! That is all that God requires.*

Plan for Salvation - Swimming the Individual Medley

Swimming the IM or the Individual Medley is when you swim all four laps in this order: butterfly, backstroke, breaststroke and then freestyle is the last lap.

As I watch that swimmer swim the **butterfly**, it reminds me of how the butterfly is the symbol of a new Christian because the caterpillar goes into his cocoon and then in God's timing comes out as a butterfly just like a new creature in Christ Jesus does. Many people receive Jesus Christ as their Savior as a child, but they often stray away from the truth and well, they swim **the backstroke**.

The **backstroke** reminds me of backslidden Christians or unbelievers who have gone through bitter hard times and have rebelled against God through peer pressure, drugs, alcohol, pre–marital sex, porn, homosexuality or some false religion. They do these sinful things to comfort themselves to fill up the void or the pain in their hearts. They have forgotten the truth of the Gospel. Then they suffer so much until they hit rock bottom. This reminds me of **the breaststroke,** the slowest stroke of all. This is where the person *opens their heart* to God and to the Word of God that breaks the lies to reveal the truth. They learn that God loves them and they need to forgive those who have hurt them and to allow God to "take revenge" or to right the wrongs done to them (Matthew 6:14; Romans 12:19.) They learn not to judge others and let it go. God shows them that He has a plan and a purpose for their life. Jeremiah 29:11

As the unbeliever or backslider surrenders their life to God and they **break free** and from the devil's lies and learn the truth becoming "free in Christ," they start swimming **the freestyle!** They learn to have faith in God and by His grace they run or swim their race for God's glory until the end!

CHAPTER TWENTY

Witnessing to
Children of Divorce

M any marriages end in divorce. I am not condemning anyone, not even pastors who should teach more often on how to have a good healthy marriage. **For those of you who are reading this book, for witnessing purposes,** I wanted to make you more aware of a couple lies that many (but not all) children of divorce believe and spouses who suffer from divorce.. These lies here **are generalities** because every person is different in their personality and in his/her past experiences that have shaped them for better or for worse.

Lie: If a child's father died or was never seen much because of a divorce situation when he or she was a young, then that child has a propensity to believe that "God does not exist" or "God does not love me" because their father did not exist in their life or was not there for them. For the same reason, they may not believe God's Word is true because of the many times their father (or their mother) lied and disappointed them and were not true to *their word*. They base their view of God in parallel with what happened to them or what they experienced in early life and because of this lie many turn away from God.

Truth to Say: The Bible really is true. God is real and He really does love you and He created the whole world, so of course He exists. God loves you and **He is your Heavenly Father.** He even now wants to be there for you like a husband. In John 10:10 Jesus says: "It is the devil who comes to kill, steal and destroy. I Am come that they may have life and have it more abundantly." It was not God's will that your father died at an early age or was not there for you. And yet, it IS God's will that you forgive him (or your mother for not being there). It is God's will for you to forgive. Unforgiveness is a sin and separates you from God, but forgiving those who hurt you draws you close to God. When you forgive, you are trusting God to "right the wrongs" that have been done to you. When you forgive, God will bring justice into your life. He will make it up to you in His way, in His timing. He will be your Heavenly Father and you can learn to be led by His Spirit. Do not be vengeful. You just have to be patient and do not take the matter into your own hands. The following scriptures are helpful:

- Romans 12:19: "Beloved, do not avenge yourselves, but rather give place to wrath; for it is written, 'Vengeance is Mine, I will repay,' says the Lord."

- Psalm 27:10: "When my father and mother forsake me, then the Lord will take me up."

- Isaiah 41:10: "Fear not, I Am with you. Do not be dismayed, I Am your God, I will strengthen you, I will help you and I will uphold you with right hand of my righteousness."

God will never leave you nor forsake you. The Holy Spirit will even hover over you like a mother. God can bring other godly father–figures and godly mother figures into your life and godly friends to help you in your walk with God. It is so important to go to

Youth group at church. Allow the "family of God" to love on you there at church and at church social events.

Lie: People who have suffered divorce because a spouse committed adultery may have bitter feelings toward God. They think, *"I cannot trust God because He did not answer my prayers. God doesn't love me nor really care about me. I prayed and prayed for him/her to be faithful and he/she still committed adultery. I prayed for him/her to come back and they are still gone, etc."* Many people turn to alcohol or drugs for comfort to dull the emotional pain and that is not the answer.

Truth: The truth is God does love you. Alcohol or drugs are not the answer. You must remember that God gave everyone a free will. Why? Because love is not truly love unless it is *freely* given. God did not want robots to worship Him. He wanted the people He created to love and worship Him, but in order for that to be true love, He had to give everyone a free will, so they could be free to choose whether they would truly love and serve God or serve the devil or be lukewarm in between, which is also serving the devil. **The truth is your spouse made a selfish sinful decision and did not listen to God's voice or God's Word.** They rebelled and chose to not listen to God. God can only change someone if they will allow Him to change them. So, it is not God's fault. It is your spouse's fault for yielding to the devil's temptation. **What you may not realize is that God is as upset as you are.** He is sad and He grieves and weeps with you. He wants to comfort you with His love, but in order to feel His loving comforting manifest presence, you must forgive your spouse, and if necessary "forgive God" (but it is not God. It's the devil's fault) so there will be no sin or unforgiveness blocking your relationship with God. If you ask Him, God will give you grace to forgive your spouse and then when you worship Him from your heart, you will feel God's manifest presence, His comfort, His love, His grace and His loving compassion will wash all over you like a river.

Index of Object
Evangelism Icebreakers

About Susan Nazarewicz

Rev. Susan Nazarewicz graduated from the University of North Carolina at Chapel Hill with a B.A. double majoring in Psychology and Political Science in 1992. She then graduated from four Bible Schools as well: RHEMA Bible Training College; Victory World Missions Training Center; Church On the Move School of Ministry and the Prophetic Age Ministry Institute. She is a full time Prayer Partner and Assistant Supervisor at Oral Roberts Ministries at the Abundant Life Prayer Group since 2004. She is ordained by John G. Lake Ministries. (www.jglm.org). She has been on mission trips to: Nicaragua, Guatemala, Sierra Leone and Liberia, West Africa, Jamaica and Pakistan and hopes to go to more nations as well. She is praying that this book will help bring in a huge harvest of souls before Jesus comes again. In June 2014, Susan Mulford married David Nazarewicz, a wonderful man of God, and changed her name to Susan Nazarewicz. See her website: www.iwanttowitness.com

To Re–Order this book

"I Want to Witness,
But What Do I Say?"

Go to:

www.iwanttowitness.com

or

www.Amazon.com

And coming soon to bookstores online and in local Christian bookstores as well.